HARCOURT
Science

Harcourt School Publishers

Orlando • Boston • Dallas • Chicago • San Diego

www.harcourtschool.com

The **blue and yellow macaw** (*Ara ararauna*) lives in the trees of the rain forest in South America and Central America. It can grow to be about 33 in. (84 cm) in length. It is the largest member of the parrot family. Its favorite food is the seed of the fruit of one rain forest tree. Blue and yellow macaws often gather at "lick" areas to eat mineral- and salt-bearing clay. The inside covers of this book show a closeup of blue and yellow macaw feathers.

Copyright © 2002 by Harcourt, Inc.

All rights reserved. No part of this publication may be reproduced or transmitted in any form or by any means, electronic or mechanical, including photocopy, recording, or any information storage and retrieval system, without permission in writing from the publisher.

Requests for permission to make copies of any part of the work should be addressed to School Permissions and Copyrights, Harcourt, Inc., 6277 Sea Harbor Drive, Orlando, Florida 32887-6777.

HARCOURT and the Harcourt Logo are trademarks of Harcourt, Inc., registered in the United States of America and/or other jurisdictions.

sciLINKS is owned and provided by the National Science Teachers Association. All rights reserved.

Smithsonian Institution Internet Connections owned and provided by the Smithsonian Institution. All other material owned and provided by Harcourt School Publishers under copyright appearing above.

The name of the Smithsonian Institution and the Sunburst logo are registered trademarks of the Smithsonian Institution. The copyright in the Smithsonian website and Smithsonian website pages are owned by the Smithsonian Institution.

Printed in the United States of America
ISBN 0-15-325383-5   UNIT A
ISBN 0-15-325384-3   UNIT B
ISBN 0-15-325385-1   UNIT C
ISBN 0-15-325386-X   UNIT D
ISBN 0-15-325387-8   UNIT E
ISBN 0-15-325388-6   UNIT F

3 4 5 6 7 8 9 10 032 10 09 08 07 06 05 04 03 02

Authors

Marjorie Slavick Frank
Former Adjunct Faculty Member
Hunter, Brooklyn, and
  Manhattan Colleges
New York, New York

Robert M. Jones
Professor of Education
University of Houston–
  Clear Lake
Houston, Texas

Gerald H. Krockover
*Professor of Earth and Atmospheric
  Science Education*
School Mathematics and
  Science Center
Purdue University
West Lafayette, Indiana

Mozell P. Lang
Science Education Consultant
Michigan Department
  of Education
Lansing, Michigan

Joyce C. McLeod
Visiting Professor
Rollins College
Winter Park, Florida

Carol J. Valenta
*Vice President—Education, Exhibits,
  and Programs*
St. Louis Science Center
St. Louis, Missouri

Barry A. Van Deman
*Program Director, Informal Science
  Education*
Arlington, Virginia

Senior Editorial Advisor

Napoleon Adebola Bryant, Jr.
Professor Emeritus of Education
Xavier University
Cincinnati, Ohio

Program Advisors

Michael J. Bell
Assistant Professor of Early Childhood Education
School of Education
West Chester University
West Chester, Pennsylvania

George W. Bright
Professor of Mathematics Education
The University of North Carolina at Greensboro
Greensboro, North Carolina

Pansy Cowder
Science Specialist
Tampa, Florida

Robert H. Fronk
Head, Science/Mathematics Education Department
Florida Institute of Technology
Melbourne, Florida

Bernard A. Harris, Jr.
Physician and Former Astronaut
(STS 55—Space Shuttle *Columbia*, STS 63—Space Shuttle *Discovery*)
President, The Harris Foundation
Houston, Texas

Lois Harrison-Jones
Education and Management Consultant
Dallas, Texas

Kenneth R. Mechling
Professor of Biology and Science Education
Clarion University of Pennsylvania
Clarion, Pennsylvania

Nancy Roser
Professor of Language and Literacy Studies
University of Texas, Austin
Austin, Texas

Program Advisor and Activities Writer

Barbara ten Brink
Science Director
Round Rock Independent School District
Round Rock, Texas

Reviewers and Contributors

Sidney Jay Abramowitz
District Administrator for Mathematics, Science & Technology
Stamford Public Schools
Stamford, Connecticut

Patricia L. Bush
Teacher
Jesse Stuart Elementary School
Madisonville, Kentucky

Kathryn Henry
Teacher Trainer
Public School CS 200
New York, New York

Jacqueline Howard
Teacher
Millard Hensley Elementary School
Salyersville, Kentucky

Faye Kelley
Teacher
Gardendale Elementary School
Gardendale, Alabama

Faye McCollum
Instructional Specialist
Muscogee County School District
Columbus, Georgia

Margie H. McCoy
Teacher
Salyer Elementary School
Salyersville, Kentucky

Chester H. Melcher
Supervisor of Curriculum and Instruction—Science
Racine Unified School District
Racine, Wisconsin

Michael F. Ryan
Educational Technology Specialist
Lake County Schools
Tavares, Florida

Michelle Bonk Severtson
Teacher
Olson Elementary
Bloomington, Minnesota

Stanley J. Wegrzynowski
Director of Science
Buffalo Public Schools
Buffalo, New York

Lee Ann White
Teacher
Morgantown Elementary School
Morgantown, Kentucky

UNIT A   LIFE SCIENCE
A World of Living Things

Unit Experiment	**A1**

CHAPTER 1 Living Things — A2
Lesson 1—What Are Cells? A4
Lesson 2—What Are Animals? A12
Lesson 3—What Are Plants with Seeds? A18
Lesson 4—What Are Fungi? A24
    Science Through Time • Discovering Cells A30
    People in Science • Gary Sayler A32
    Activities for Home or School A33
Chapter Review and Test Preparation A34

CHAPTER 2 Animal Growth and Adaptations — A36
Lesson 1—What Are the Basic Needs of Animals? A38
Lesson 2—How Do Animals' Body Parts Help Them Meet Their Needs? ... A46
Lesson 3—How Do Animals' Behaviors Help Them Meet Their Needs? ... A54
    Science and Technology • Robot Roaches and Ants ... A62
    People in Science • Jane Goodall A64
    Activities for Home or School A65
Chapter Review and Test Preparation A66

CHAPTER 3 Plant Growth and Adaptations — A68
Lesson 1—What Do Plants Need to Live? A70
Lesson 2—How Do Leaves, Stems, and Roots Help Plants Live? ... A76
Lesson 3—How Do Plants Reproduce? A82
    Science and Technology • Superveggies A88
    People in Science • Mary Agnes Meara Chase A90
    Activities for Home or School A91
Chapter Review and Test Preparation A92

CHAPTER 4 Human Body Systems — A94
Lesson 1—How Do the Skeletal and Muscular Systems Work? ... A96
Lesson 2—How Do the Respiratory and Circulatory Systems Work? ... A102
Lesson 3—How Do the Nervous and Digestive Systems Work? ... A108
    Science and Technology • Skin Adhesive A114
    People in Science • Rosalyn Sussman Yalow A116
    Activities for Home or School A117
Chapter Review and Test Preparation A118

Unit Expeditions — **A120**

UNIT B

LIFE SCIENCE
Looking at Ecosystems

Unit Experiment	**B1**

CHAPTER 1
Ecosystems	**B2**
Lesson 1—What Are Systems?	B4
Lesson 2—What Makes Up an Ecosystem?	B10
Lesson 3—What Are Habitats and Niches?	B18
Lesson 4—What Are Tropical Rain Forests and Coral Reefs?	B26
Lesson 5—What Are Some Saltwater Communities?	B34
Science and Technology • Computer Models of Ecosystems	B42
People in Science • Henry Chandler Cowles	B44
Activities for Home or School	B45
Chapter Review and Test Preparation	B46

CHAPTER 2
Protecting Ecosystems	**B48**
Lesson 1—What Kinds of Changes Occur in Ecosystems?	B50
Lesson 2—How Do People Change Ecosystems?	B58
Lesson 3—What Is Conservation?	B66
Science Through Time • National Parks	B74
People in Science • Ruth Patrick	B76
Activities for Home or School	B77
Chapter Review and Test Preparation	B78

Unit Expeditions	**B80**

v

UNIT C
EARTH SCIENCE
Earth's Surface

Unit Experiment	**C1**

CHAPTER 1
Earthquakes and Volcanoes	**C2**
Lesson 1—What Are the Layers of the Earth?	C4
Lesson 2—What Causes Earthquakes?	C12
Lesson 3—How Do Volcanoes Form?	C18
Science and Technology • Dante, Robot Volcano Explorer	C26
People in Science • Hiroo Kanamori	C28
Activities for Home or School	C29
Chapter Review and Test Preparation	C30

CHAPTER 2
Fossils	**C32**
Lesson 1—How Do Fossils Form?	C34
Lesson 2—What Can We Learn from Fossils?	C40
Lesson 3—How Do Fossil Fuels Form?	C50
Science Through Time • Buried in Time	C58
People in Science • Lisa D. White	C60
Activities for Home or School	C61
Chapter Review and Test Preparation	C62

Unit Expeditions	**C64**

UNIT D

EARTH SCIENCE
Patterns on Earth and in Space

Unit Experiment	**D1**

CHAPTER 1 — Weather Conditions — D2
Lesson 1—What Makes Up Earth's Atmosphere? D4
Lesson 2—How Do Air Masses Affect Weather? D10
Lesson 3—How Is Weather Predicted? D18
    Science and Technology • Red Sprites, Blue Jets, and E.L.V.E.S. D24
    People in Science • Denise Stephenson-Hawk D26
    Activities for Home or School D27
Chapter Review and Test Preparation D28

CHAPTER 2 — The Oceans — D30
Lesson 1—What Role Do Oceans Play in the Water Cycle? D32
Lesson 2—What Are the Motions of Oceans? D38
Lesson 3—What Is the Ocean Floor Like? D46
    Science and Technology • Deep Flight II D54
    People in Science • Rachel Carson D56
    Activities for Home or School D57
Chapter Review and Test Preparation D58

CHAPTER 3 — Planets and Other Objects in Space — D60
Lesson 1—How Do Earth and Its Moon Move? D62
Lesson 2—How Do Objects Move in the Solar System? D68
Lesson 3—What Are the Planets Like? D74
Lesson 4—How Do People Study the Solar System? D82
    Science Through Time • Discovering the Planets D90
    People in Science • Clyde Tombaugh D92
    Activities for Home or School D93
Chapter Review and Test Preparation D94

Unit Expeditions — **D96**

UNIT E
PHYSICAL SCIENCE
Matter and Energy

Unit Experiment	**E1**

CHAPTER 1 — Matter and Its Changes — E2
Lesson 1—What Are Three States of Matter? E4
Lesson 2—How Can Matter Be Measured and Compared? E10
Lesson 3—What Are Some Useful Properties of Matter? E16
Lesson 4—What Are Chemical and Physical Changes? E24
    Science and Technology • Plastics You Can Eat. E32
    People in Science • Shirley Ann Jackson E34
    Activities for Home or School E35
Chapter Review and Test Preparation E36

CHAPTER 2 — Heat—Energy on the Move — E38
Lesson 1—How Does Heat Affect Matter? E40
Lesson 2—How Can Thermal Energy Be Transferred? E46
Lesson 3—How Is Thermal Energy Produced and Used? E54
    Science and Technology • Refrigerants E60
    People in Science • Frederick McKinley Jones E62
    Activities for Home or School E63
Chapter Review and Test Preparation E64

CHAPTER 3 — Sound — E66
Lesson 1—What Is Sound? E68
Lesson 2—Why Do Sounds Differ? E76
Lesson 3—How Do Sound Waves Travel? E82
    Science and Technology • Active Noise Control E90
    People in Science • Amar Gopal Bose E92
    Activities for Home or School E93
Chapter Review and Test Preparation E94

CHAPTER 4 — Light — E96
Lesson 1—How Does Light Behave? E98
Lesson 2—How Are Light and Color Related? E108
    Science Through Time • Discovering Light and Optics E114
    People in Science • Lewis Howard Latimer E116
    Activities for Home or School E117
Chapter Review and Test Preparation E118

Unit Expeditions   **E120**

UNIT F

PHYSICAL SCIENCE
Forces and Motion

Unit Experiment	F1

CHAPTER 1 — Electricity and Magnetism — F2
Lesson 1—What Is Static Electricity? F4
Lesson 2—What Is an Electric Current? F10
Lesson 3—What Is a Magnet? F16
Lesson 4—What Is an Electromagnet? F22
    Science Through Time • Discovering Electromagnetism F30
    People in Science • Raymond V. Damadian F32
    Activities for Home or School F33
Chapter Review and Test Preparation F34

CHAPTER 2 — Motion—Forces at Work — F36
Lesson 1—What Is Motion? F38
Lesson 2—What Effects Do Forces Have on Objects? F44
Lesson 3—What Are Some Forces in Nature? F54
    Science and Technology • High-Speed Human-Powered Vehicles ... F60
    People in Science • Ellen Ochoa F62
    Activities for Home or School F63
Chapter Review and Test Preparation F64

CHAPTER 3 — Simple Machines — F66
Lesson 1—How Does a Lever Help Us Do Work? F68
Lesson 2—How Do a Pulley and a Wheel and Axle Help Us Do Work? ... F76
Lesson 3—How Do Some Other Simple Machines Help Us Do Work? ... F82
    Science Through Time • Simple Machines and Water Transportation .. F90
    People in Science • Wilbur and Orville Wright F92
    Activities for Home or School F93
Chapter Review and Test Preparation F94

Unit Expeditions — F96

References   Using Science Tools R2
                      Glossary R6
                      Index R16

HOW SCIENTISTS WORK

Planning an Investigation

How do scientists answer a question or solve a problem they have identified? They use organized ways called **scientific methods** to plan and conduct a study. They use science process skills to help them gather, organize, analyze, and present their information.

Nathan is using this scientific method for experimenting to find an answer to his question. You can use these steps, too.

STEP 1 Observe, and ask questions.

- Use your senses to make observations.
- Record **one** question that you would like to answer.
- Write down what you already know about the topic of your question.
- Decide what other information you need.
- Do research to find more information about your topic.

What soil works best for planting marigold seeds?
I need to find out more about the different kinds of soils.

STEP 2 Form a hypothesis.

- Write a possible answer, or hypothesis, to your question. A **hypothesis** is a possible answer that can be tested.
- Write your hypothesis in a complete sentence.

My hypothesis is: Marigold seeds sprout best in potting soil.

STEP 3 Plan an experiment.

- Decide how to conduct a fair test of your hypothesis by controlling variables. **Variables** are factors that can affect the outcome of the investigation.
- Write down the steps you will follow to do your test.
- List the equipment you will need.
- Decide how you will gather and record your data.

I'll put identical seeds in three different kinds of soil. Each flowerpot will get the same amount of water and light. So, I'll be controlling the variables of water and light.

STEP 4 Conduct the experiment.

- Follow the steps you wrote.
- Observe and measure carefully.
- Record everything that happens.
- Organize your data so you can study it carefully.

I'll measure each plant every 3 days. I'll record the results in a table and then make a bar graph to show the height of each plant 21 days after I planted the seeds.

xi

HOW SCIENTISTS WORK

STEP 5 Draw conclusions and communicate results.

- Analyze the data you gathered.
- Make charts, tables, or graphs to show your data.
- Write a conclusion. Describe the evidence you used to determine whether your test supported your hypothesis.
- Decide whether your hypothesis was correct.

> Hmmm. My hypothesis was not correct. The seeds sprouted equally well in potting soil and sandy soil. They did not sprout at all in clay soil.

INVESTIGATE FURTHER

If your hypothesis was correct . . .

You may want to pose another question about your topic that you can test.

If your hypothesis was incorrect . . .

You may want to form another hypothesis and do a test of a different variable.

> I'll test this new hypothesis: Marigold seeds sprout best in a combination of clay, sandy, and potting soil. I will plan and conduct a test using potting soil, sandy soil, and a combination of clay, sandy, and potting soil.

Do you think Nathan's new hypothesis is correct? Plan and conduct a test to find out!

Using Science Process Skills

When scientists try to find an answer to a question or do an experiment, they use thinking tools called **process skills.** You use many of the process skills whenever you speak, listen, read, write, or think. Think about how these students use process skills to help them answer questions, do experiments, and investigate the world around them.

HOW SCIENTISTS WORK

What Sarah plans to investigate

Sarah collects seashells on her visit to the beach. She wants to make collections of shells that are alike in some way. She looks for shells of different sizes and shapes.

Process Skills

Observe—use the senses to learn about objects and events.

Compare—identify characteristics of things or events to find out how they are alike and different.

Classify—group or organize objects or events in categories based on specific characteristics.

How Sarah uses process skills

She **observes** the shells and **compares** their sizes, shapes, and colors. She **classifies** the shells first into groups based on their sizes and then into groups based on their shapes.

What Ling plans to investigate

Ling is interested in learning what makes the size and shape of a rock change. He plans an experiment to find out whether sand rubbing against a rock will cause pieces of the rock to flake off and change the size or shape of the rock.

How Ling uses process skills

He collects three rocks, **measures** their masses, and puts the rocks in a jar with sand and water. He shakes the rocks every day for a week. Then he measures and **records** the mass of the rocks, the sand, and the container. He interprets his data and concludes that rocks are broken down when sand rubs against them.

Process Skills

Measure—Compare an attribute of an object, such as mass, length, or capacity, to a unit of measure, such as gram, centimeter, or liter.

Gather, Record, Display, or Interpret Data

- Gather data by making observations that will be useful for inferences or predictions.
- Record data by writing down the observations in a table, graph, or notebook.
- Display data by making tables, charts, or graphs.
- Interpret data by drawing conclusions about what the data shows.

HOW SCIENTISTS WORK

Process Skills

Use a Model—make a representation to help you understand an idea, an object, or an event, such as how something works.

Predict—form an idea of an expected outcome, based on observations or experience.

Infer—use logical reasoning to explain events and draw conclusions based on observations.

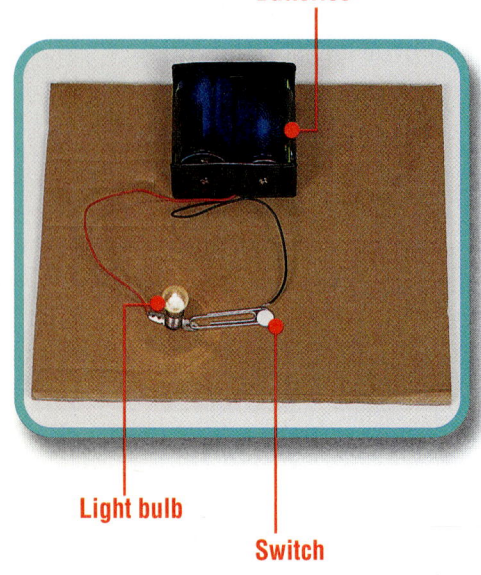

Batteries

Light bulb

Switch

What Justin plans to investigate

Justin wants to find out how the light switch in his bedroom works. He uses batteries, a flashlight bulb, a bulb holder, thumbtacks, and a paper clip to help him.

How Justin uses process skills

He decides to **use a model** of the switch and the wires in the wall. He **predicts** that the bulb, wires, and batteries have to be connected to make the bulb light. He **infers** that moving the paper clip interrupts the flow of electricity and turns off the light. Justin's model verifies his prediction and inference.

xvi

What Kendra plans to investigate

Kendra wants to know what brand of paper towel absorbs the most water. She plans a test to find out how much water different brands of paper towels absorb. She can then tell her father which brand is the best one to buy.

How Kendra uses process skills

She chooses three brands of paper towels. She **hypothesizes** that one brand will absorb more water than the others. She **plans and conducts an experiment** to test her hypothesis, using the following steps:

- Pour 1 liter of water into each of three beakers.
- Put a towel from each of the three brands into a different beaker for 10 seconds.
- Pull the towel out of the water, and let it drain back into the beaker for 5 seconds.
- Measure the amount of water left in each beaker.

Kendra **controls variables** by making sure each beaker contains exactly the same amount of water and by timing each step in her experiment exactly.

Process Skills

Hypothesize—make a statement about an expected outcome.

Plan and Conduct an Experiment—identify and perform the steps necessary to test a hypothesis, using appropriate tools and recording and analyzing the data collected.

Control Variables—identify and control factors that affect the outcome of an experiment so that only one variable is changed in a test.

HOW SCIENTISTS WORK

Reading to Learn

Scientists use reading, writing, and numbers in their work. They read to find out everything they can about a topic they are investigating. So it is important that scientists know the meanings of science vocabulary and that they understand what they read. Use the following strategies to help you become a good science reader!

Before Reading

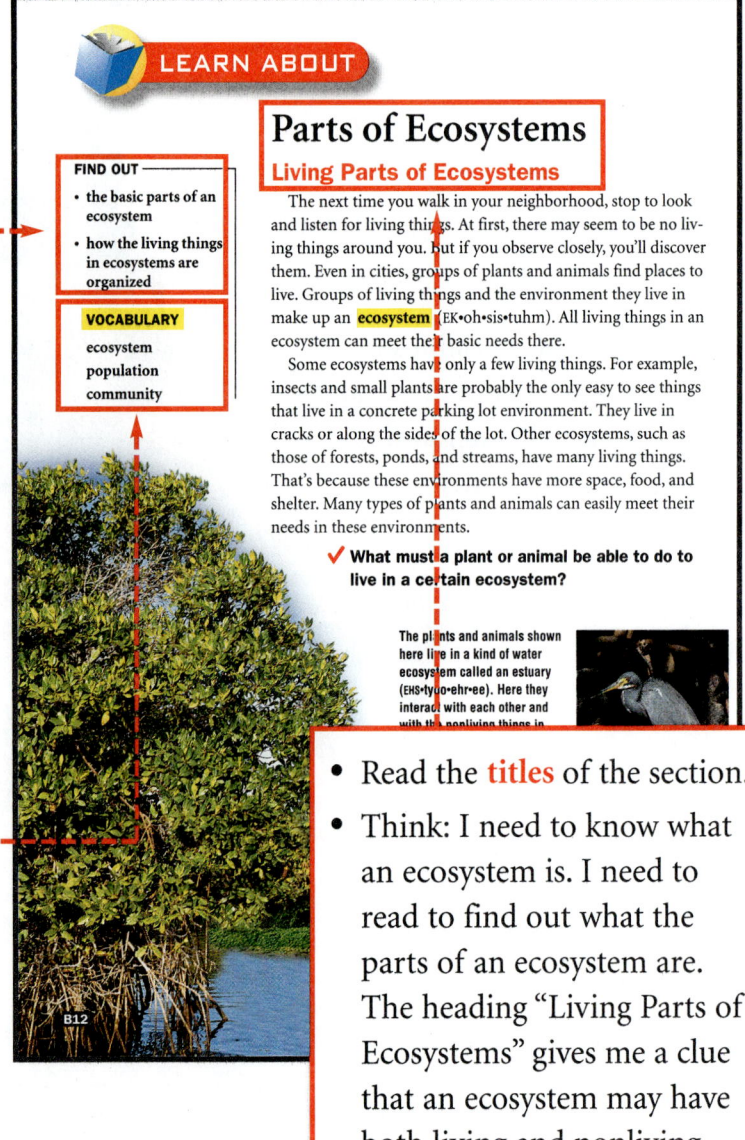

- Read the **Find Out** statement to help you know what to look for as you read.
- Think: I need to find out what the parts of an ecosystem are and how they are organized.

- Look at the **Vocabulary** words.
- Be sure that you can pronounce each word.
- Look up each word in the Glossary.
- Say the definition to yourself. Use the word in a sentence to show its meaning.

- Read the **titles** of the section.
- Think: I need to know what an ecosystem is. I need to read to find out what the parts of an ecosystem are. The heading "Living Parts of Ecosystems" gives me a clue that an ecosystem may have both living and nonliving parts.

During Reading

Find the **main idea** in the first paragraph.
- Groups of living things and their environment make up an ecosystem.

Find **details** in the next paragraph that support the main idea.
- Some ecosystems have only a few living things.
- Environments that have more space, food, and shelter have many living things.
- Plants and animals in an ecosystem can meet all their basic needs in their ecosystem.

Check your understanding of what you have read.
- Answer the question at the end of the section.
- If you're not sure of the answer, reread the section and look for the answer to the question.

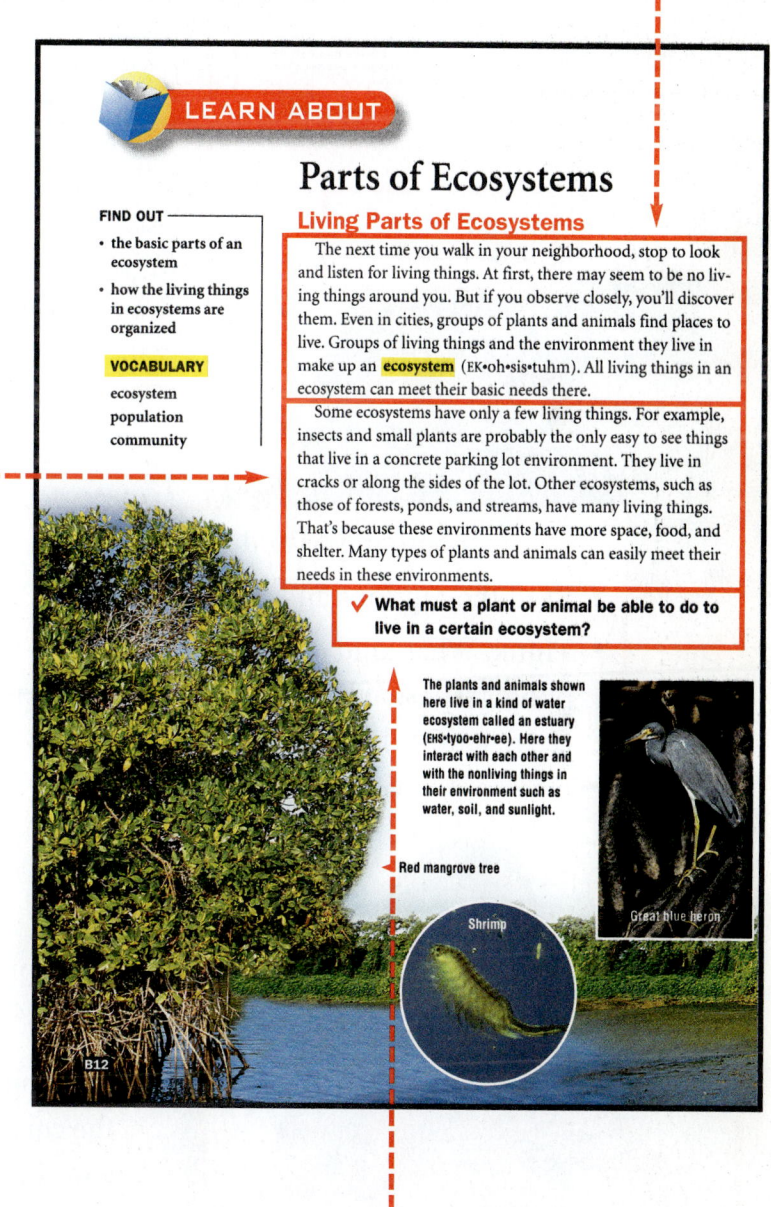

After Reading

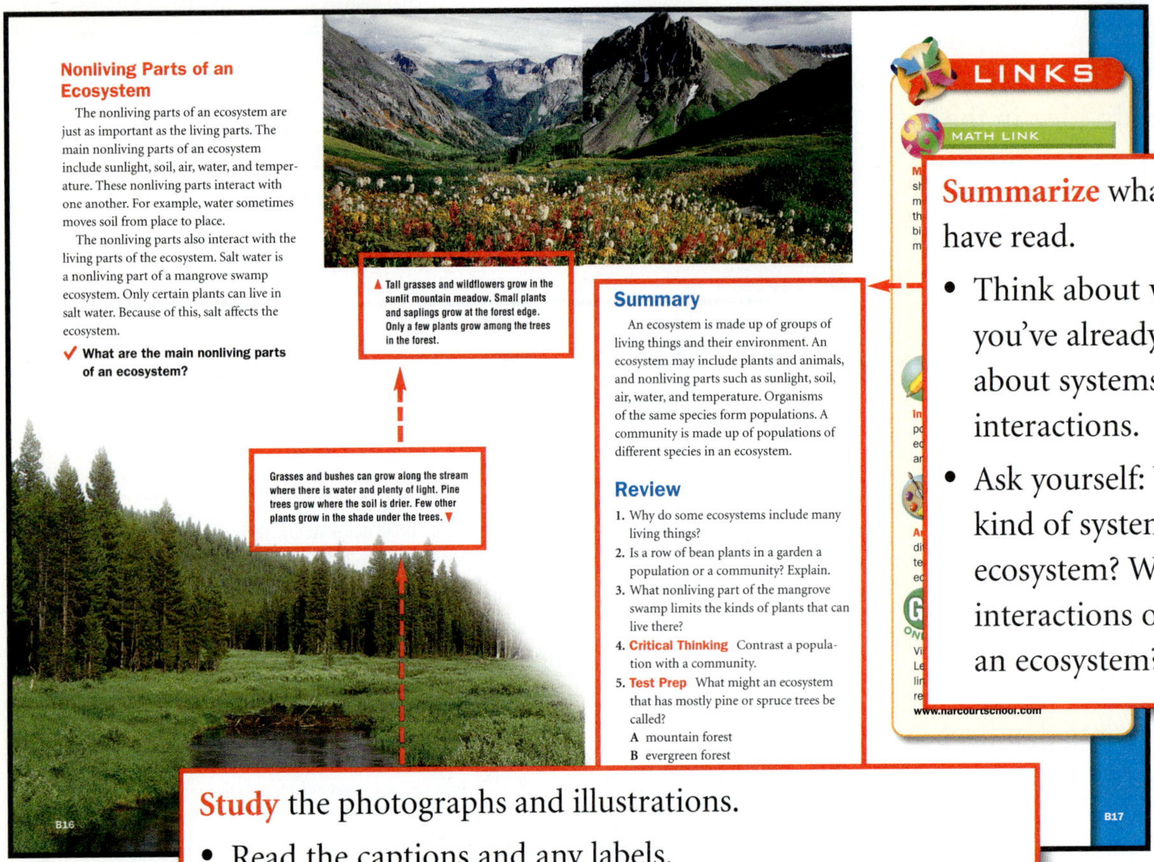

Nonliving Parts of an Ecosystem

The nonliving parts of an ecosystem are just as important as the living parts. The main nonliving parts of an ecosystem include sunlight, soil, air, water, and temperature. These nonliving parts interact with one another. For example, water sometimes moves soil from place to place.

The nonliving parts also interact with the living parts of the ecosystem. Salt water is a nonliving part of a mangrove swamp ecosystem. Only certain plants can live in salt water. Because of this, salt affects the ecosystem.

✓ **What are the main nonliving parts of an ecosystem?**

▲ Tall grasses and wildflowers grow in the sunlit mountain meadow. Small plants and saplings grow at the forest edge. Only a few plants grow among the trees in the forest.

Grasses and bushes can grow along the stream where there is water and plenty of light. Pine trees grow where the soil is drier. Few other plants grow in the shade under the trees. ▼

B16

Summary

An ecosystem is made up of groups of living things and their environment. An ecosystem may include plants and animals, and nonliving parts such as sunlight, soil, air, water, and temperature. Organisms of the same species form populations. A community is made up of populations of different species in an ecosystem.

Review

1. Why do some ecosystems include many living things?
2. Is a row of bean plants in a garden a population or a community? Explain.
3. What nonliving part of the mangrove swamp limits the kinds of plants that can live there?
4. **Critical Thinking** Contrast a population with a community.
5. **Test Prep** What might an ecosystem that has mostly pine or spruce trees be called?
   A mountain forest
   B evergreen forest

LINKS

MATH LINK

www.harcourtschool.com

B17

Summarize what you have read.

- Think about what you've already learned about systems and interactions.
- Ask yourself: What kind of system is an ecosystem? What interactions occur in an ecosystem?

Study the photographs and illustrations.

- Read the captions and any labels.
- Think: What kind of ecosystem is shown in the photographs? What are the nonliving parts of the ecosystem? What living parts of the ecosystem are shown?

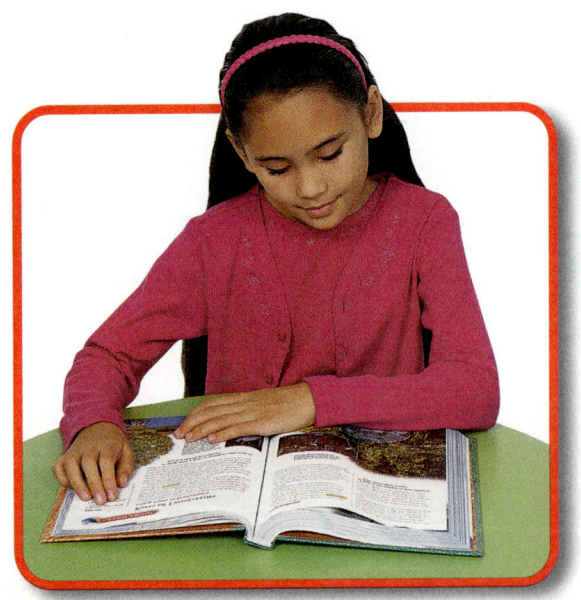

For more reading strategies and tips, see pages R38–R49.

Reading about science helps you understand the conclusions you have made based on your investigations.

Writing to Communicate

Writing about what you are learning helps you connect the new ideas to what you already know. Scientists **write** about what they learn in their research and investigations to help others understand the work they have done. As you work like a scientist, you will use the following kinds of writing to describe what you are doing and learning.

In **informative writing,** you may
- describe your observations, inferences, and conclusions.
- tell how to do an experiment.

In **narrative writing,** you may
- describe something, give examples, or tell a story.

In **expressive writing,** you may
- write letters, poems, or songs.

In **persuasive writing,** you may
- write letters about important issues in science.
- write essays expressing your opinions about science issues.

Writing about what you have learned about science helps others understand your thinking.

xxi

HOW SCIENTISTS WORK

Using Numbers

Scientists **use numbers** when they collect and display their data. Understanding numbers and using them to show the results of investigations are important skills that a scientist must have. As you work like a scientist, you will use numbers in the following ways:

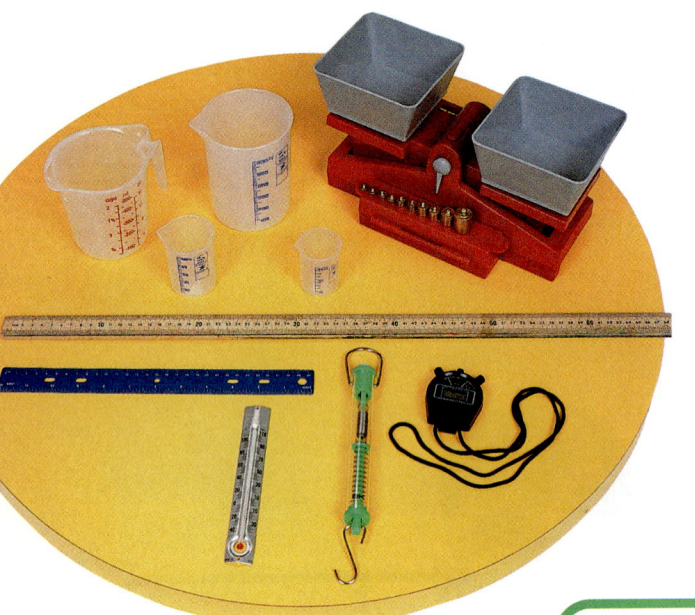

Measuring

Scientists make accurate measurements as they gather data. They use many different measuring instruments, such as thermometers, clocks and timers, rulers, a spring scale, and a balance, and they use beakers and other containers to measure liquids.

For more information about using measuring tools, see pages R2–R6.

Interpreting Data

Scientists collect, organize, display, and interpret data as they do investigations. Scientists choose a way to display data that helps others understand what they have learned. Tables, charts, and graphs are good ways to display data so that it can be interpreted by others.

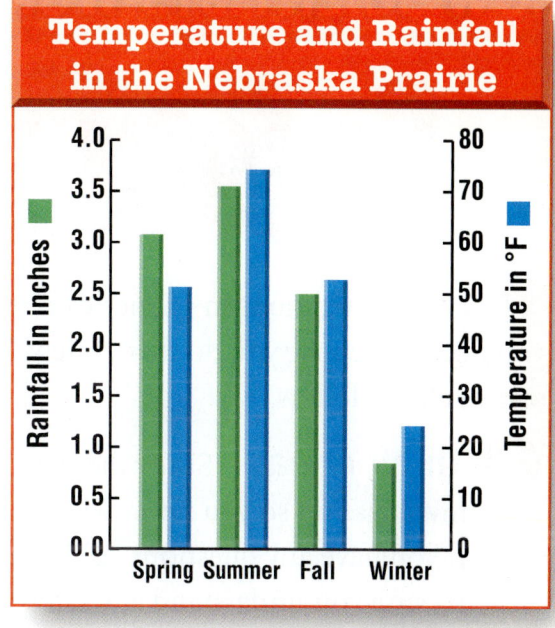

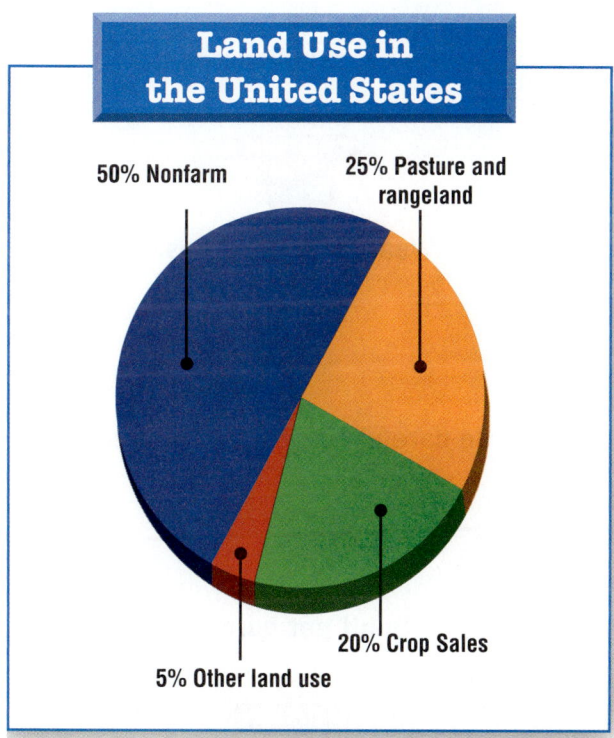

Using Number Sense

Scientists must understand what the numbers they use represent. They compare and order numbers, compute with numbers, read and understand the numbers shown on graphs, and read the scales on thermometers, measuring cups, beakers, and other tools.

Good scientists apply their math skills to help them display and interpret the data they collect.

In Harcourt Science you will have many opportunities to work like a scientist. An exciting year of discovery lies ahead!

xxiii

HOW SCIENTISTS WORK

Safety in Science

Doing investigations in science can be fun, but you need to be sure you do them safely. Here are some rules to follow.

① **Think ahead.** Study the steps of the investigation so you know what to expect. If you have any questions, ask your teacher. Be sure you understand any safety symbols that are shown.

② **Be neat.** Keep your work area clean. If you have long hair, pull it back so it doesn't get in the way. Roll or push up long sleeves to keep them away from your experiment.

③ **Oops!** If you should spill or break something or get cut, tell your teacher right away.

④ **Watch your eyes.** Wear safety goggles anytime you are directed to do so. If you get anything in your eyes, tell your teacher right away.

⑤ **Yuck!** Never eat or drink anything during a science activity unless you are told to do so by your teacher.

⑥ **Don't get shocked.** Be especially careful if an electric appliance is used. Be sure that electric cords are in a safe place where you can't trip over them. Don't ever pull a plug out of an outlet by pulling on the cord.

⑦ **Keep it clean.** Always clean up when you have finished. Put everything away and wipe your work area. Wash your hands.

In some activities you will see these symbols. They are signs for what you need to act safely.

Be especially careful.

Wear safety goggles.

Be careful with sharp objects.

Don't get burned.

Protect your clothes.

Protect your hands with mitts.

Be careful with electricity.

UNIT E — PHYSICAL SCIENCE

Matter and Energy

CHAPTER 1	Matter and Its Changes	E2
CHAPTER 2	Heat—Energy on the Move	E38
CHAPTER 3	Sound	E66
CHAPTER 4	Light	E96
	Unit Expeditions	E120

UNIT EXPERIMENT

Color and Energy Absorption

Everything around you is made of matter. Part of science is studying properties of matter, such as how matter and energy interact. While you study this unit, you can conduct a long-term experiment about color and light energy. Here are some questions to think about. How does color affect the amount of energy absorbed from light? Does one color warm up or cool down faster than others? Do different light sources produce different results? Does insulation affect the results? Plan and conduct an experiment to find answers to these or other questions you have about matter and energy. See pages x–xix for help in designing your experiment.

CHAPTER 1

Matter and Its Changes

Vocabulary Preview

matter
mass
solid
liquid
gas
volume
density
solution
dissolve
solubility
buoyancy
physical change
chemical change
chemical reaction

How heavy? How light? How big? How small? How much? These are some of the questions that help us measure and compare matter. People had to answer most of these questions before they could decide how to make the shelves in your kitchen, the food products you buy in the store, and many of the other inventions you use every day!

Fast Fact

The ancient Greeks believed that Atlas carried Earth on his shoulders. They must have thought he was pretty strong! The mass of the Earth is 5.97 trillion trillion kilograms (about 13.2 trillion trillion lb)!

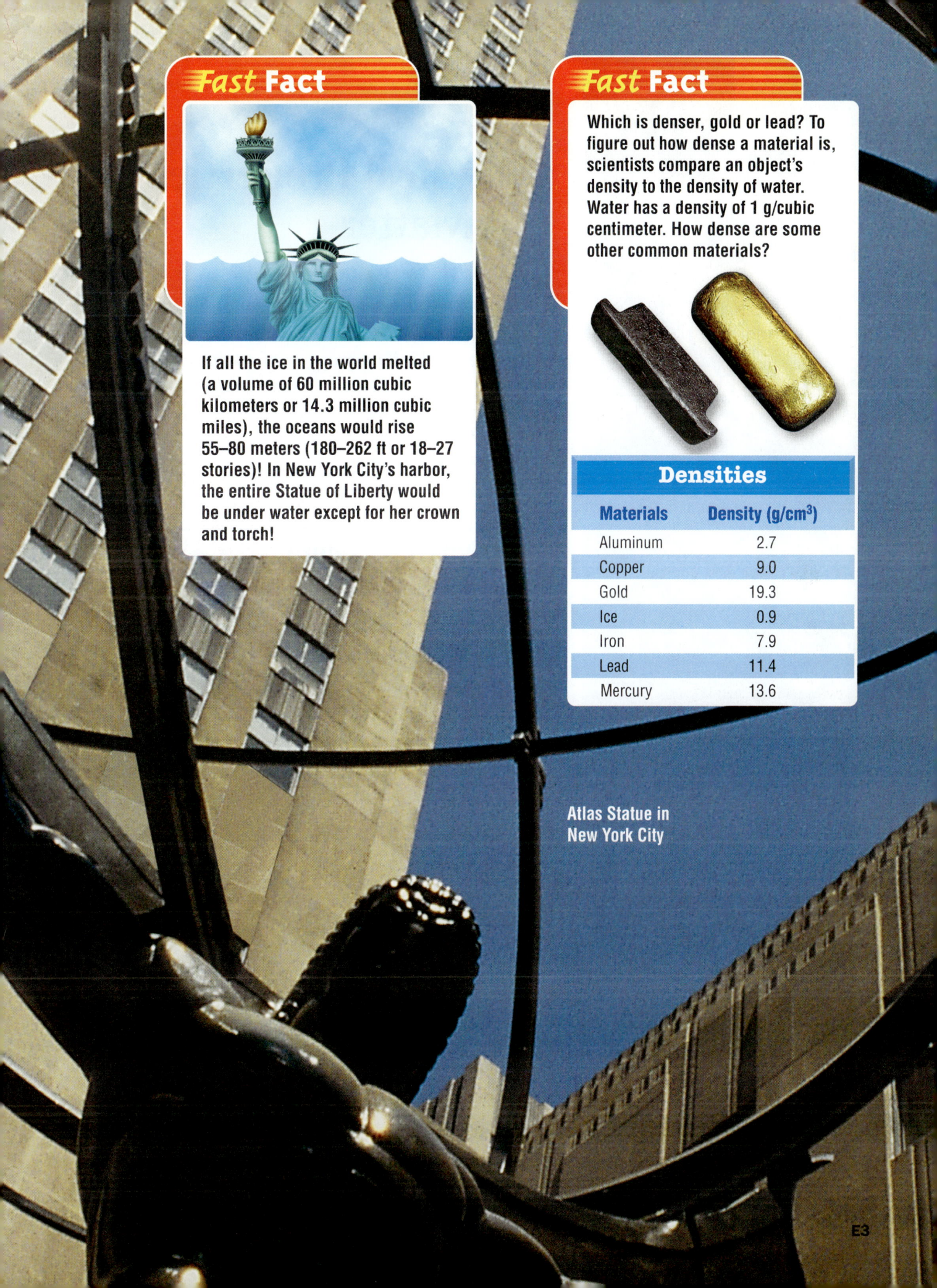

Fast Fact

If all the ice in the world melted (a volume of 60 million cubic kilometers or 14.3 million cubic miles), the oceans would rise 55–80 meters (180–262 ft or 18–27 stories)! In New York City's harbor, the entire Statue of Liberty would be under water except for her crown and torch!

Fast Fact

Which is denser, gold or lead? To figure out how dense a material is, scientists compare an object's density to the density of water. Water has a density of 1 g/cubic centimeter. How dense are some other common materials?

Densities

Materials	Density (g/cm^3)
Aluminum	2.7
Copper	9.0
Gold	19.3
Ice	0.9
Iron	7.9
Lead	11.4
Mercury	13.6

Atlas Statue in New York City

LESSON 1

What Are Three States of Matter?

In this lesson, you can . . .

INVESTIGATE a physical property of matter.

LEARN ABOUT solids, liquids, and gases.

LINK to math, writing, technology, and other areas.

INVESTIGATE

Physical Properties of Matter

Activity Purpose You can't see it. Often you can't even feel it. But air is all around you. In this investigation you will **observe** one way air behaves and you will **infer** a property of matter.

Materials
- plastic bag
- plastic drinking straw
- book

Activity Procedure

1. Wrap the opening of the plastic bag tightly around the straw. Use your fingers to hold the bag in place. (Picture A)

2. Blow into the straw. **Observe** what happens to the bag.

◀ After a while this horse carving made of ice will melt into a puddle of water. How are the carving and a puddle alike? How are they different?

Picture A

Picture B

3. Empty the bag. Now place a book on the bag. Again wrap the opening of the bag tightly around the straw and use your fingers to hold the bag in place. (Picture B)

4. **Predict** what will happen when you blow into the straw. Blow into it and **observe** what happens to the book.

Draw Conclusions

1. What happened to the bag when you blew air into it? What happened to the book?

2. What property of air caused the effects you observed in Steps 2 and 4?

3. **Scientists at Work** Scientists **draw conclusions** after they think carefully about observations and other data they have collected. What data supports your answer to Question 2 above?

Investigate Further In a sink, place a filled 1-L bottle on an empty plastic bag. Use a tube connected to a faucet to slowly fill the bag with water. What happens to the bottle when the bag fills with water? What property of water do you **observe**?

Process Skill Tip

When you **draw a conclusion,** you make a statement of what you know based on all the data you have collected. Unlike an inference, a conclusion is supported, or shown to be likely, by results of tests.

E5

LEARN ABOUT

States of Matter

Solids

FIND OUT

- how particles are arranged in matter
- how three states of matter are different

VOCABULARY

matter
mass
solid
liquid
gas

One way you know about the world around you is from your sense of touch. A tree trunk stops your finger. Water changes its shape as you poke your finger into it. You feel the moving air of a breeze. By touch you know that wood, water, and air have different properties. Yet they are all matter. Everything in the universe that has mass and takes up space is classified as **matter**.

In the investigation you saw that air takes up space. Matter also has mass. **Mass** is the amount of matter something contains. A large, heavy object such as an elephant has a lot of mass. A small, light maple leaf has much less mass. Even though an elephant and a leaf are very different, each is an example of matter.

All matter is made up of small bits called *particles*. The particles are so small that they can be seen only with the strongest microscopes. These tiny particles are always moving quickly.

The arrangements of particles give matter properties. Each arrangement is called a *state of matter*. A door key is an example of matter in the solid state. When you touch a door key, it stops your finger. A **solid** is matter that has a definite shape and takes up a definite amount of space. The particles in a solid are close together, like neat and even stacks of tiny balls. Each particle moves back and forth around one point. This arrangement of particles gives a solid its definite shape.

✓ How are particles arranged in a solid?

This old key is a solid. It keeps its shape when you put it into a lock. ▶

▼ The particles in this metal key are arranged in a tight, regular pattern.

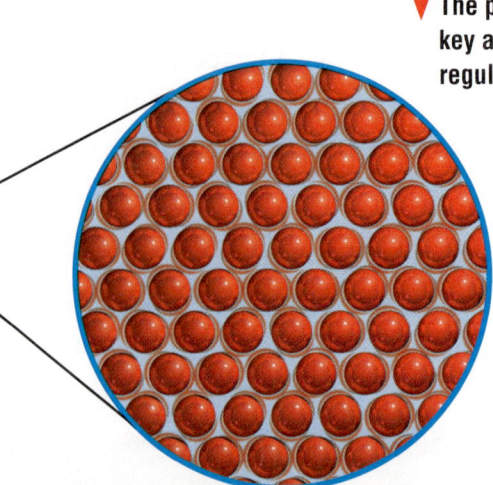

E6

Liquids

A frozen ice cube keeps its shape. But when you heat the ice cube in a pan, the ice becomes liquid water. The water changes shape and fills the bottom of the pan. If you spill the water onto a table, the water will spread out to cover the tabletop. The water still takes up the same amount of space as in the pan. It just has a new shape. A **liquid** is matter that takes the shape of its container and takes up a definite amount of space.

When matter is a liquid, its particles slip and slide around each other. The particles don't keep the same neighbors, as particles in a solid do. They move from place to place. But they still stay close to each other.

As the particles in a liquid move, they bump into the walls of their container. The solid walls of the container don't change shape. The particles of the liquid can't move past the walls, and the liquid particles stay close together. So, the liquid takes the shape of its container.

If you pour a liquid from one container into another, the amount of matter in the liquid stays the same. The amount of space the liquid takes up also stays the same.

✓ Why does a liquid have the same shape as its container?

▲ The particles in a liquid move past each other easily. They are still close together but are not in a neat, even arrangement, as particles in a solid are.

As these straws show, a liquid always takes the shape of its container. ▶

E7

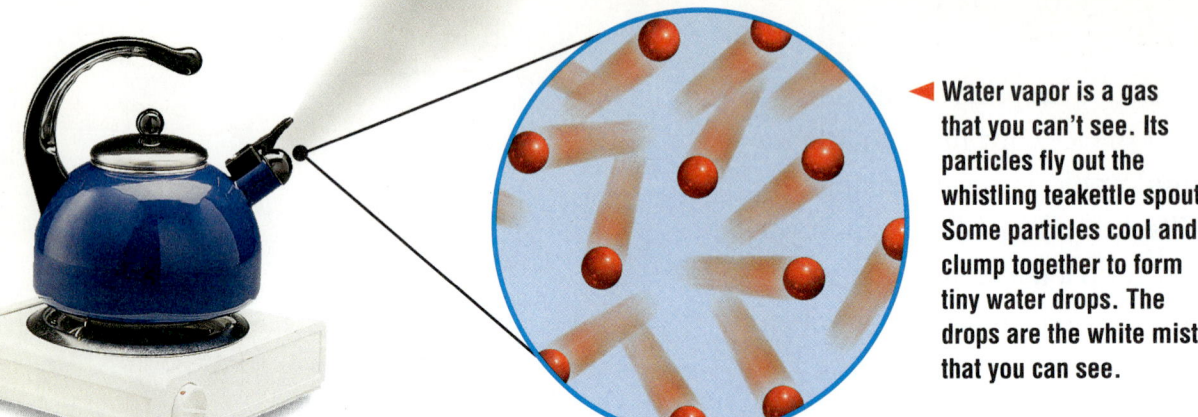

◀ Water vapor is a gas that you can't see. Its particles fly out the whistling teakettle spout. Some particles cool and clump together to form tiny water drops. The drops are the white mist that you can see.

Gases

A **gas** is matter that has no definite shape and takes up no definite amount of space. Like particles in liquids, the particles in gases are not arranged in any pattern. Unlike particles in liquids, however, particles in gases don't stay close together. This is because particles in gases are moving much faster than particles in liquids.

The amount of space a gas takes up depends on the amount of space inside its container. A gas always fills the container it is in. If the container is open, the gas particles move out.

Most matter can change state from a solid to a liquid to a gas. You can see this when you leave an ice cube in a pan on a hot stove. In a few minutes, the cube changes from a solid to a liquid. Minutes later the liquid is gone—the water has become a gas called *water vapor*. The gas particles have moved off in all directions.

Heating matter makes particles move faster. When ice is heated, some particles begin to move fast enough to break away from their neighbors. As the regular arrangement of particles breaks down, the ice melts. Heated particles of liquid water move faster and faster. After a while they move fast enough to bounce away from each other. The liquid boils, or changes quickly into a gas.

✓ **How does heating matter change its state?**

◀ A lot of air is squeezed into the tank carried by this diver. The tank valve is open. Particles of gases move out of the tank as the diver breathes in.

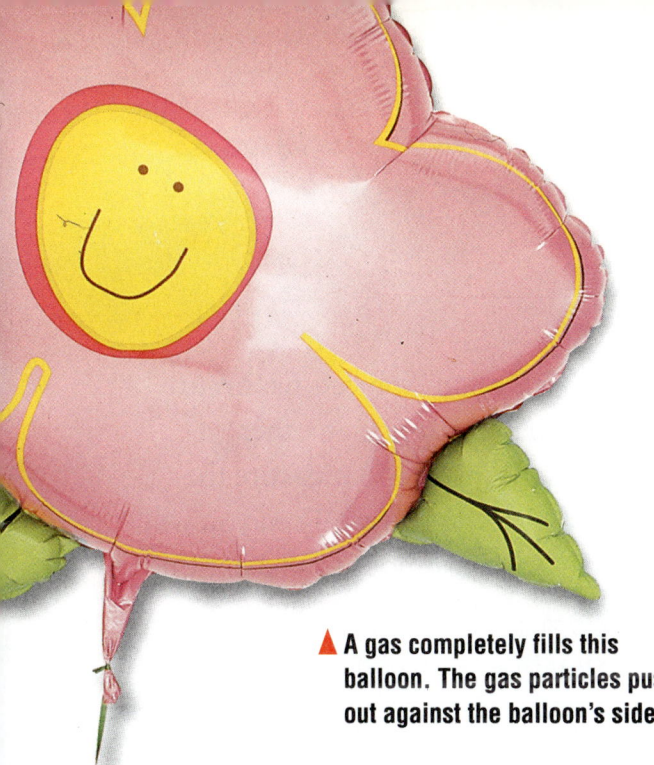

▲ A gas completely fills this balloon. The gas particles push out against the balloon's sides.

Summary

Matter takes up space. Matter is made up of particles. Particles in solid matter stay close together and move back and forth around one point. Particles in liquid matter stay close together but move past each other. Particles in a gas are spread far apart.

Review

1. What are three states of matter?
2. Which state of matter keeps its shape?
3. Which states of matter take the shapes of their containers?
4. **Critical Thinking** How can matter be changed from a liquid to a solid?
5. **Test Prep** Which sentence describes a liquid?
   A Particles slide past each other.
   B Particles stay near their neighbors.
   C Particles are arranged in a pattern.
   D Particles bounce away from each other.

LINKS

MATH LINK

Solve a Problem Mercury is a metal that becomes a solid at 39° *below* 0°C. It becomes a gas at 357° *above* 0°C. What is the total number of degrees Celsius at which mercury is a liquid?

WRITING LINK

Narrative Writing—Story Suppose that you are a particle in a solid that melts and then becomes a gas. Write a story for your teacher about your experiences.

HEALTH LINK

States of Matter in the Body Find out which organ in the body is a liquid. Name some of the organs that bring a gas into the body. Plan and make a model of one body system that uses a liquid or a gas.

ART LINK

Using Matter in Art Find and describe in your own words one example each of a work of art that uses a solid, a liquid, and a gas.

TECHNOLOGY LINK

Visit the Harcourt Learning Site for related links, activities, and resources.
www.harcourtschool.com

E9

LESSON 2

How Can Matter Be Measured and Compared?

In this lesson, you can . . .

 **INVESTIGATE** the densities of some types of matter.

 **LEARN ABOUT** measuring and comparing matter.

 **LINK** to math, writing, health, and technology.

 INVESTIGATE

Density

Activity Purpose Some objects have more matter packed into a smaller space than other objects. In this investigation you will **measure** the mass of raisins and of breakfast cereal. Then you will **compare** their masses and the amounts of space they take up.

Materials
- 3 identical plastic cups
- raisins
- breakfast cereal
- pan balance

Activity Procedure

1. Fill one cup with raisins. Make sure the raisins fill the cup all the way to the top. (Picture A)

2. Fill another cup with cereal. Make sure the cereal fills the cup all the way to the top.

3. **Observe** the amount of space taken up by the raisins and the cereal.

◀ The gold coin is only slightly larger than the quarter. However, it has more then five times the quarter's mass.

E10

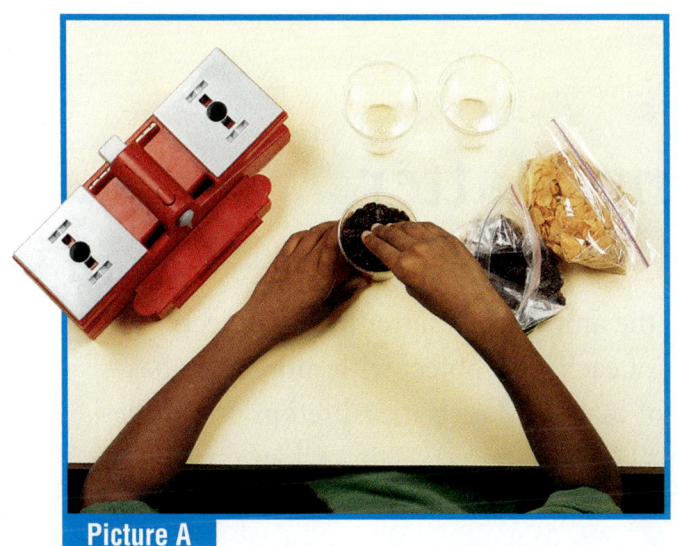

Picture A

Picture B

4. Adjust the balance so the pans are level. Place one cup on each pan. **Observe** what happens. (Picture B)

5. Fill the third cup with a mixture of raisins and cereal. **Predict** how the mass of the cup of raisins and cereal will compare with the masses of the cup of raisins and the cup of cereal. Use the pan balance to check your predictions.

Draw Conclusions

1. **Compare** the amount of space taken up by the raisins with the space taken up by the cereal.

2. Which has more mass, the cup of raisins or the cup of cereal? Explain your answer.

3. Which cup has more matter packed into it? Explain your answer.

4. **Scientists at Work** It is important to know the starting place when you measure. What would happen if you **measured** without making the balance pans equal? Explain your answer.

Investigate Further Write step-by-step directions to **compare** the masses of any two materials and the space they take up. Exchange sets of directions with a classmate. Test the directions and suggest revisions.

Process Skill Tip

A balance **measures** by comparing two masses. To make sure the comparison is accurate, you must make both sides of the balance equal before you measure. This is what you did in Step 4.

E11

LEARN ABOUT

Measuring Matter

Measuring Mass

You can compare the amount of matter in two objects by measuring the mass of each. The object with more mass has the greater amount of matter. Mass is measured in units called grams and kilograms (KIL•uh•gramz). Half a kilogram, or $\frac{1}{2}$ kg, is about the same mass as four sticks of margarine. A medium-sized paper clip has a mass of about 1 gram, or 1 g.

One way to compare two masses is by using a pan balance. Put an object in each pan. When the pans of the balance are level, the matter in the two pans has the same mass. In the investigation, you used a pan balance to find out that a cup of raisins has more mass than a cup of cereal.

If you know the mass of the matter in one pan, you can find the mass of the matter in the other pan. This is one way scientists measure mass. They have objects with masses that are known—for example, 50 grams, 200 grams, and 1 kilogram. These objects are known as *standard masses*. Scientists put an object whose mass they don't know in one pan and put standard masses in the other pan. Then they add or remove standard masses until the two pans balance. The total of the standard masses equals the mass of the object.

✔ **Name one way you can measure mass.**

FIND OUT

- about mass and volume and how to measure them
- a way to use measurements of mass and volume to describe density

VOCABULARY

volume
density

When the pans of a balance are level, the pieces of matter on the two pans have the same mass. These cotton balls have the same mass as the wood block. ▼

E12

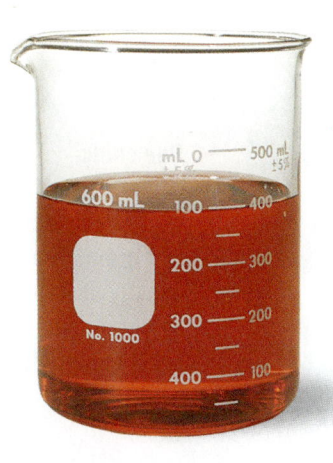

◀ It is easy to measure the volume of a liquid by using this container marked in milliliters, or mL. This container is called a beaker, and it has about 400 mL of red liquid.

Volume

Matter has mass and takes up space. The amount of space that matter takes up is called its **volume** (VAHL•yoom). You can measure the amount of space a solid or liquid takes up. You also can measure a container such as a box and calculate its volume. Volume often is measured in cubic centimeters. A *cubic centimeter* is the space taken up by a cube that has each side equal to 1 centimeter. A cubic centimeter is the same as a milliliter.

Cooks use measuring cups and measuring spoons to find the volume of ingredients for a recipe. Scientists measure volume with a beaker or a graduate, a tall cylinder with measuring marks on the side.

A solid keeps its shape, so it is easy to see that its volume stays the same. A liquid changes shape to match its container. But it does not change its volume. A gas has no definite volume. However, the mass of a gas sample doesn't change when the volume of the gas changes.

✓ **What is volume?**

▲ You can find the volume of odd-shaped solid objects, such as these marbles, by sinking them in water. They push away some of the water, and the water level rises. The change in water level gives the volume of the solids.

▲ The level in this graduate changed from 250 mL to 285 mL when the marbles were added. Therefore, the volume of the marbles is 285 mL − 250 mL = 35 mL.

To find the volume of a box, first measure its height, width, and length. Then multiply the three numbers together. This box is about 6 cm thick, 20 cm wide, and 30 cm tall. Its volume is 6 cm × 20 cm × 30 cm = 3600 cubic centimeters. ▶

E13

Density

Some matter takes up a large space but has a small mass. A balloon filled with gas may take up 10,000 cubic centimeters. But it may have such a small mass that it floats in the air. Other matter takes up very little space and has a large mass. A brick is smaller than the balloon, but it has much more mass.

The property of matter that compares the amount of matter to the space taken up is called **density** (DEN•suh•tee). The gas in a balloon has a low density. The density of a brick is much higher.

You can find the density of an object by dividing the mass of the object by its volume. For example, an apple may have a mass of 200 grams and a volume of 200 cubic centimeters. Its density is 200 grams ÷ 200 cubic centimeters, or 1 gram per cubic centimeter.

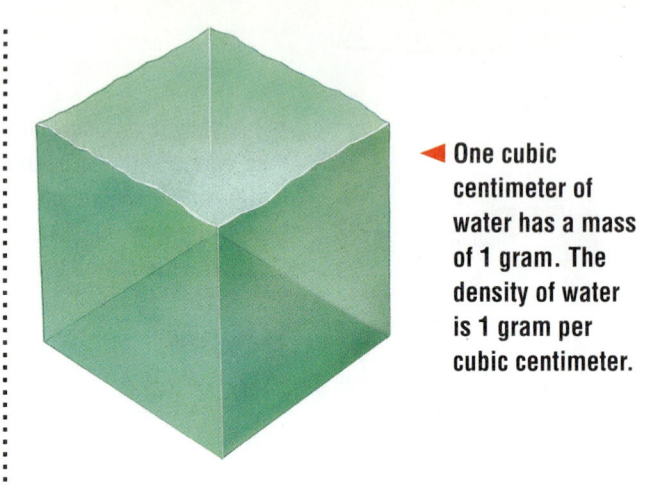

◄ One cubic centimeter of water has a mass of 1 gram. The density of water is 1 gram per cubic centimeter.

In the investigation you saw that cereal is less dense than raisins. You also found that a mixture of cereal and raisins is denser than cereal and less dense than raisins. Whenever you mix two kinds of matter, the density of the mixture is between the densities of the two separate materials.

✓ **Which material in the table has the greatest density?**

Density of Some Common Materials

Materials	Density (g per cubic centimeter)	Relative Size of 1-kg Disk
Pine	0.40	
Motor oil	0.90	
Plastic (HDPE)	0.96	
Lead	11.30	

◄ The disks show the volume needed to make up one kilogram of each material. Notice how the size of the disks compares to the density of the materials.

Summary

All matter has mass and volume. Mass is the amount of matter in an object. The space that matter takes up is called volume. Density compares the amount of matter in an object to the amount of space it takes up. You can find the density of an object by dividing its mass by its volume.

Review

1. What is one way to measure mass?
2. What word is used to describe the amount of space that matter takes up?
3. What property of matter compares the amount of matter to the space that the matter takes up?
4. **Critical Thinking** You are shopping for cereal. How does estimating density help you find a good buy?
5. **Test Prep** If a black ball is denser than a white ball of the same size, the black ball has —
   A less volume
   B more volume
   C more matter taking up the same space
   D less matter taking up the same space

LINKS

MATH LINK

Compare Volumes Use a pan balance and three cups to measure 100 g, 200 g, and 300 g of water. Use a beaker or a graduate to measure and compare the volumes of water.

WRITING LINK

Informative Writing—Narration You are making a short video for younger students. It will show how to measure volume and mass. Decide what you will show. Then, write a script to explain what you are showing.

HEALTH LINK

Your Density Find out how to measure and compare the mass of a person's muscles and body fat. Make a comic strip that shows how this is done.

TECHNOLOGY LINK

Learn more about measuring matter by visiting this Internet site.
www.scilinks.org/harcourt

LESSON 3

What Are Some Useful Properties of Matter?

In this lesson, you can . . .

INVESTIGATE what happens to some solids in water.

LEARN ABOUT ways to group kinds of matter.

LINK to math, writing, technology, and other areas.

INVESTIGATE

Floating and Sinking

Activity Purpose Some solids sink in liquid water, and others float. But even solids that sink can be made to float. In this investigation you will see what happens to two solid materials when they are placed in water. Then you will make boats from the materials. You will **infer** some of the things that affect floating and sinking.

Materials
- plastic shoe box
- water
- sheet of aluminum foil
- modeling clay

Activity Procedure

1. Fill the plastic shoe box halfway with water.

2. Take a sheet of aluminum foil about 10 cm long and 10 cm wide. Squeeze it tightly into a ball. Before placing the ball in the shoe box, **predict** whether it will sink or float. Test your prediction and **record** your **observations.**

3. Take a thin piece of modeling clay about 10 cm long and 10 cm wide. Squeeze it tightly into a ball. Place the ball in the shoe box. **Observe** whether it sinks or floats.

◀ This sailing ship is made to float, but its black metal anchor is made to sink.

E16

Picture A

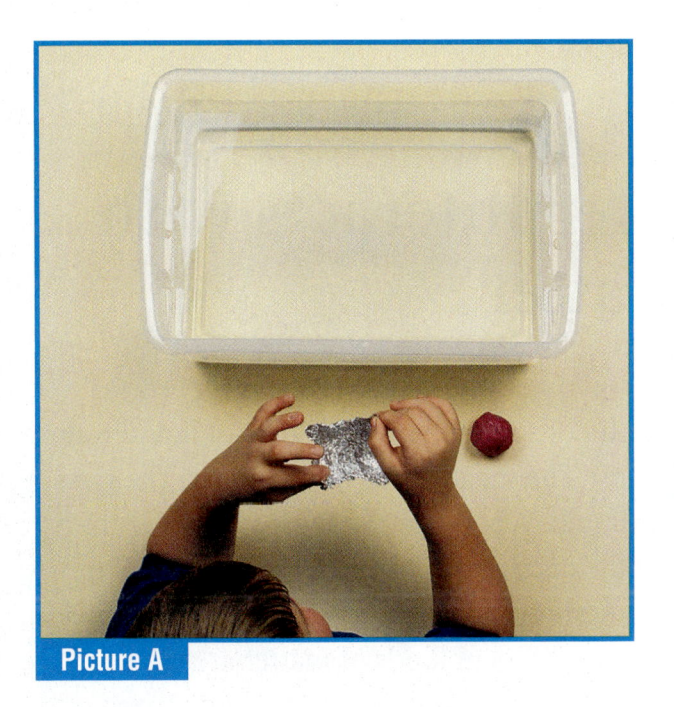

Picture B

4 Uncurl the foil. Use it to make a boat. (Picture A) Before placing the boat on the water, **predict** whether it will sink or float. Test your prediction and **record** your **observations.**

5 Make a boat out of the modeling clay. Before placing the boat on the water, **predict** whether it will sink or float. Test your prediction and **record** your **observations.** (Picture B)

Draw Conclusions

1. Which objects floated? Which objects sank?

2. Which do you think has the greater density, the ball of aluminum foil or the ball of modeling clay? Explain.

3. **Scientists at Work** Scientists often look at two situations in which everything is the same except for one property. What property was the same in Step 3 as in Step 5? What property was different in Step 3 and Step 5? What can you **infer** about how that difference changed the results?

Investigate Further How fast do you think each boat would sink if you put a hole in the bottom of it? **Form a hypothesis** about how the size and material of a boat affect its rate of sinking. Then **plan and conduct an experiment** to test your hypothesis. Be sure to **control,** or keep the same, all the variables except the one you are changing and the one you are observing.

Process Skill Tip

Usually in an investigation, only one property is changed at a time. This makes it easier to **infer** the causes of the results. This is called controlling variables.

LEARN ABOUT

How Water Interacts with Other Matter

Water and Sugar

If you put a spoonful of solid sugar into a glass of liquid water and stir, what happens? The sugar seems to disappear. The glass still contains a clear liquid. Where did the sugar go?

The answer is that the sugar and the water formed a kind of mixture called a solution. A **solution** (suh•LOO•shuhn) is a mixture in which the particles of different kinds of matter are mixed evenly with each other. In this case the sugar particles mixed with the water particles. You can't see the sugar, but you can tell it is there because the solution tastes sweet. Another way to show that the sugar is still there is to let the water evaporate, or dry up. After all the water is gone, solid sugar will be left at the bottom of the glass.

FIND OUT

- how solids dissolve in water
- why objects float or sink

VOCABULARY

solution
dissolve
solubility
buoyancy

When you mix sugar and water, they form a solution. What is happening to the sugar as you stir the water? ▼

Dissolving

1. When a lump of sugar dissolves in water, water particles pull sugar particles away from the solid sugar.
2. Moving water particles spread sugar particles to all parts of the solution.
3. After a while all the sugar particles are pulled away by water particles. The sugar is completely dissolved. It can't be seen because the particles are too small and spread out.

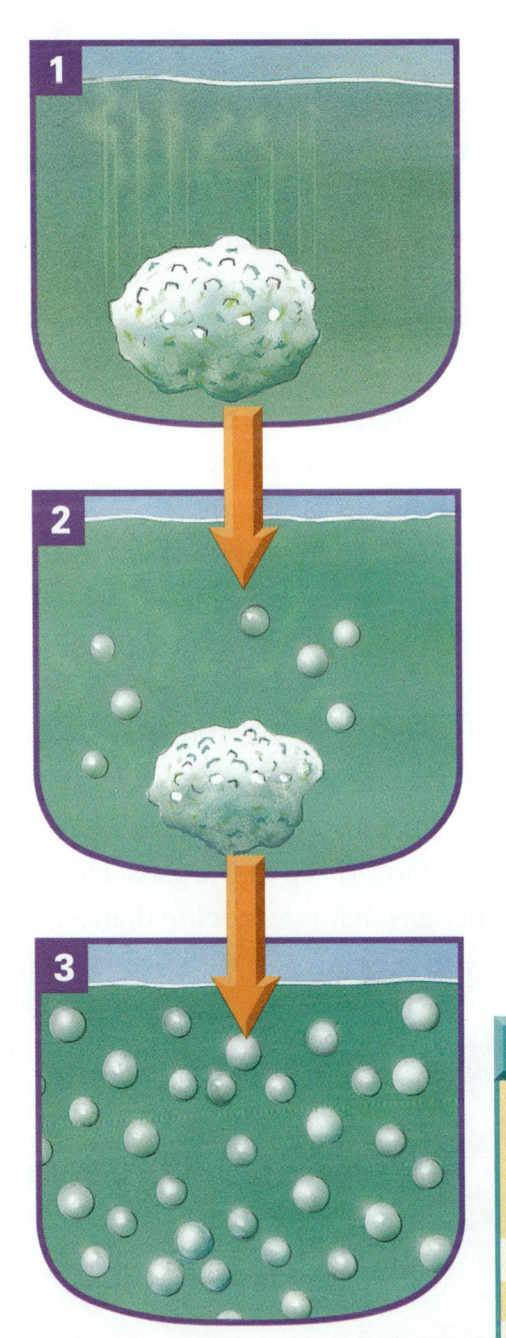

When one material forms a solution with another material, we say it **dissolves** (dih•ZAHLVZ). As sugar dissolves in water, particles of solid sugar are pulled away from each other by water particles. The water particles bump into and move the sugar. Very quickly the sugar particles spread to all parts of the solution. You can no longer see the sugar because the very small sugar particles are mixed evenly with the water particles.

If you add more and more sugar to a glass of water, at some point the sugar particles can't mix evenly with the water particles. The extra sugar doesn't dissolve. When you stop stirring, the extra sugar falls to the bottom of the glass.

Some solids dissolve in water. Other solids do not. Try stirring sand into water. While you are stirring, the sand mixes with the water but does not dissolve. When you stop stirring, the sand falls to the bottom of the jar. **Solubility** (sahl•yoo•BIL•uh•tee) is a measure of the amount of a material that will dissolve in another material. The solubility of sand in water is zero. No amount of sand dissolves in water.

✓ **What happens to a solid when it forms a solution with water?**

Solubility in Water

Material	Volume of Water (mL)	Mass of Materials That Can Be Dissolved in Water at 25°C (g)
Sugar	100	105
Salt	100	36
Baking soda	100	7
Sand	100	0

Floating and Sinking

If you put a coin, such as a penny, into water, it doesn't dissolve. It sinks. A chip of wood doesn't dissolve in water, either. It floats. The ability of matter to float in a liquid or gas is called **buoyancy** (BOY•uhn•see).

A solid object denser than water sinks in water. Lead is more than 11 times as dense as water, so a lead fishing weight rapidly sinks. A solid object less dense than water floats in water. Pine wood is about half as dense as water. So a plank of pine floats.

▲ Most humans have a density that is a little less than 1 gram per cubic centimeter, so they float in water.

If you tied several pine planks together to form a raft, the raft would float because it is made of a material that is less dense than water.

Liquids can also float or sink. Have you ever seen rainbow streaks on puddles on a road or sidewalk? Motor oil floating on the water causes the streaks. The oil floats because it is less dense than water.

Some liquids sink in water. Maple syrup is mostly a sugar solution. It is denser than pure water. Maple syrup sinks to the bottom when you pour it into a glass of water.

Gases can also sink or float. All the gases in the air you breathe are much less dense than liquid water. When you blow through a drinking straw into water, air bubbles are pushed up, or buoyed up, by the water. They rise to the top of the glass. Helium is another gas that is less dense than air. When you fill a balloon with helium, it is buoyed up by the air and rises.

◄ A scuba diver wears a belt or vest with dense pieces of lead. This makes the diver's density about the same as that of water. With the belt on, the diver can swim up or down easily.

The density of the cup and air is less than water so the cup floats.

Most rocks sink. But pumice (PUHM•is) is a kind of rock that contains a lot of air, so pumice floats.

Diet soft drink is less dense than water, so this can of diet soft drink floats. A can of regular soft drink would sink.

Most wood floats, but most metal, like this can opener, sinks.

Remember from Lesson 2 that you can change the density of a material by mixing it with material that has a different density.

Air is not very dense. A good way to lower the density of an object is to add air to it. If you add enough air, the object will become less dense than water. Then it will float. Clay is denser than water. In the investigation you got clay to float by making it into a boat. A boat contains air. The sides and bottom of a boat keep water out and hold air in. The clay boat floated because it contained a lot of air. Even a heavy metal boat will float if it contains enough air.

Most human bodies are a little less dense than water. So, most people float on water. Scuba divers don't want to float or sink. If they floated, they would have to swim hard to stay under water. If they sank, they would have to swim hard to get back to the water's surface. Scuba divers control their buoyancy by wearing a belt or vest loaded with dense lead pieces. While wearing the lead weights, a diver has about the same density as water.

✓ **What is buoyancy?**

Each liquid layer in this beaker has a different density. The densest layer is liquid mercury on the bottom. Even a steel bolt floats on mercury. The less dense materials float on the more dense materials. ▶

E21

Floating Transportation

Humans use machines to control buoyancy and to move from place to place. Submarines, hot-air balloons, and blimps all use buoyancy to help move people. Hot-air balloons are buoyed up by air, so they rise. This is because hot air is less dense than cool air. Blimps are big, football-shaped balloons. They are filled with helium, a gas that is less dense than air. Submarines control their density to float and to sink in the water.

✓ **How is buoyancy used for travel?**

THE INSIDE STORY

How Submarines Work

Submarines can float on top of the ocean or dive down and travel deep under water. They do this by adding or removing water to control their density.

1. When a submarine floats on the surface of the water, it is like any other metal boat. It is filled with enough air to make it float.

2. Tanks inside the submarine have air in them when the submarine is at the surface. To make the submarine float just below the surface, some of the air is taken out and the tanks are partly filled with water. The combination of the submarine, the water, and the air has about the same density as water.

3. The submarine can dive to the bottom by squeezing air in its tanks into smaller tanks. Because the air's volume is now smaller, its density is greater. The original tanks are then filled with water. This makes the metal submarine denser than water. To allow the submarine to return to the surface, water is pumped out of the tanks. Air is allowed to expand back into them. The submarine becomes less dense than water. It is buoyed up and rises to the surface.

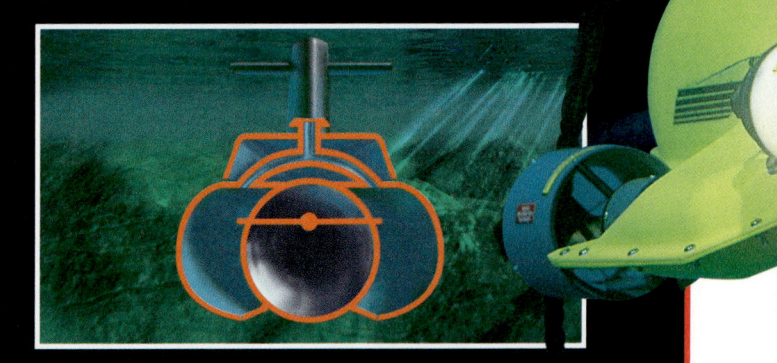

Summary

Solutions are mixtures in which the particles are mixed evenly. Some matter dissolves in water and some does not. Matter that is less dense than water floats on water. Buoyancy can be controlled by changing density.

Review

1. What changes happen to sugar when it dissolves in water? What stays the same?
2. What happens when you add more of a material to water than the water will dissolve?
3. How can you float a piece of solid material that is denser than water?
4. **Critical Thinking** What could you do to make an object float in air?
5. **Test Prep** Any material that floats in water —
   A is denser than water
   B has the same density as water
   C is less dense than water
   D is made of metal

LINKS

MATH LINK

Use Mental Math The greatest amount of sugar you can dissolve in 100 milliliters of water is 105 grams. How much sugar can you dissolve in 1000 milliliters of water?

WRITING LINK

Informative Writing—Explanation Find out what the ancient Greek scientist Archimedes discovered about density. Write an explanation of what you learn for a younger student.

PHYSICAL EDUCATION LINK

Floating and Swimming Find out what survival floating is. Use a model to demonstrate it for your class, or make a poster that explains it.

LITERATURE LINK

Submarine Predictions Read *20,000 Leagues Under the Sea* to find out what French science-fiction writer Jules Verne predicted about the modern submarine.

TECHNOLOGY LINK

Learn more about physical properties of matter by viewing *Peep Science* on the **Harcourt Science Newsroom Video.**

LESSON 4

What Are Chemical and Physical Changes?

In this lesson, you can . . .

- **INVESTIGATE** a chemical change.
- **LEARN ABOUT** physical and chemical changes.
- **LINK** to math, writing, art, and technology.

◀ The bright colors and booming sounds of fireworks are caused by chemical changes.

INVESTIGATE

Changes in a Penny

Activity Purpose A bright, shiny new bicycle looks great. An older, used bicycle looks dull, scratched, and may be rusty. The bicycle looks different because of changes to metal, paint, and other materials. In this activity, you will investigate a change of another metal object. You will **observe, compare,** and **predict** changes of a penny.

Materials
- safety goggles
- 2 paper clips
- foam cup
- vinegar
- 3 pennies
- plastic wrap

CAUTION

Procedure

1. **CAUTION Put on the safety goggles.** Make a coin holder. Bend the paper clip into the shape shown in Picture A.

2. Place one penny flat on the bottom of the cup at one side. Use the second paper clip to attach a penny to the top of the coin holder. Put the coin holder on the bottom of the plastic cup.

3. Carefully pour vinegar down the side of the cup until the flat penny is just covered. The vinegar should be about 1 cm deep at most. (Picture B)

4. Cover the cup tightly with a piece of plastic wrap. Lay the third penny on top of the plastic wrap. Place the cup where it will not be bumped or spilled.

5. **Observe** each penny carefully. Record your observations.

E24

Picture A

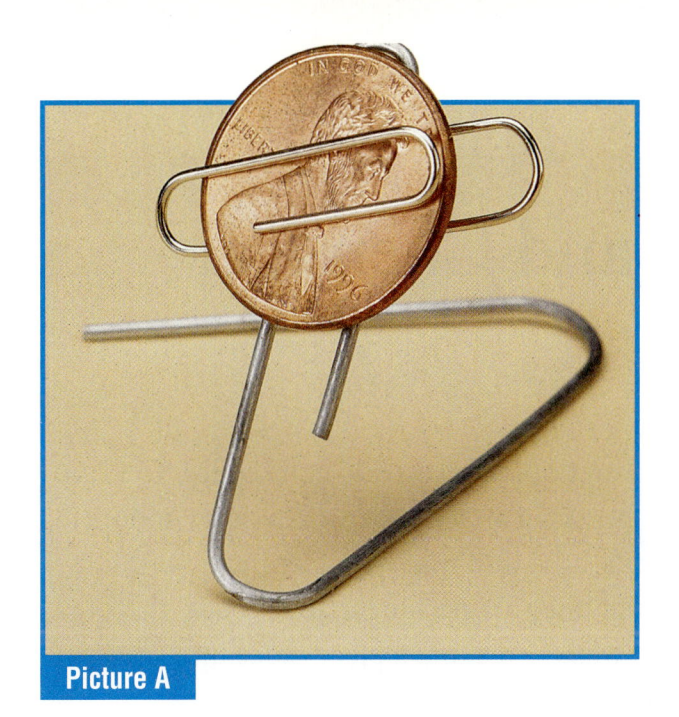

Picture B

6 **Observe** each penny after four hours. **Record** your observations.

7 **Predict** what will happen to each penny after one day.

8 Test your prediction and **record** your observations.

Draw Conclusions

1. **Compare** your observations of the pennies in Steps 5 and 6.

2. Do your observations in Step 8 match the prediction you made in Step 7? Explain.

3. What is the purpose of the penny on the top of the plastic wrap?

4. **Scientists at Work** Scientists **predict** new observations using what they have learned from their past observations. Explain how you used past observations to make your prediction in Step 7.

Investigate Further What will happen if the pennies are replaced by dimes? **Form a hypothesis** about the effect of vinegar on dimes. Then **design and conduct an experiment** to test your hypothesis.

> **Process Skill Tip**
>
> You can tell that a substance has changed by **comparing observations** made at different times. If the observations are different, then the substance has changed.

E25

Physical and Chemical Changes

FIND OUT

- some examples of physical and chemical changes
- how to distinguish between physical and chemical changes

VOCABULARY

physical change
chemical change
chemical reaction

Physical Changes

To cool a glass of water quickly, you add cracked ice. You can make cracked ice by breaking an ice cube with a heavy spoon. The ice changes from a cube into many smaller pieces with different shapes. Although they are no longer an ice cube, the pieces still are frozen water. Breaking a piece of ice into smaller pieces is an example of a change in shape.

An ice cube can change in another way—you can melt it in your hand. In Lesson 1, you learned that melting is a change of state. The melted ice still is water. If you wanted, you could refreeze it and make a new ice cube. These changes of state are physical changes. Any change in the size, shape, or state of a substance is called a **physical change**.

✓ What is a physical change?

How do you change a sheet of paper when you cut it, fold it, or wad it up? Does it change colors? Does it become a piece of cloth? No, of course not. You change only the shape and size of the paper. These changes are examples of physical changes.

Sugar can undergo many physical changes. Even though each form is different, they are all still sugar.

▲ Rock candy is a large crystal of sugar. It is a clear solid with many smooth, flat surfaces.

▲ Sugar cubes are made by pressing together many small grains of sugar. The cubes are not clear or smooth like rock candy, but they still taste sweet.

▲ Table sugar is made up of many separate, tiny crystals. Unlike rock candy or cubes, you can pour and scoop it. It is still sugar.

▲ Confectioners' sugar is made by grinding sugar crystals into powder. It looks different than rock candy, cubes, or grains but it is still sugar.

Heat from the waffle melts the butter. In cold butter, the butter particles move slowly. As butter warms, the particles move faster and can slide past each other. The change from a solid to a liquid is a physical change. ▼

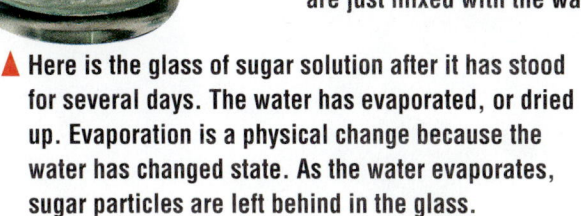

▲ Dissolving is another physical change. When you mix sugar and water, the sugar dissolves in the water. Water particles pull apart the solid sugar into particles of sugar that are too small to be seen. The particles of sugar still taste sweet. They are just mixed with the water.

▲ Here is the glass of sugar solution after it has stood for several days. The water has evaporated, or dried up. Evaporation is a physical change because the water has changed state. As the water evaporates, sugar particles are left behind in the glass.

E27

Chemical Changes

Did you ever bite into an apple and then lay it down? When you picked it up later, parts of it were brown. A change of color is a sign that a new substance formed. A change that produces one or more new substances and may release energy is called a **chemical change**. Remember the color change of the penny in the activity? The dark material was a new substance formed by a chemical reaction. **Chemical reaction** is another term for chemical change.

The sweet smell of baking bread is another sign that a chemical reaction is taking place. The odor is a property of a new substance. The substance forms as the bread dough is cooked. If you watch the dough bake, you also can see it change color from pale white to brown.

When someone strikes a match, you can see light and feel warmth as the match head burns and slowly turns black. Light, energy release, and color change are all signs of a chemical change. Where does the light energy come from? A match head has *potential*, or stored, energy because of the arrangement of its particles. This stored energy is changed to light and heat when the match head burns. Potential energy that can be released by a chemical change is called *chemical energy*. Fuels such as gasoline have chemical energy.

✓ **What are some signs of a chemical change?**

The dark areas on the teapot are a thin layer of a new substance called tarnish. The tarnish is not bright and shiny like silver. A new substance formed when silver and substances in the air combined. Polishing rubs away the tarnish and uncovers the shiny silver again. ▶

◄ The bottle contains vinegar. The snugly fitting balloon contains some baking soda. When vinegar and baking soda mix, the balloon fills with a gas. The filled balloon shows that a new substance formed. A chemical reaction made a gas called carbon dioxide.

◄ The burning gas in a Bunsen burner produces warmth, light, carbon dioxide, and water vapor.

Rust results from a slower chemical change than burning. It is made by a chemical reaction between the metal iron and oxygen, a gas in the air. Rust is a different color and weaker than iron. A new anchor is strong, but this rusty anchor crumbles easily. ▼

◄ Burning is a chemical change. Light and warmth are released. Smoke, ash, and hot gases are produced.

Using Physical and Chemical Changes

Making steel is an important industry because steel is a useful substance. Steel sheets are used to make the outside of washers, dryers, stoves, and refrigerators. Steel beams help support buildings and bridges. Metal spoons, forks, and knives are made of a kind of steel.

The steel industry uses physical and chemical changes. Steel is made in a large furnace. Burning fuel heats iron and other materials until they melt. The melted materials mix to form liquid steel.

Liquid steel is poured into smaller containers, where it cools. The cooled steel is slowly moved into a giant machine. Rows of large, heavy rollers squeeze the steel into long slabs. Sprays of water cool the steel. It slowly hardens.

To make thin sheet steel, the hardened slabs are reheated. Then the hot slabs move through another rolling machine. These rollers squeeze the slabs, making them thinner and thinner. Finally, the thin sheet steel is cut and rolled up for shipment.

✓ **How is a chemical change used to make steel?**

▲ Burning provides the energy to melt the iron and other substances that form steel. The light and thermal energy released show chemical changes are taking place.

To form these rolls of thin sheet steel, large steel bars were heated, partially melted, and rolled thinner and thinner (below left). These changes of state and changes of size and shape are physical changes. ▼

Summary

Physical changes are changes to the size or shape of a substance such as cutting or folding; and changes of state such as melting, freezing, and boiling. During physical changes, no new substances are formed. Chemical changes, or chemical reactions, form new substances. Changes in color or releases of energy show chemical changes have taken place. Burning and rusting are examples of chemical changes.

Review

1. What changes happen to a substance during a physical change?
2. What is a chemical change?
3. Describe one physical change in the production of steel.
4. **Critical Thinking** Is an explosion a slow or fast chemical reaction? Explain your thinking.
5. **Test Prep** Which of the following is a chemical change?
   A boiling some water
   B frying a hamburger
   C sawing a board
   D grinding wheat into flour

LINKS

MATH LINK

Solve a Two-Step Problem Some knife blades are made of hard, high-carbon steel, which can be made very sharp. High-carbon steel is made up mostly of iron with a little carbon. Suppose a block of high-carbon steel contains 396 grams of iron and 4 grams of carbon. What fraction of the block is carbon?

WRITING LINK

Expressive Writing—Song Lyrics You see physical and chemical changes happening all around you. Set them to music. Choose a tune you know. Then write words for a song that will help someone else see these changes, too.

HEALTH LINK

Food Changes Food gives your body energy. To get this energy, your body must change food physically and chemically. Use library resources to find out more about one of these changes. Then report to the class to share what you learned.

TECHNOLOGY LINK

Visit the Harcourt Learning Site for related links, activities, and resources.
www.harcourtschool.com

E31

SCIENCE AND TECHNOLOGY

Plastics You Can Eat

The two inventors of edible plastic

Plastics are artificial materials, or substances that are made by people. They can be shaped into different objects, such as bottles, chairs, or notebook covers. There are hundreds of different plastics, each with its own properties. One new type has an unusual property for a plastic. It dissolves in a special way, so it can be eaten!

Why Would Anyone Want to Eat Plastic?

You wouldn't want to eat regular plastic. It could be harmful. But the people who invented plastic that can be eaten weren't thinking about making it edible. Two students were trying to make green slime in their high-school laboratory for a Halloween trick. But something went wrong.

There was a small explosion. Green slime flew everywhere, covering the laboratory floor, ceiling, and walls. The students cleaned up the mess before anyone found out. But they missed a little bit of slime that landed in a jar.

The next day, their teacher found the green slime in the jar. It was stuck to a glass stirring rod. It looked like a lollipop. It even looked edible, and it really was.

Plastic Coated Medicine

It turned out that the green slime dissolves in the saliva in your mouth, but it doesn't dissolve in just water. This makes it perfect as a coating for pills. It protects the medicine in the pills from moisture in the air, but still is digested easily in the stomach. Other pill coatings take in moisture from the air. This can make the medicine less effective.

Green slime works well for coating medicine that can be absorbed in the stomach. But some medicines, such as the insulin needed by people who have diabetes, are destroyed by the digestive juices in the stomach. For that reason, these medicines are usually given as shots instead of pills. But no one likes to get shots.

Another Edible Plastic

Scientists have invented another kind of edible plastic that won't dissolve in the mouth, the stomach, or even the small intestine. Medicine that has been coated with this plastic gets all the way to the large intestine. There, the plastic absorbs water and gets larger. Tiny holes in the plastic open up as that happens. The medicine gets out through the holes, and the patient gets the medicine without getting a shot.

THINK ABOUT IT

1. What other uses can you think of for edible plastic?
2. Do you know of any other medicines that can't be swallowed that edible plastic could be used for?

CAREERS
INDUSTRIAL ENGINEER

What They Do Industrial engineers design and build machines for factories. They solve problems to help people make things and put things together easily and quickly. For example, they might design the machines to make pills and coat them with plastic. They also might decide what shapes work best for plastic or metal car parts.

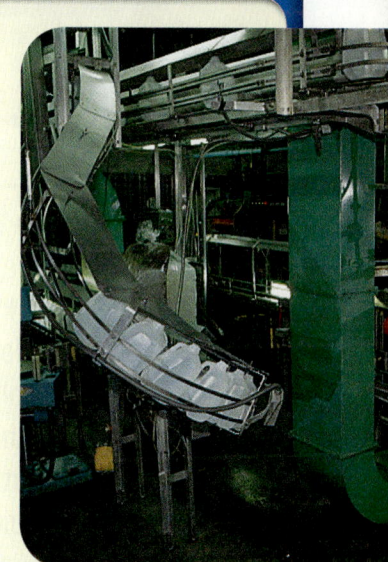

Education and Training

Industrial engineers need a college degree. They may be licensed as a professional engineer by the state they live in. For that, they will need four years of experience and a passing grade on a state test.

WEB LINK
For Science and Technology updates, visit the Harcourt Internet site.
www.harcourtschool.com

PEOPLE IN SCIENCE

Shirley Ann Jackson
PHYSICIST

This is a view downward into the core of a nuclear reactor.

As a little girl in Washington, D.C., Shirley Jackson collected live hornets, bumblebees, and wasps to study. She kept the animals in old mayonnaise jars under the back porch. She also studied fungi and molds around her home. Her father helped her with these science projects. She won first place at a science fair with an experiment on how different environments affect the growth of bacteria.

Jackson graduated first in her class at Roosevelt High School. She won scholarships for college and decided to go to the Massachusetts Institute of Technology (MIT). She became the first African-American woman to receive a doctoral degree, or advanced degree, from MIT.

From 1995 to 1999, she was chairperson of the five-member U.S. Nuclear Regulatory Commission (NRC). NRC makes sure nuclear reactors and radioactive materials are used safely.

In 1998, Jackson was inducted into the National Women's Hall of Fame. She was included because of her work in education, science, and public policy.

In 1999, Jackson became president of Rensselaer Polytechnic Institute, a university in Troy, New York.

THINK ABOUT IT

1. What areas of science first interested Jackson when she was young? What area of science most interests her now?
2. What skills and talents do you think a person needs to work for NRC?

ACTIVITIES FOR HOME OR SCHOOL

LIQUID LAYERS

How does density help you predict which liquids float?

Materials
- 3 clear plastic cups
- water
- corn oil
- maple syrup

Material	Density
water	1 g/mL
corn oil	< 1 g/mL
maple syrup	> 1 g/mL

Procedure
1. Fill one cup about one-fourth full of water.
2. Repeat Step 1 for the corn oil and for the maple syrup.
3. Slowly pour the maple syrup down the inside of the cup containing water. Observe what happens.
4. Predict what will happen when you pour the corn oil into the same cup. Slowly pour the corn oil down the side of the cup. Observe what happens.

Draw Conclusions
What can you conclude about the buoyancy of these liquids?

SOLUBILITY

How can you determine solubility?

Materials
- safety goggles
- rubber gloves
- 200-mL beaker
- water
- balance
- 40 g alum
- small scrap of paper
- stirring stick

Procedure
1. **CAUTION** Put on the goggles and gloves. 
2. Fill the beaker to the 100-mL mark with cold tap water.
3. Measure 25 g of alum on the paper. Use the paper to pour the alum into the water.
4. Stir until the alum dissolves.
5. Measure 1 g of alum, and add it to the beaker. Stir. Observe the solution.
6. Repeat Step 5 until no more alum will dissolve.

Draw Conclusions
What is the solubility of alum?

CHAPTER 1 Review and Test Preparation

Vocabulary Review

Use the terms below to complete the sentences. The page numbers in ( ) tell you where to look in the chapter if you need help.

matter (E6) **solution** (E18)
mass (E6) **dissolve** (E19)
solid (E6) **solubility** (E19)
liquid (E7) **buoyancy** (E20)
gas (E8) **physical change** (E26)
volume (E13) **chemical change** (E28)
density (E14) **chemical reaction** (E28)

1. The ___ of a solid cube is the amount of space it takes up.
2. In a ___, the particles are far away from each other and move quickly.
3. You can't see a solid when you ___ it, because its particles become separated by water particles.
4. If the particles of matter move back and forth around one point, the matter is in the ___ state.
5. The amount of matter in an object is its ___.
6. ___ is a measure of whether an object floats or sinks in a gas or liquid.
7. Particles of matter in the ___ state can slip and slide past each other.
8. When the particles of a mixture are evenly mixed and can't be seen, the mixture is a ___.
9. Air and pine wood each have a ___ that is less than that of water.
10. ___ is a measure of the amount of a material that will dissolve in another material.
11. ___ is anything that takes up space and has mass.
12. Melting is an example of a ___ change.
13. Rusting is an example of a ___ change, which is another name for a ___.

Connect Concepts

Some of the substances and objects mentioned in the chapter are listed in the Word Bank. In the table below, list each substance or object under each of its properties. Use each item as often as necessary.

air   lead weight   water vapor   brick
wood   sugar cube   ice   water

Properties of Matter

Dissolves in Water	Floats in Water	Density About 1 g/mL
14. ___	15. ___	17. ___
	16. ___	

Takes Shape of Container	Sinks in Water	Has No Definite Volume
18. ___	21. ___	23. ___
19. ___	22. ___	24. ___
20. ___		

E36

Check Understanding

Write the letter of the best choice.

25. A boat made from matter that is denser than water can float on water if it is filled with enough —
    A water
    B air
    C salt
    D salt water

26. When two materials are mixed, the ____ of the mixture is between those of the separate materials.
    F mass
    G volume
    H density
    J state

27. Which of the following properties of sugar does **NOT** change when sugar dissolves in water?
    A color
    B shape
    C texture
    D taste

28. The volume of a ____ depends on the size of its container.
    F liquid
    G solid
    H gas
    J solution

29. Formation of a new substance shows that a ____ has happened.
    A physical change
    B change of state
    C solution
    D chemical reaction

Critical Thinking

30. Compare the relationships between particles in ice, water, and water vapor.

31. When a solid dissolves completely in water, what happens to the particles that made up the solid?

Process Skills Review

32. You measure the temperature of four pans of boiling water. Your measurements are 99°C, 100°C, 100°C, and 101°C. What **conclusion** can you **draw** about the temperature at which water boils? Explain your answer.

33. You use the same pan balance to **measure** the mass of a rock on two days. Your measurement is larger on the second day. The rock hasn't changed. How do you explain the difference in measurements?

34. You take a sip from a glass of clear water, and it tastes salty. What can you **infer** about what is in the glass?

35. Suppose that you **observe** a fresh scratch on a bicycle. A few weeks later, you notice that the area under the scratch has changed color. What are two things you can infer by **comparing** your observations?

Performance Assessment

Maximum Float

Use a piece of aluminum foil to make a shape that will float in water. Experiment to find the boat shape that will support the largest number of pennies. Explain the reasons you changed the boat's shape.

E37

CHAPTER 2
Heat—Energy on the Move

Vocabulary Preview

energy
kinetic energy
thermal energy
temperature
heat
conduction
convection
radiation
infrared radiation
fuel
solar energy

You push and shove! Finally the door opens! In summer, doors often stick. This is because materials expand and contract as they get hot and cold. For the same reason, if you put a jar with a stuck lid under hot water, the lid will loosen!

Fast Fact

If you add enough heat, almost anything will boil. If you take away enough heat, things freeze. Water freezes at 0°C (32°F) and boils at 100°C (212°F). Substances freeze and boil at different temperatures.

Freezing and Boiling

Substance	Freezes at °C (°F)	Boils at °C (°F)
Iron	1538 (2800)	2862 (5184)
Mercury	-39 (-38)	357 (675)
Nitrogen	-209 (-344)	-196 (-321)
Oxygen	-218 (-360)	-183 (-297)

Molten iron

Fast Fact

When a light bulb is on, the temperature of the glowing wire inside is a sizzling 2500°C (about 4500°F). That's why the outside of a light bulb gets hot while the bulb is on. The empty space around the wire keeps the bulb from melting and the wire from burning up.

Fast Fact

The temperature of a lightning bolt is estimated to be 30,000°C (54,000°F)! If people could harness the energy from a single lightning bolt, they could light up an average-size town for a year.

LESSON 1

How Does Heat Affect Matter?

In this lesson, you can . . .

INVESTIGATE how heat affects air in a balloon.

LEARN ABOUT thermal energy.

LINK to math, writing, social studies, and technology.

◀ Icicles form when water melts, flows, and freezes again.

E40

INVESTIGATE

Changes in a Heated Balloon

Activity Purpose Have you ever wondered why a hot-air balloon rises? Or how a thermometer measures temperature? The answers have something in common—a property of matter. In this investigation you will **measure** changes in a balloon as it is heated. Then you'll **infer** what caused the changes.

Materials
- desk lamp
- bulb
- safety goggles
- 3 rubber balloons
- string
- ruler
- stopwatch or clock with second hand

CAUTION

Activity Procedure

1. Turn on the lamp, and let the light bulb get warm.

2. **CAUTION** **Put on your safety goggles.** Blow up a rubber balloon just enough to stretch it. Tie it closed.

3. **Measure** the length of the balloon with the ruler. **Record** the measurement. (Picture A)

4. Carefully hold the balloon by its tied end about 3 cm above the lamp. Hold it there for two minutes. (Picture B) **CAUTION** **The light bulb is hot. Do not touch it with your hands or with the balloon. Observe** what happens to the balloon. **Record** your observations.

Picture A

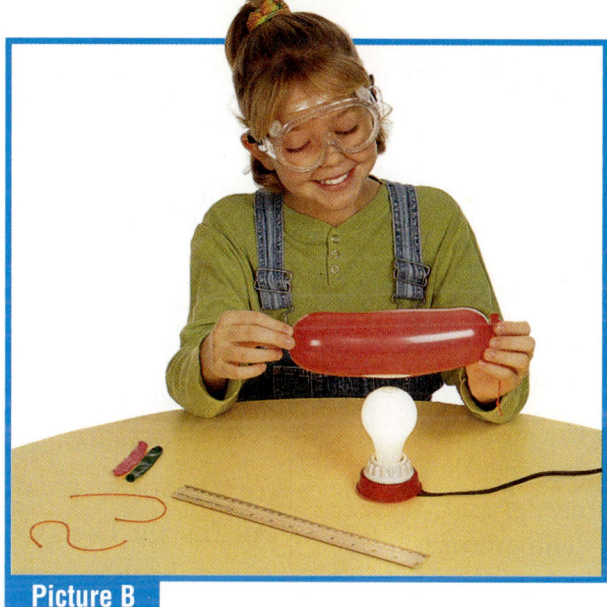

Picture B

5. **Measure** the length of the balloon while it is still over the lamp. **Record** the measurement.

6. Repeat Steps 2 through 5 using a new balloon each time.

Draw Conclusions

1. What did you **observe** as you warmed the balloons?

2. **Compare** the lengths of the heated balloons with the lengths of the unheated balloons.

3. What can you **infer** happened to the air inside the balloons as you heated it?

4. **Scientists at Work** Scientists often **measure** several times to make sure the measurements are accurate. In this investigation you measured the lengths of three different balloons. Were the measurements all the same? Explain.

Investigate Further Fill a balloon with water that is at room temperature. Put the balloon on a desk and **measure** its length. Heat the balloon by putting it in a bowl of hot tap water for 15 minutes. Take the balloon out of the bowl and measure its length. **Compare** these lengths with those you measured with the air-filled balloons in the investigation.

Process Skill Tip

Scientists often observe and **measure** an object or an event several times. Patterns among measurements may show something important in an investigation.

LEARN ABOUT

Matter and Energy

Thermal Energy

Have you ever thrown a ball? Pushed a grocery cart? Run in a race? All these activities need energy. **Energy** is the ability to cause a change. In each of these cases, you transferred energy to the object and its motion changed. The ball flew through the air. The grocery cart rolled through the store. You moved along the racetrack. Each of these three objects gained **kinetic** (kih•NET•ihk) **energy**, or energy of motion.

The much smaller particles in matter are always moving from one place to another at random. The particles in a solid jiggle back and forth like balls on a spring. The particles in a liquid slide past each other. The particles in a gas move quickly in many directions. All of this movement requires energy. The kinetic energy of particles in matter is called **thermal energy**. The word *thermal* means "heat." We feel the thermal energy of the particles in matter as heat.

✓ What is thermal energy?

FIND OUT

- what thermal energy is
- the difference between thermal energy and temperature

VOCABULARY

energy
kinetic energy
thermal energy
temperature

Water boils when its particles are moving so fast that many begin to fly away from its surface. This happens when the water's temperature is 100°C (212°F). ▼

When liquid water freezes, its particles settle into an arrangement as a solid. This happens when the temperature of the water is 0°C (32°F). The ice cubes and lemonade are at 0°C. ▼

1. These balls stand for particles in a solid. The springs stand for the forces holding the solid together. Particles in a solid keep their arrangement, but they move back and forth around a point.

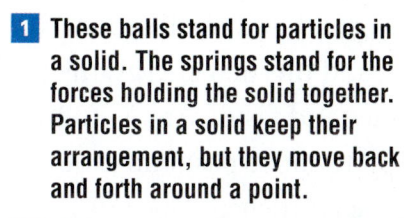

2. When you add thermal energy, the particles move faster. The solid gets hotter.

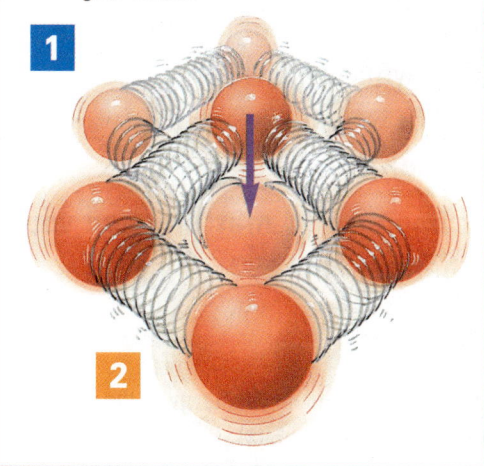

▲ The water in this cup is the same temperature as the nearly boiling water in the hot spring. But the water in the spring has more thermal energy because it has more water and, therefore, more moving particles of matter.

Temperature

Most people think that temperature is a measure of heat. Actually, **temperature** is a measure of the average energy of motion of the particles in matter. At 50°F (about 10°C) the particles in the air move more slowly than they do at 80°F (about 27°C). They have less thermal energy.

In the investigation you heated a balloon and observed how its volume changed. You can measure temperature by observing how the volume of a liquid changes as it is heated or cooled. One kind of thermometer has liquid in a narrow tube. When the liquid gets hotter, its volume changes and it moves up the tube. When it gets colder, it moves back down the tube.

✓ What does temperature measure?

Temperature and Thermal Energy

Two pieces of matter can be at the same temperature but not have the same amount of thermal energy. Temperature measures the *average* amount of motion of the particles in a piece of matter. Thermal energy is the *total* energy of motion of the particles in a piece of matter. More matter equals more particles. More particles equals more energy of motion.

When a drop of cold water falls into a hot pan or skillet, the water boils away in a second or two. Its particles speed up and fly off. Little thermal energy is needed to warm the drop to 100°C (212°F). A pan full of cold water has many more particles. It takes much more thermal energy to boil the water.

✓ What is the difference between temperature and thermal energy?

Adding Thermal Energy

▲ When thermal energy is added to frozen water, the water slowly changes from a solid to a liquid and then from a liquid to a gas. When thermal energy is removed from water vapor, this process is reversed.

Adding Thermal Energy

When thermal energy is added to matter, the particles in the matter move faster. Below 0°C (32°F) water is solid ice. The particles move back and forth around one point. As you add thermal energy, the particles move faster and faster. At 0°C (32°F) the particles begin to move past and around each other. The ice melts.

After ice melts, adding energy causes the particles of liquid water to move faster and faster. The temperature of the liquid water rises. After a while, particles begin to fly away from the water's surface. The water boils, or rapidly becomes a gas.

✔ **What happens to matter when you add thermal energy?**

Water vapor in the air loses energy to the cold air outside the window. First, it becomes small water droplets on the glass. Then, it becomes a solid and forms these ice crystals. ▼

Summary

Energy is the ability to cause change. Energy is needed to move something from one place to another. The total energy of motion of the particles in matter is thermal energy. More particles mean more total thermal energy. Temperature is a measure of the average motion of the particles in matter. Adding thermal energy causes the particles of matter to move faster.

Review

1. What does temperature measure?
2. If all particles in a metal spoon start moving faster, how has the spoon's temperature changed?
3. When you add thermal energy to matter, what happens?
4. **Critical Thinking** The water in two glasses has the same average energy of motion. One glass holds 250 mL, and one holds 400 mL. Which glass of water has more thermal energy? Why?
5. **Test Prep** The particles in two pieces of chocolate have the same average energy of motion. One piece has more mass than the other. Which piece is at a higher temperature?

   A the piece with more mass
   B the piece with less mass
   C the piece with more thermal energy
   D They are the same temperature.

LINKS

MATH LINK

Measure Temperature On a Fahrenheit temperature scale, water freezes at 32°F and boils at 212°F. How many Fahrenheit degrees are between the two temperatures? Now think about the boiling and freezing temperatures in Celsius degrees. Are Celsius degrees bigger or smaller units of measure than Fahrenheit degrees?

WRITING LINK

Expressive Writing—Poem Write a poem for your family that describes a hot day and a cold day. You could describe how your neighborhood looks, things people do, and how you feel.

SOCIAL STUDIES LINK

Early Thermometers Find out who invented the first thermometers and temperature scales and how the thermometers worked. Make a time line that shows what you learned.

TECHNOLOGY LINK

Visit the Harcourt Learning Site for related links, activities, and resources.
www.harcourtschool.com

LESSON 2

How Can Thermal Energy Be Transferred?

In this lesson, you can . . .

INVESTIGATE one way thermal energy is transferred.

LEARN ABOUT the three ways thermal energy is transferred.

LINK to math, writing, art, and technology.

INVESTIGATE

Hot Air

Activity Purpose Have you ever watched a hawk soaring high in the sky? The hawk rides on air that is moving up. But what makes the air move up? In this investigation you will **observe** the effects of air moving up and **infer** why the air is moving up.

Materials
- sheet of construction paper
- scissors
- straight pin
- 20-cm piece of thread
- desk lamp
- bulb

Activity Procedure

1. **CAUTION** **Be careful when using scissors.** Cut out a spiral strip about 2 cm wide from the sheet of construction paper. (Picture A)

2. **CAUTION** **Be careful with the pin.** With the pin, carefully make a small hole through the center of the paper spiral. Tie the thread through the hole.

◀ A glass blower uses a tube to blow air into hot glass. The long tube keeps heat from the glass away from his face. How can you tell the glass is hot?

E46

Picture A

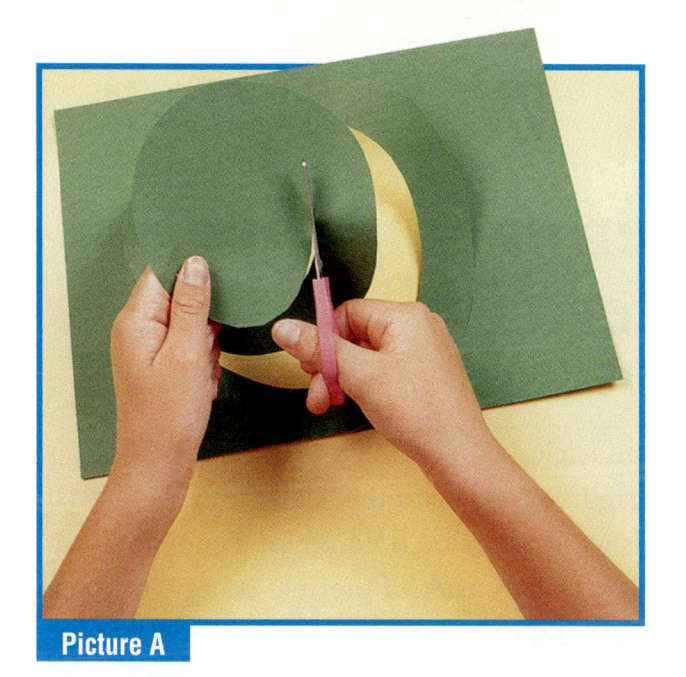

Picture B

3 Hold the spiral above your head by the thread. Blow upward on it. **Observe** the spiral.

4 Carefully hold the spiral a few centimeters above the unlighted desk lamp. **Observe** the spiral.

5 Turn on the desk lamp. Let the bulb warm up for a few minutes.

6 Carefully hold the spiral a few centimeters above the lighted desk lamp. **Observe** the spiral. (Picture B)

Draw Conclusions

1. What did you **observe** in Steps 3, 4, and 6?
2. What caused the result you **observed** in Step 3?
3. What was different about Steps 4 and 6?
4. **Scientists at Work** Scientists often **infer** from **observations** a cause that they can't see directly. What do you think caused the result you observed in Step 6?

Investigate Further Hold the spiral a few centimeters away from the side of the lighted desk lamp. **Observe** the spiral. What can you **infer** from your observation?

Process Skill Tip

You need to **observe** what an object does in different situations before you can **infer** the causes of what it does.

E47

LEARN ABOUT

How Thermal Energy Is Transferred

FIND OUT

- what heat is
- three ways thermal energy is transferred

VOCABULARY

heat
conduction
convection
radiation
infrared radiation

Heat

When you touch an icicle, some of the thermal energy in your hand is transferred, or moved, to the icicle. Your hand gets colder. The icicle gets warmer. If you hold on long enough, the icicle melts completely. This transfer of thermal energy from one piece of matter to another is called **heat**.

Thermal energy is transferred naturally from hot matter to cold matter. When you walk in warm sand, some of the thermal energy from the sand moves to your feet. The soles of your feet get warmer. When your lips touch a cold can of soft drink, thermal energy is transferred from your lips to the can. Your lips lose thermal energy and get cooler. The can gains thermal energy and gets warmer.

Thermal energy is transferred in three ways—conduction, convection, and radiation. You will learn more about these processes on the next pages.

✓ **What is heat?**

◀ The burning gases from the artist's torch are very hot. A large amount of thermal energy moves to the metal where the gases touch it. The metal glows and quickly melts.

Conduction

You can tell if tap water is hot by touching the metal faucet it is running through. This works because the particles of hot water are moving fast and bump into the particles of the faucet, causing them to start moving fast as well. In other words, the particles of hot water transfer thermal energy to the faucet. Soon the faucet and the water are the same temperature. The transfer of thermal energy by particles bumping into each other is called conduction (kuhn•DUHK•shuhn).

Conduction is how thermal energy moves from an electric stove burner to a metal pan. Conduction is also how you can get a painful burn if you touch the pan.

Most metals conduct thermal energy well. They are good *conductors*. But some kinds of matter do not conduct thermal energy so well. A foam cup, for example, is a very poor conductor of thermal energy. If a foam cup were filled with hot cocoa, the cocoa would get cold long before the outside of the cup became hot to the touch. Materials that don't conduct thermal energy well are called *insulators*.

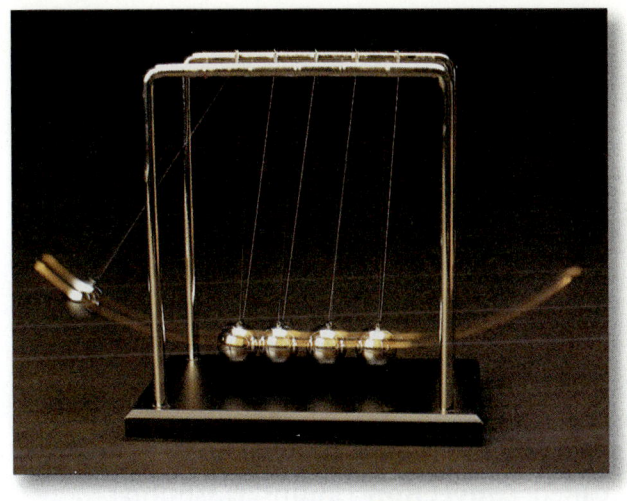

▲ A moving ball transfers motion energy when it bumps into its neighbor. A particle in matter transfers motion energy when it bumps into a nearby particle.

✓ **What is conduction?**

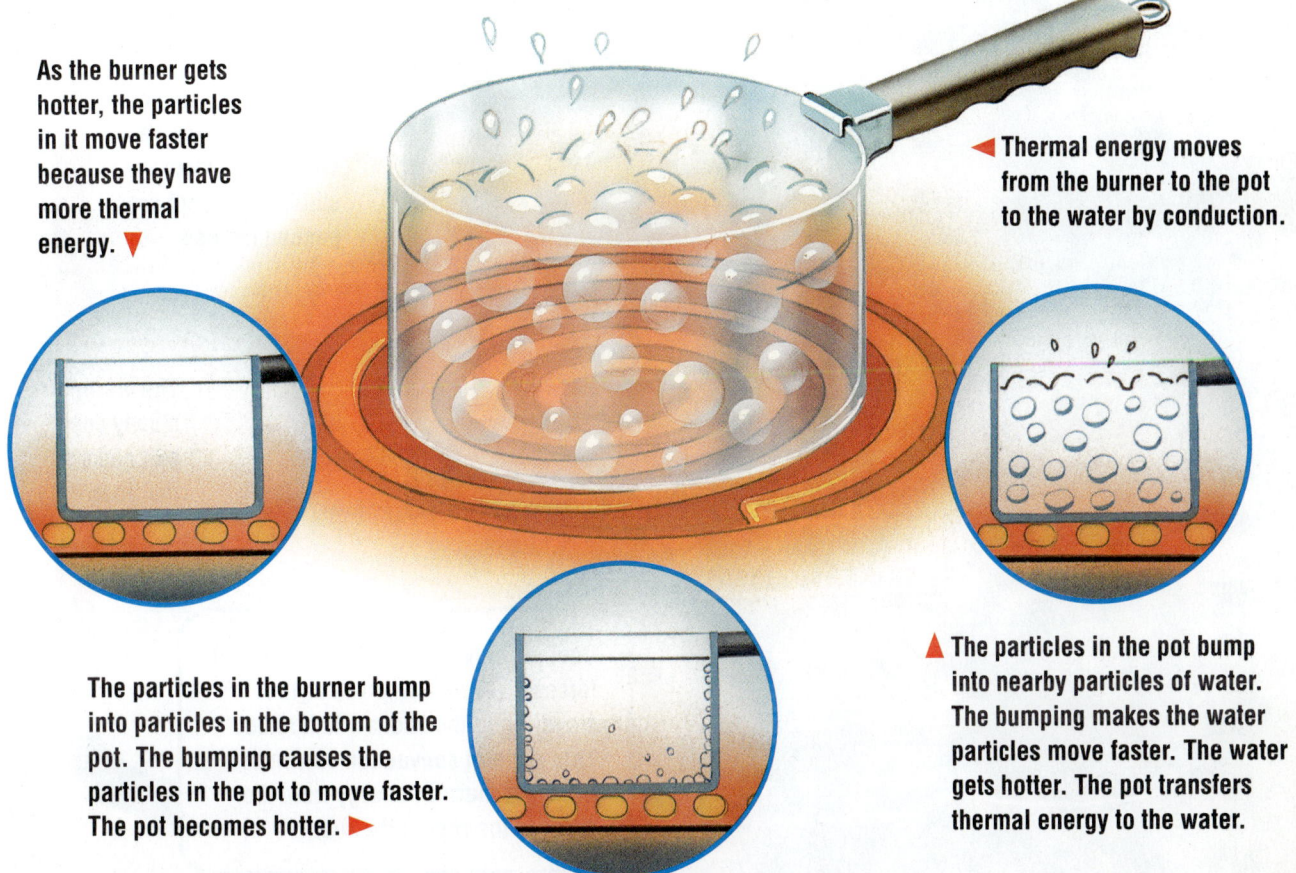

As the burner gets hotter, the particles in it move faster because they have more thermal energy. ▼

◀ Thermal energy moves from the burner to the pot to the water by conduction.

The particles in the burner bump into particles in the bottom of the pot. The bumping causes the particles in the pot to move faster. The pot becomes hotter. ▶

▲ The particles in the pot bump into nearby particles of water. The bumping makes the water particles move faster. The water gets hotter. The pot transfers thermal energy to the water.

Convection

Unlike particles in solids, particles in liquids and gases move from one place to another. In the investigation, you held a paper spiral above a lighted bulb. The heated air above the light bulb moved enough to cause the spiral to twirl. In this case, a large group of hot particles of air moved and transferred thermal energy. This type of energy transfer in a liquid or a gas is called **convection** (kuhn•VEK•shuhn).

As the air near a hot object gets hot, it takes up more space, or expands. You saw a balloon expand in the investigation on pages E40–E41. Because the hot air is less dense, it is forced up by the cooler, denser air around it.

As the hot air is forced up, it warms the air around it. As the hot air cools, its density increases, and it sinks. This process can repeat. The air can move in a circle—warming, being pushed up, cooling, sinking, and then warming again. This pattern of movement is called a *convection current*.

✓ **What is convection?**

The air above the stove gets warm. Cool air pushes in and forces the warm air up. The warm air moves through the room and transfers energy to the things around it.

◀ As cooler air pushes up air warmed by a campfire, sparks, smoke, and soot are pushed up also.

The warm air slowly cools and sinks to the floor.

Cool air moves toward the stove and forces up the warm air near the stove. Then the cool air is heated. This cycle of convection currents transfers thermal energy from the stove to the rest of the room.

THE INSIDE STORY

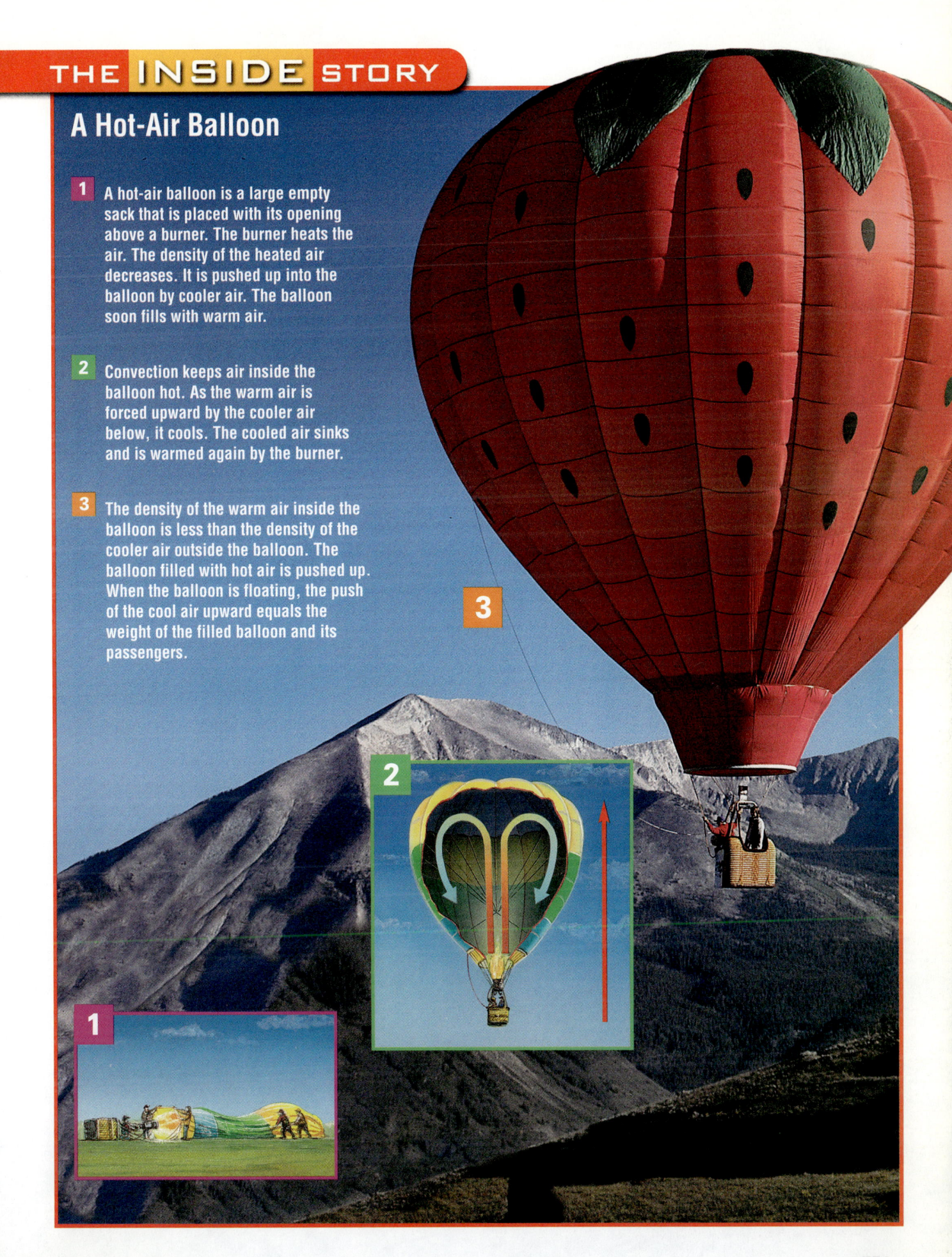

A Hot-Air Balloon

1 A hot-air balloon is a large empty sack that is placed with its opening above a burner. The burner heats the air. The density of the heated air decreases. It is pushed up into the balloon by cooler air. The balloon soon fills with warm air.

2 Convection keeps air inside the balloon hot. As the warm air is forced upward by the cooler air below, it cools. The cooled air sinks and is warmed again by the burner.

3 The density of the warm air inside the balloon is less than the density of the cooler air outside the balloon. The balloon filled with hot air is pushed up. When the balloon is floating, the push of the cool air upward equals the weight of the filled balloon and its passengers.

Radiation

The sun produces great amounts of thermal energy. But there's no matter between Earth and the sun to which it can transfer that energy. So energy can't reach Earth by conduction or convection. The sun transfers bundles of energy that can move through matter and empty space. Bundles of energy that move through matter and empty space are called **radiation** (ray•dee•AY•shuhn).

You sense some bundles of energy with your eyes. This radiation is visible light. You sense other bundles of energy with your skin. These bundles of energy are carrying heat. Bundles of energy that carry heat are called **infrared** (in•fruh•RED) **radiation**. Outside on a sunny day, your skin feels warm because of infrared radiation from the sun.

Some things can transfer energy by conduction, convection, and radiation at the same time. For example, the air above a campfire is warmed by convection. This hot air quickly warms your hands by conduction. You can warm your hands around the sides of a campfire, too. But it is radiation, not hot air, that is warming them.

✓ **How is thermal energy transferred from the sun?**

▼ A gila (HEE•luh) monster warms its body by moving to a sunny place where its skin absorbs infrared radiation.

E52

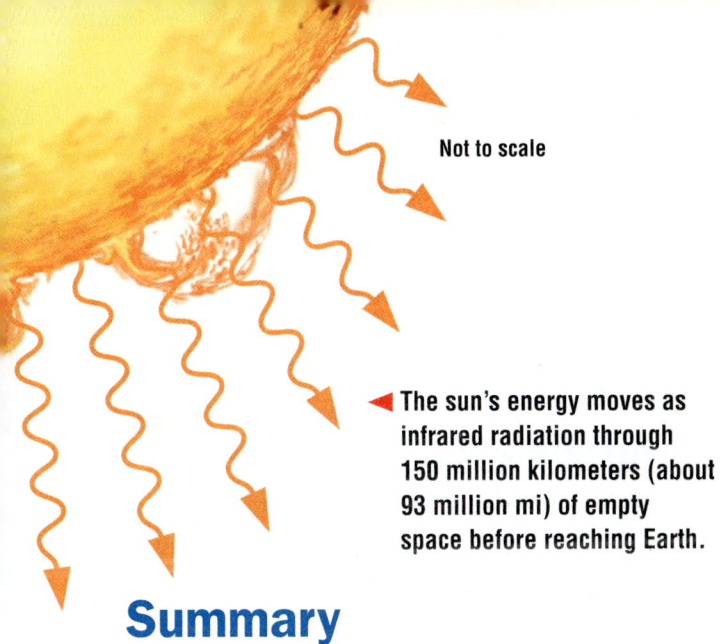

◀ The sun's energy moves as infrared radiation through 150 million kilometers (about 93 million mi) of empty space before reaching Earth.

Not to scale

Summary

Heat is the transfer of thermal energy from one piece of matter to another. Thermal energy naturally moves from warm matter to cool matter. Conduction and convection need moving particles of matter to transfer thermal energy. Energy is transferred as infrared radiation through matter and empty space.

Review

1. Which type of thermal-energy transfer requires moving liquids and gases?
2. How is energy transferred through empty space?
3. How is thermal energy transferred when particles are touching?
4. **Critical Thinking** Which type of thermal-energy transfer is prevented when a baker uses a potholder to remove hot cookie sheets from an oven?
5. **Test Prep** What property must be different between two pieces of matter for thermal energy to be transferred between them?
   A density
   B mass
   C temperature
   D volume

LINKS

MATH LINK

Solve a Two-Step Problem The ability of air conditioners to cool air is rated in British thermal units (Btus). It takes about 12,000 Btus to cool a room that measures 500 square feet. How many Btus are needed to cool a room with 100 square feet of floor space?

WRITING LINK

Persuasive Writing—Business Letter Imagine that you are selling a furnace for a house to a homeowner. Write a letter describing the furnace and giving reasons for the homeowner to buy it.

ART LINK

Icons A "don't walk" sign that shows a walking person inside a circle with a slanted line across it is an icon. So is a smiley face. Design icons that show (1) heating by conduction, (2) heating by convection, and (3) heating by radiation.

TECHNOLOGY LINK

Learn more about how thermal energy is used to shape glass by viewing *Glass Blowing* on the **Harcourt Science Newsroom Video.**

E53

LESSON 3

How Is Thermal Energy Produced and Used?

In this lesson, you can . . .

- **INVESTIGATE** temperatures in a solar cooker.
- **LEARN ABOUT** ways to produce and use thermal energy.
- **LINK** to math, writing, literature, and technology.

INVESTIGATE

Temperatures in a Solar Cooker

Activity Purpose You know that heat from a campfire can cook hot dogs. Heat from the sun can cook them, too. A solar cooker uses a mirror to reflect, or bounce, infrared radiation from the sun to the food. In this activity you will make a mirror to reflect infrared radiation onto a thermometer. You will then **gather, record, display,** and **interpret data** about the temperatures in the cooker.

Materials
- 2 sheets of graph paper
- shoe-box lid
- aluminum foil
- thermometer
- clock or watch
- scissors
- poster board
- glue
- string

Activity Procedure

1. Label the two sheets of graph paper like the example shown on page E55.

2. Place the thermometer in the shoe-box lid. (Picture A)

3. Place the lid in sunlight. **Record** the temperature immediately. Then record the temperature each minute for 10 minutes.

4. In the shade, remove the thermometer from the shoe-box lid.

◀ Most people like pizza best when it is crisp and fresh from the oven. This pizza oven burns wood to produce thermal energy for baking. In what other ways is thermal energy produced and used?

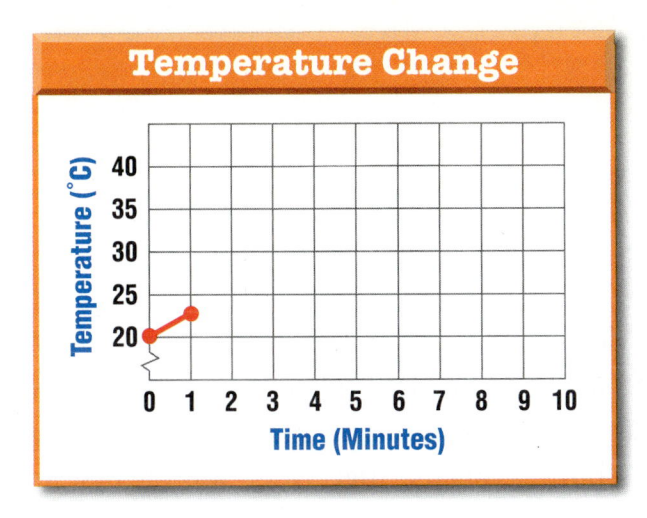

Temperature Change

Picture A

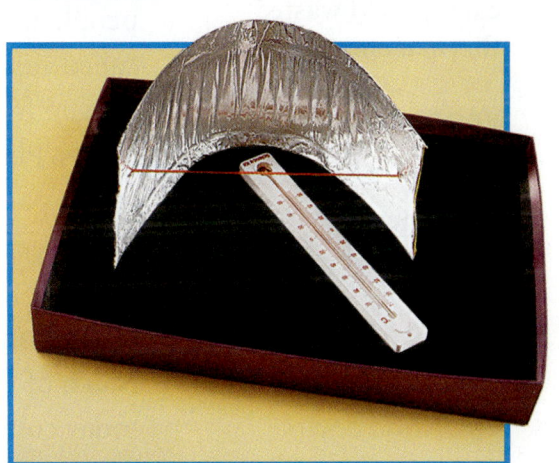

Picture B

5. Cut a rectangle of poster board 10 cm by 30 cm. Glue foil to one side. Let the glue dry for 10 minutes.

6. **CAUTION** **Be careful when using scissors.** Use scissors to punch a hole about 2 cm from each end of the rectangle. Make a curved reflector by drawing the poster board ends toward each other with string until they are about 20 cm apart. Tie the string.

7. Put the curved reflector in the shoe-box lid. Put the thermometer in the center of the curve. Repeat Step 3. (Picture B)

8. Make a line graph of the measurements in Step 3. Make another line graph of the measurements in Step 7.

Draw Conclusions

1. Describe the temperature changes shown on each graph.
2. **Compare** the temperature changes shown on the two graphs.
3. **Infer** what may have caused the differences in the temperatures on the two graphs.

Investigate Further Use what you observed in the activity to **form a hypothesis** about how quickly a different size cooker would warm up. **Plan and conduct an experiment** to test your hypothesis.

Process Skill Tip

When scientists **interpret data** shown on graphs, they look at the slants of the lines on the graphs. In your graphs a line with a steep slant means a fast change in the temperature. A line with a less steep slant means a slower temperature change.

LEARN ABOUT

FIND OUT
- ways to produce thermal energy
- uses of the sun's energy
- examples of wasted thermal energy

VOCABULARY
fuel
solar energy

Using Thermal Energy

Burning Fuel

When something burns, it gets hot. Burning releases thermal energy and light. Many homes are heated by furnaces that burn oil or natural gas. Some cooking stoves burn natural gas. Any material that can burn is called a **fuel**. Wood was the first fuel people used, and it is still used today. Wood contains a substance called carbon. When wood burns, the carbon combines with oxygen from the air. A new substance called carbon dioxide forms. Plants use carbon dioxide to make food. Carbon dioxide is also part of the *greenhouse effect*, which helps keep Earth warm. (See page D12.)

Many fuels contain carbon. Coal is mainly carbon. Fuel oil and natural gas both contain carbon. Much of the thermal energy people use today comes from burning fuels that contain carbon.

✓ **What happens when a fuel burns?**

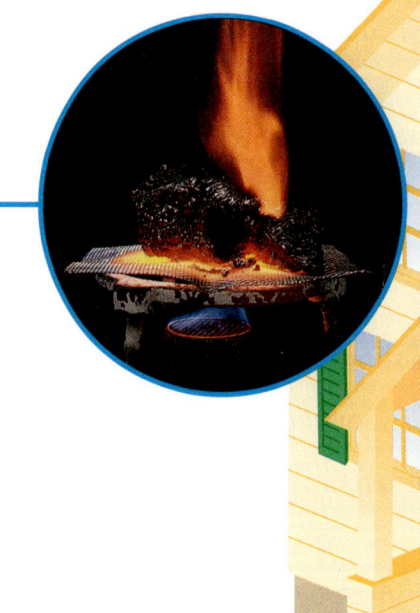

Burning coal releases thermal energy. In some houses the energy is used to warm air directly. In others it is used to heat water in radiators. Like the burner below the coal, a gas stove burns natural gas. The thermal energy released from the flame is used for cooking and baking.

Most of the electricity used in the United States is produced by energy stations that burn fuels.

E56

Solar Energy

The energy given off by the sun is called **solar energy**. People use solar energy to heat water. They put solar panels on top of their roofs. The panels absorb infrared radiation from the sun. The radiation heats water flowing through the panels. The hot water can be used for washing. Solar energy also heats some homes and businesses.

Solar energy can also be used to cook. A solar cooker gathers infrared radiation from the sun and reflects it onto food. You know this works because you measured temperature change in a solar cooker in the investigation.

The sun is the source of most energy on Earth. Even the thermal energy in fossil fuels, such as coal and oil, came from the sun. These fuels have stored energy from plants and animals that lived long ago. The plants used the sun's energy to make food by photosynthesis. The animals got their energy by eating plants or other animals.

✓ **What is solar energy?**

▲ Rooftop solar panels like these are used to heat water.

▲ An electric water heater contains a tank of water. Under the tank is an electric heating coil.

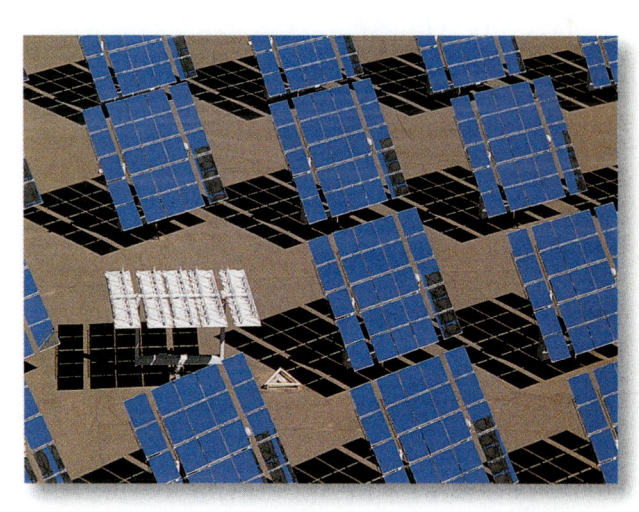

▲ These mirrors focus the sun's thermal energy on a target. The thermal energy gathered in the target is used to produce electricity.

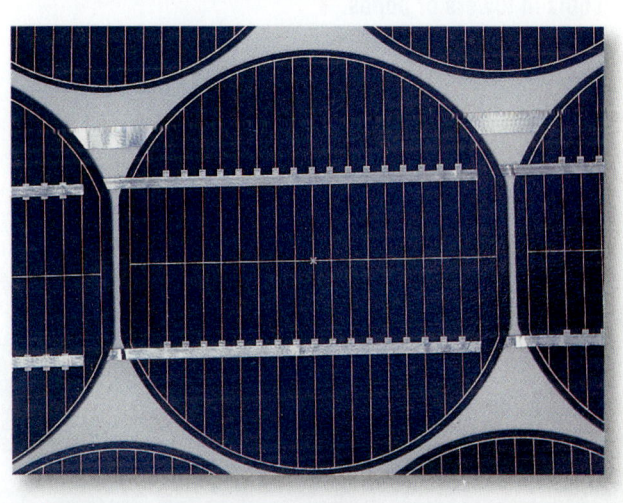

▲ Small appliances such as calculators and watches often use solar cells such as these to supply electricity. Solar cells can also keep batteries charged.

Waste Heat

Using fuel for energy has a side effect. It often makes thermal energy that no one wants or needs. This unneeded thermal energy is called *waste heat*. For example, a campfire produces thermal energy even if the campers need it only for light. Even a campfire used for warmth sends most of its thermal energy straight up, where it is not useful to campers.

Common light sources such as candles and bulbs also make waste heat. So do car engines, electric energy stations, computers, and people. Almost any time energy is produced or used, thermal energy is a part of the process. Much of that thermal energy is not useful, and it can even be harmful. It must be gotten rid of. For example, cars have radiators to carry thermal energy that is not needed away from the engine.

✓ **What is waste heat?**

▲ Light bulbs give off both light and heat. But most of the thermal energy from light bulbs in your home is waste heat.

A candle produces less light than a light bulb but can produce more thermal energy. Most of the thermal energy from candles is not used. ▶

Electric energy stations can't change all thermal energy from fuel into electricity. There is always some waste heat produced. One way to remove this waste heat is to let it heat water. The hot water then cools in towers or ponds. ▼

Fans and radiators carry waste heat away from a car engine. If either the fan or the radiator stops working, the engine soon overheats and stops working as well. ▼

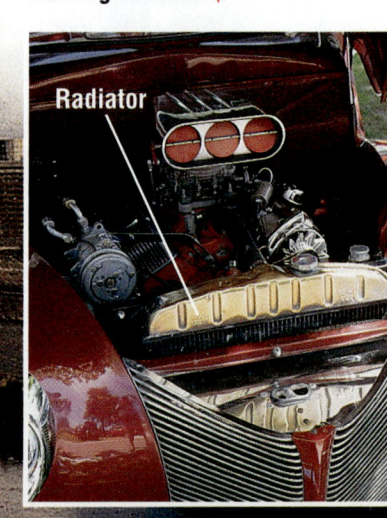

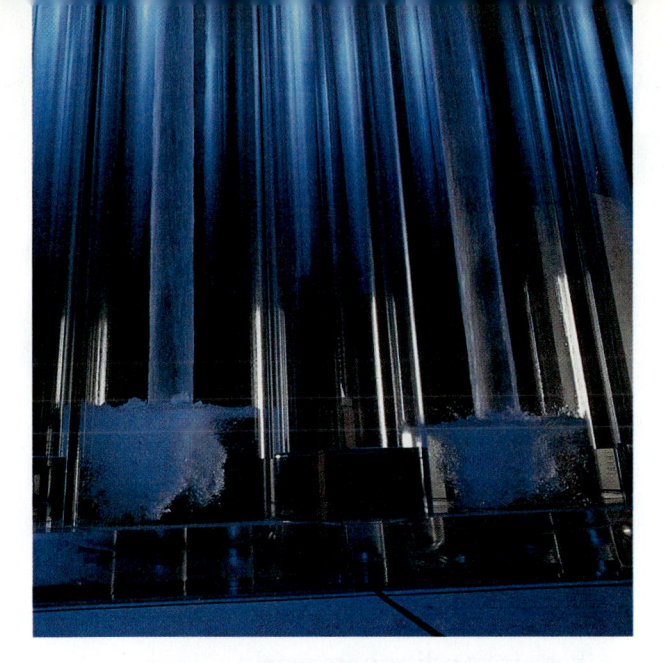

▲ Large, very fast computers need special cooling systems such as this one to get rid of waste heat from wiring and circuits.

Summary

Much of the thermal energy used by people today comes from burning fuels that contain carbon. Energy given off by the sun is called solar energy. Solar energy can be used to heat homes and businesses, heat water, and cook food. Most processes that use energy also produce thermal energy. If this thermal energy isn't useful, it is waste heat.

Review

1. What is a fuel?
2. What happens when a fuel burns?
3. What do we call energy given off by the sun?
4. **Critical Thinking** What happens to most waste heat?
5. **Test Prep** Which of the following removes waste heat?
   A car radiator
   B solar cell
   C stove burner
   D windmill

LINKS

MATH LINK

Solve a Two-Step Problem A water heater produces a total of 500 Btus of thermal energy each hour. Only 400 Btus go to heat water. How much waste heat is produced per hour? How much waste heat is produced in a 24-hour day?

WRITING LINK

Persuasive Writing—Opinion A new kind of light bulb, called a compact fluorescent bulb, produces less waste heat than an incandescent light bulb. Write an ad telling consumers why you think they should use this new bulb.

LITERATURE LINK

A Cold Time in the North In Jack London's short story "To Build a Fire," a man lost in the wilderness has a lot of trouble getting thermal energy. Read the story and suggest other ways the man might have kept warm.

TECHNOLOGY LINK

Learn more about fossil fuels and thermal energy by visiting this Internet site.
www.scilinks.org/harcourt

SCIENCE AND TECHNOLOGY
REFRIGERANTS

Hot weather and high humidity can be unpleasant. For some people, such as older people or those with lung diseases, heat can even be dangerous. Their bodies don't work well enough to stay cool. They need to be kept cool by air conditioning.

Air Conditioning

You already know that when thermal energy moves from one place to another, the place it moves *to* gets hotter. The place it moves *from* gets colder. That's part of what makes air conditioners work.

An air conditioner is a machine that uses energy to move heat in the opposite direction from where it would flow on its own. An air conditioner moves heat from inside a house to the outdoors, where it's hotter. To do this, an air conditioner uses a material called a *refrigerant* (ree•FRIJ•er•uhnt).

In an air conditioner, liquid refrigerant is pumped under pressure through tubes. In the part of the air conditioner that is inside

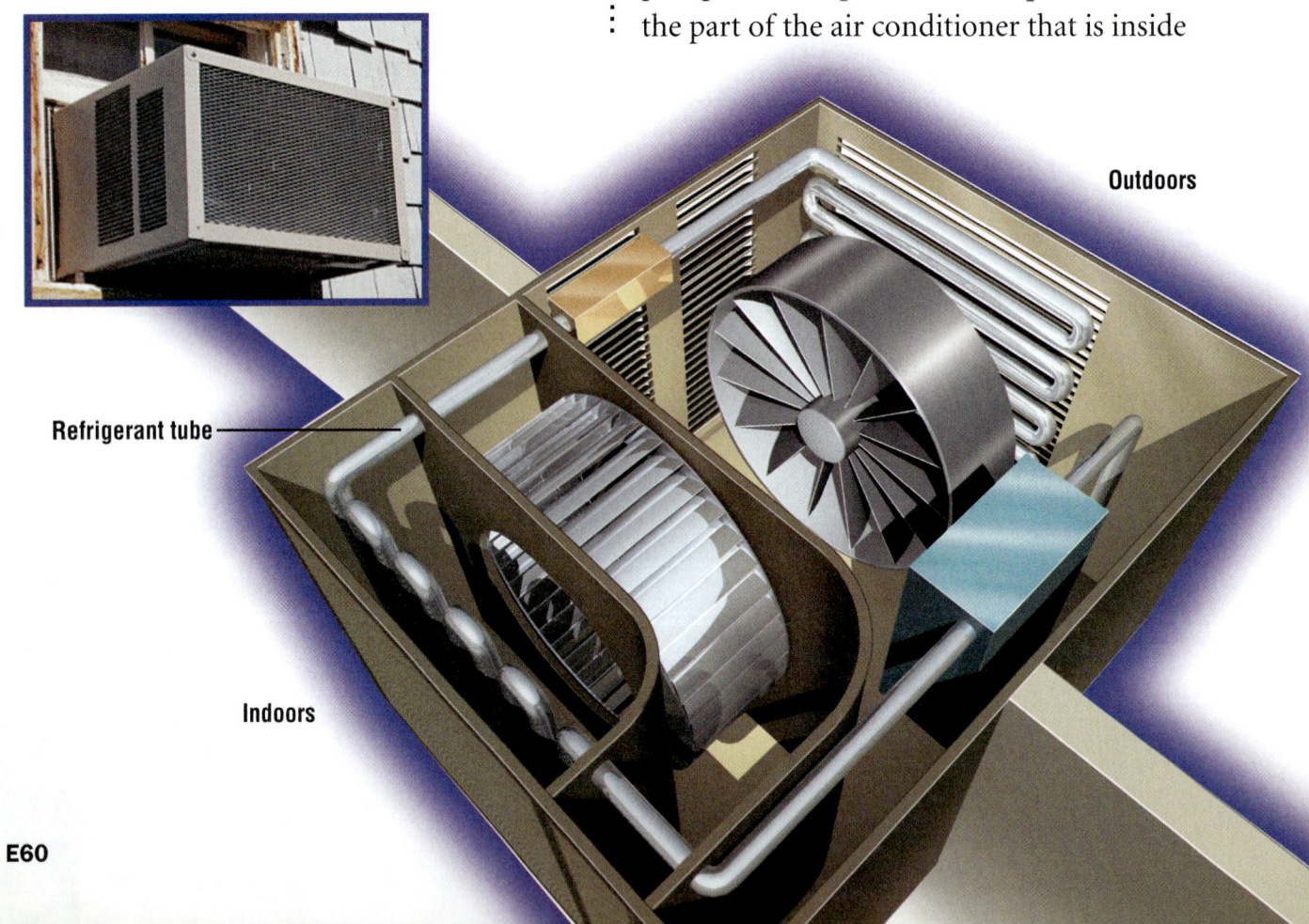

Outdoors

Refrigerant tube

Indoors

E60

the house, the refrigerant gets thermal energy from the air. This causes it to boil. The refrigerant, which is now a gas, is pumped to the part of the air conditioner that is outside the house. There the gas is squeezed and changed back to a liquid. It must lose thermal energy to do this. The thermal energy moves to the outside air.

The first refrigerant used was ammonia (uh•MOHN•yuh). It's still used for large refrigerators in factories. It has an unpleasant smell, however, and it is a poison. Leaks of ammonia, common in the first air conditioners, can cause breathing problems for any people nearby. The second refrigerant used was methyl chloride (METH•uhl KLOR•eyed). But when methyl chloride leaked into the air, it exploded.

Freon

Freon (FREE•ahn) is a colorless, tasteless, odorless gas that doesn't explode or make people ill. It also boils at a temperature that works best for refrigerants. So when Thomas Midgley discovered Freon, he thought he'd found the perfect refrigerant.

Freon made home air conditioners and modern refrigerators possible. From its discovery in the 1930s until the 1990s, Freon was almost the only refrigerant used. In the 1970s, however, scientists discovered that Freon and similar refrigerants harm Earth's protective ozone layer. So the use of Freon as a refrigerant was banned in the United States. Scientists started looking for other materials to use.

Old and New Refrigerants

Ammonia and other "old" refrigerants may be used to replace Freon in refrigerators and home air conditioners. New machines use less ammonia and are sealed more tightly. Other substances that are like Freon but are less damaging are being developed. However, none of these materials work very well in cars, where refrigerants sometimes must both heat and cool the air. Scientists at the University of Illinois are testing ordinary carbon dioxide gas as a refrigerant for cars. So, some of the gas that you breathe out may end up cooling you off!

THINK ABOUT IT

1. Why do you think refrigerant leaks were so common in early air conditioners?
2. Where does the thermal energy that leaves an air-conditioned home go?

CAREERS
HVAC Technician

What They Do HVAC (heating, ventilation, and air conditioning) technicians install, repair, and maintain heating and cooling systems. These systems may be in buildings, vehicles, or machinery such as the refrigerator in your home.

Education and Training Most HVAC technicians need a high-school education that includes math, electricity, and technical drawing. Most employers prefer technicians to have also finished either a two-year apprenticeship or a technical program.

WEB LINK For Science and Technology updates, visit the Harcourt Internet site. www.harcourtschool.com

E61

PEOPLE IN SCIENCE

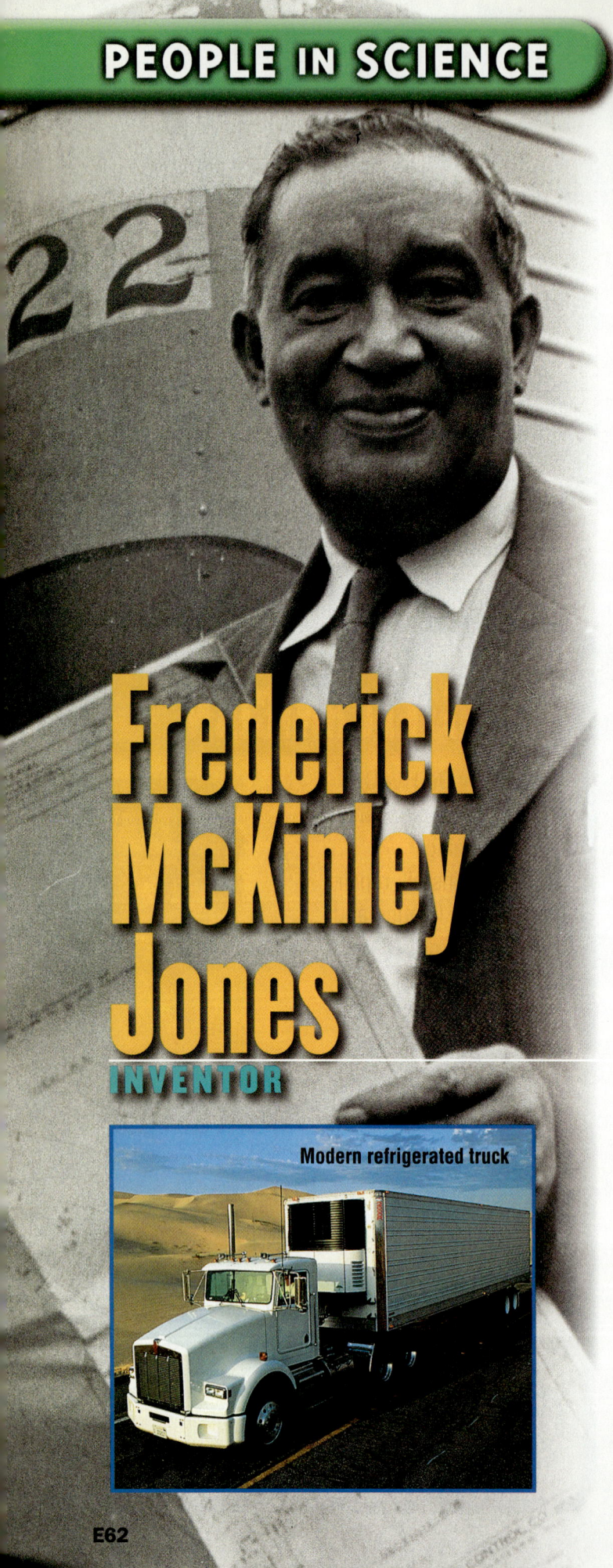

Frederick McKinley Jones
INVENTOR

Frederick Jones was an orphan by the age of nine and quit school after sixth grade. He was sent to live with a Catholic priest in Kentucky. As an older teenager, he moved to Minnesota and began a job fixing farm machinery. He studied electricity and mechanical engineering when he wasn't working.

Jones served in World War I. When he came back from the war, he built a radio transmitter in his town. He also invented machine parts so that movies with sound could be run on small projectors. During the early 1930s, he heard a man who owned trucks telling his boss that a whole shipment of chicken had spoiled because of the heat. Jones began to design a refrigeration unit for trucks.

Earlier ways to keep trucks cold took up too much room. Most also fell apart quickly because of being shaken during travel. Jones built his first refrigeration unit by using odds and ends of machine parts. It was small, shake-proof, and lightweight. But it was made to go beneath the truck and broke down often because mud and dirt from roads got inside.

After a time, Jones designed and made a unit that went on top of a truck. He and his boss formed a partnership to build the trucks. Jones was vice-president of the company.

The refrigerated trucks could ship more than food. During World War II, Jones's invention saved lives. Because the units were portable, badly needed blood and medicine could be shipped safely to battlefields.

Jones continued to work on his inventions. He eventually received more than 60 patents. More than 40 of them were for refrigeration products.

THINK ABOUT IT

1. What were some design problems that Jones solved to make a working truck-refrigerator?
2. What foods do you eat that might be shipped in a refrigerated truck?

Modern refrigerated truck

ACTIVITIES FOR HOME OR SCHOOL

COMPARE CONDUCTORS

Which material conducts thermal energy fastest?

Materials
- 3 thermometers
- warm tap water
- tape
- jar
- plastic, wood, and metal spoons of about the same size

Procedure
1. Carefully tape the bulb of a thermometer to the handle of each spoon.
2. Fill the jar with warm tap water to a level that will cover only the bottoms of the spoons. Carefully place the spoons in the jar.
3. Measure and record the temperature of each spoon every minute for 5 minutes.

Draw Conclusions
Which spoon conducted thermal energy most quickly? How do you know?

THERMAL ENERGY

How do different amounts of water affect melting?

Materials
- warm tap water
- 2 jars, 1 large and 1 small
- 4 ice cubes that are the same size
- clock or watch

Procedure
1. Fill each container almost full with warm tap water.
2. Put two ice cubes in each container.
3. Measure the time it takes for each pair of cubes to melt completely.

Draw Conclusions
Did one pair melt faster than the other pair? Why were the times different?

E63

CHAPTER 2 Review and Test Preparation

Vocabulary Review

Use the terms below to complete the sentences. The page numbers in ( ) tell you where to look in the chapter if you need help.

energy (E42)
kinetic energy (E42)
thermal energy (E42)
temperature (E43)
heat (E48)
conduction (E49)
convection (E50)
radiation (E52)
infrared radiation (E52)
fuel (E56)
solar energy (E57)

1. ____ is the transfer of thermal energy.
2. The ability to cause a change is ____.
3. A material that is burned to produce thermal energy is ____.
4. ____ is a measure of the average energy of motion of particles in matter.
5. The total energy of motion of particles of matter is ____.
6. ____ is the transfer of thermal energy by particles bumping into each other.
7. Radiation that carries thermal energy is called ____.
8. ____ is bundles of energy that can travel through empty space.
9. Energy given off by the sun is called ____.
10. ____ is the transfer of thermal energy that can occur only in a liquid or gas.
11. Because an object such as a bicycle is moving, it has ____.

Connect Concepts

Fill in the blanks in the diagram below to correctly describe some of the main concepts of this chapter.

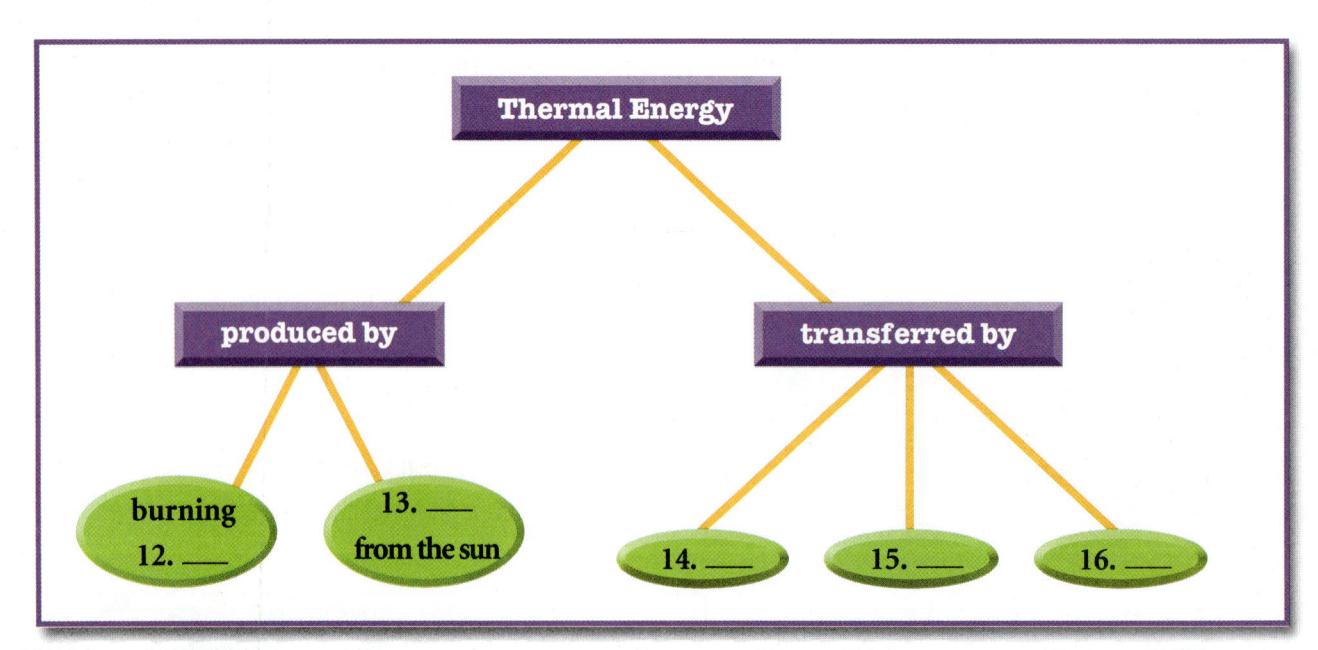

Thermal Energy
- produced by
  - burning 12. ____
  - 13. ____ from the sun
- transferred by
  - 14. ____
  - 15. ____
  - 16. ____

E64

Check Understanding

Write the letter of the best choice.

17. Most thermometers work because matter ____ when it is heated.
    A disappears
    B collects radiation
    C expands
    D loses mass

18. A thermometer measures the ____ energy of motion of particles of matter.
    F total   H solar
    G long-term   J average

19. Two pieces of the same kind of matter have the same temperature. The one with the larger mass has more —
    A conduction
    B thermal energy
    C convection
    D solar energy

20. When thermal energy moves from one piece of matter to another, the transfer is called —
    F solar energy   H temperature
    G heat   J fuel

21. Thermal energy can be transferred by conduction from one piece of matter to another only if the two pieces are —
    A liquids   C solids
    B touching   D fuel

22. Convection takes place only in liquids and —
    F gases   H solids
    G energies   J states

23. Energy that travels from the sun to Earth is being transferred by —
    A conduction   C convection
    B fuel   D radiation

Critical Thinking

24. You put a pot of water on the burner of an electric stove and turn the burner on high heat. The water soon boils. Describe how the heat from the stove gets to the water in the pot.

25. A solar panel on a roof collects solar energy to warm water for a house. Describe how the heat is transferred from the sun to the panel, and then from the panel to the water.

Process Skills Review

26. What property of particles of matter do you **measure** with a thermometer?

27. Suppose a thermometer is hanging from a thread inside a jar completely empty of gases or liquids. You **infer** that infrared radiation is falling on the thermometer. What observation would lead you to this inference? Explain.

28. A line graph has the temperature scale on the left and the time scale on the bottom. If the line is level, what can you conclude by **interpreting** the temperature **data** shown?

Performance Assessment

Temperature Balance

Your teacher will give you a thermometer, a straw, a full glass of warm water, a full glass of cool water, and an empty glass. Your goal is to use the materials to end up with a glass that is half full of water that is about room temperature. You can't wait for the two full glasses to cool and warm naturally. Explain what you did and why it worked.

E65

CHAPTER 3

Sound

Have you ever heard nothing at all? Probably not. Even in a space suit while orbiting Earth, you can still hear the sound of your blood flowing and your heart beating!

Vocabulary Preview

sound
compression
sound wave
amplitude
wavelength
loudness
pitch
speed of sound
echo
sonic boom

Fast Fact

Bats don't use their eyes to catch prey. They use their ears! Bats send out high-pitched squeaks and clicks that bounce off objects. The returning echoes direct them to their prey. Using echoes, some bats can find an insect as thin as a human hair in total darkness!

Fast Fact

When a volcano on the island of Krakatau, Indonesia, erupted in 1883, it made the loudest natural sound ever observed. Heard 4500 km (2796 mi) away, the eruption was so strong that it blew the island apart!

Fast Fact

Every type of animal has a different hearing and voice range. When the Canadian Pacific Railroad switched to air-driven horns, large numbers of female moose were killed by trains. Biologists determined that the low-pitched horns sounded like the calls of male moose! Changing the pitch of the horns has greatly reduced the number of moose on the tracks.

Sound and Hearing

	Hearing Range (Vibrations per Second)	Voice Range (Vibrations per Second)
Bats	1,000–120,000	10,000–120,000
Cats	60–65,000	750–1500
Dogs	15–50,000	452–1080
Dolphins	150–150,000	7000–120,000
Humans	20–20,000	80–1500
Robins	250–20,000	2000–15,000

LESSON 1

What Is Sound?

In this lesson, you can . . .

- **INVESTIGATE** making and hearing sounds.
- **LEARN ABOUT** the way sound travels.
- **LINK** to math, writing, social studies, and technology.

INVESTIGATE

Sound from a Ruler

Activity Purpose Sit still a moment and listen. What do you hear? People talking, car horns honking, dogs barking, the refrigerator humming? We hear different kinds of sounds all day long. In this investigation you will **observe** how a sound is made. You will also observe some ways to change sound.

Materials
- plastic ruler

Activity Procedure

1. Place the ruler on a tabletop. Let 15 to 20 cm stick out over the edge of the table.

2. Hold the ruler tightly against the tabletop with one hand. Use the thumb of your other hand to flick, or strum, the free end of the ruler. (Picture A)

3. **Observe** the ruler with your eyes. **Record** your observations.

4. Repeat Step 2. **Observe** the ruler with your ears. **Record** your observations.

◀ Hitting cymbals together produces a loud sound that can be heard over that of an entire band or orchestra.

E68

Picture A

Picture B

5. Flick the ruler harder. **Observe** the results. **Record** your observations.

6. Change the length of the ruler sticking over the edge of the table, and repeat Steps 2 through 5. **Observe** the results. **Record** your observations. (Picture B)

Draw Conclusions

1. What did you **observe** in Step 3?

2. What did you **observe** in Step 4?

3. **Make a hypothesis** to explain what you **observed** in Steps 3 and 4. How could you test your explanation?

4. **Scientists at Work** When scientists want to learn more about an experiment, they change one part of it and **observe** the effect. What did you change in Step 6? What effect did you observe?

Investigate Further Place one ear on the tabletop. Cover the other ear with your hand. Have a partner repeat Steps 1 and 2. What do you **observe? Plan and conduct an experiment** to test this **hypothesis**: Sounds are louder if you listen through a solid material than if you listen through air.

Process Skill Tip

When people use the word *observe*, they usually think of seeing. But you can use all your senses to **observe**. In this investigation you also used your sense of hearing to observe the effects of the movements of the ruler.

E69

LEARN ABOUT

Characteristics of Sound

Vibrations

FIND OUT

- causes of sounds
- how sound travels
- how your ears help you hear

VOCABULARY

sound
compression
sound wave
amplitude
wavelength

In the investigation, you saw the ruler make quick back-and-forth movements after you snapped it. These back-and-forth movements are called *vibrations* (vy•BRAY•shuhnz). After you strum a guitar string, it vibrates for a while and slowly stops. You hear the guitar note start and then slowly fade away. When you hum, you can feel the vibrations of your larynx (LAIR•inks), or voice box, by putting your fingers on the outside of your throat. When you stop humming, the vibration also stops. **Sound** is vibrations that you can hear. An object vibrates to make sounds. This vibration causes particles in the air around the object to vibrate as well. You can see and feel the object vibrate, but not the particles in the air.

✓ What is sound?

As the ruler vibrates, the particles in air are pushed closer together. The areas where air is pushed together are called compressions (kuhm•PRESH•uhnz). ▶

When one end of the ruler is snapped, it vibrates, or moves back and forth. The ruler pushes against the air around it. ▼

Each compression moves away from the ruler, in the same way that ripples move away from a pebble thrown into a pond. ▶

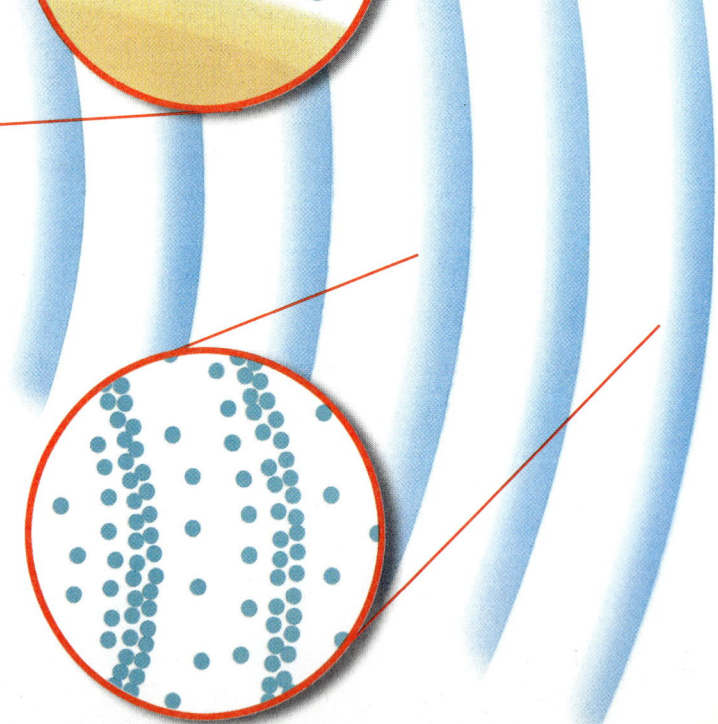

E70

Traveling Waves

The vibrations of the guitar string, the ruler, and your voice box push and then pull on the particles of air around them. As they push, they increase the pressure in the air. The area where air is pushed together is called a **compression**. As the vibrations pull, they decrease the pressure in the air. This results in alternating areas of high and low pressure in the air. **Sound waves** are quickly moving areas of high and low pressure. All sound is carried through matter as sound waves.

Sound waves move out in all directions from a vibrating object. You can hear something making sound all around you, above you, or below you. As the sound waves move away from their source, their energy is spread over a larger area. The farther you are from the source of a sound, the softer the sound will be.

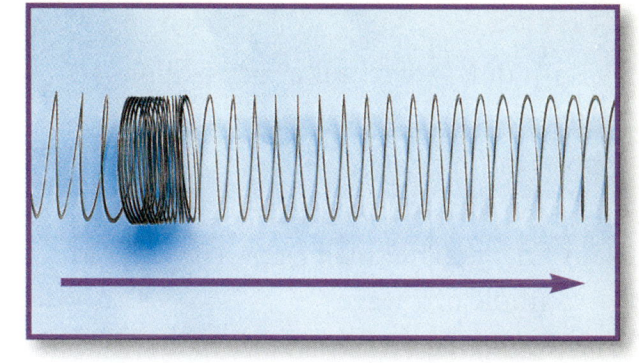

▲ A wave travels through this spring toy just as a sound wave travels through the air. The places where the springs are close together are like compressions, or areas of high pressure, in the air. The places where the springs are far apart are like areas of low pressure in the air.

Most of the sound we hear travels through the air. In the investigation you found that sound waves travel through other materials, too. Sound waves can move through each state of matter.

✓ **In what direction do sound waves travel?**

1 Each instrument in a marching band makes a sound by vibrating something. For example, the head of a bass drum vibrates when it is hit. The vibrations cause sound waves in the air. The audience watching and listening to the parade hears the drumbeat.

2 Sound waves can also travel through liquids. These underwater swimmers could hear the band play if it marched by the pool.

3 Someone behind a closed door could hear the band, too, because sound waves can also travel through solids.

E71

Waves

Ka-plunk—you hear a rock fall into a pond. You turn toward the sound and see ripples on the water. You put your hand in the water and feel the ripples lap against your fingers. The small ripples in water are an example of a wave.

How did the rock form the ripples? The rock transferred kinetic energy to the water as it fell into the pond. This caused a wave to form. As the energy moved through the water, it made the water's surface rise and fall.

▼ This picture shows a snapshot of a wave on a pond. When a rock falls into a calm pond, it pushes the nearby water particles. These particles then push on their neighbors. The movement of the particles is a wave that moves through the water.

You can use how a wave rises and falls to describe it. The greatest distance that the water rises from its rest, or calm, position is called **amplitude** (AM•pluh•tood). The more energy a wave carries, the greater its amplitude. **Wavelength** is the distance in a straight line from one place on a ripple to the same place on the next ripple.

✓ **What causes a wave to form?**

When you drop a rock into a calm pond, it causes ripples. Each ripple forms a ring that gets wider as it moves through the water. The source of the rings is the place where the rock was dropped into the water. ▼

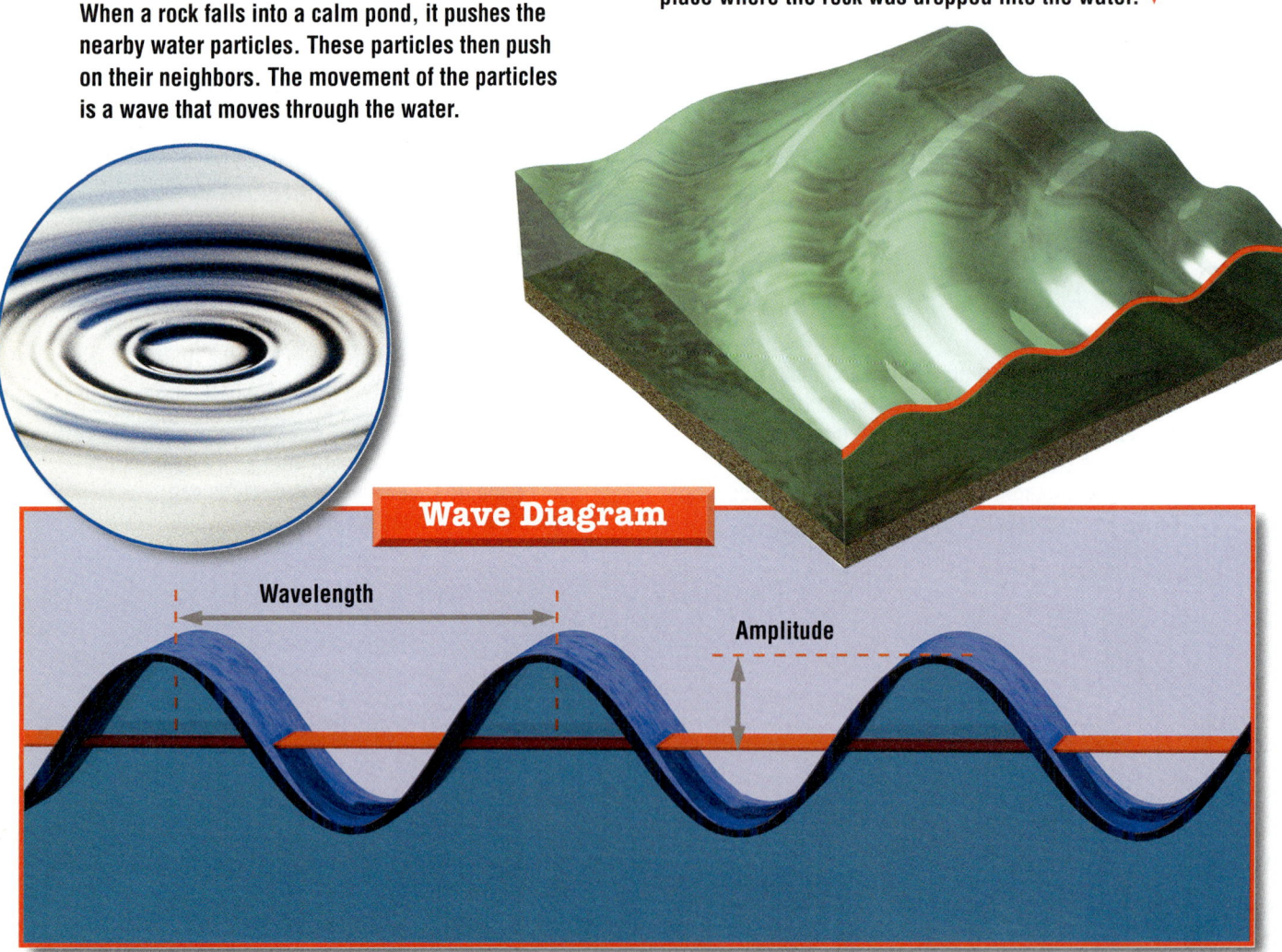

Wave Diagram

▲ The straight, dark-red ribbon shows where the calm, smooth surface of the pond would normally be. It is called the *rest position* of the water. As you can see, part of the wave is above the rest position and part of the wave is below it. A drawing of the ripple shape is called a wave diagram. You can use a wave diagram to show wavelength and amplitude.

E72

The jangle of an alarm clock is a sound. The sound wave moves out from the alarm in all directions, much like ripples on a pond. ▶

The ripples of this wave model the areas of high and low pressure in the sound wave further below. The peaks, or high points, show where pressure is greatest. The valleys, or low points, show where pressure is lowest. ▼

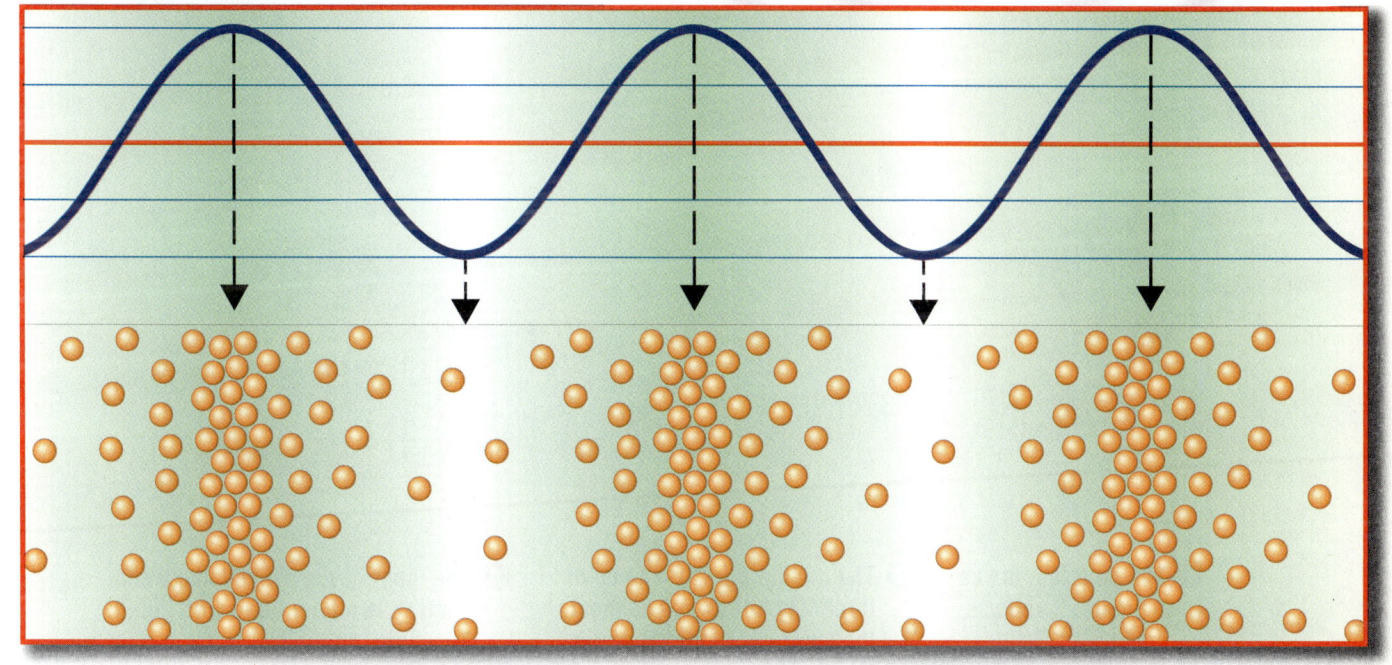

▲ A sound wave is moving areas of high and low pressure. The high pressure occurs where particles are bunched together. The low pressure occurs where they are spread apart. Suppose you could stack the particles in each thin slice of this sound wave. The stacks would form a pattern of peaks and valleys just like the wave shown above.

Waves and Sound

Waves on a pond are like sound waves. They both move out in all directions from the source. When you trace the ripple shape of a wave with your finger, your finger's back and forth movements are like the vibrations that cause sounds. In fact, scientists use the ripple shapes of waves to model sound waves.

The peaks and valleys of a wave stand for the areas of high and low pressure in a sound wave. The peaks match where pressure is highest. The valleys match where pressure is lowest. If the source of the sound is vibrating faster, the peaks will be closer together.

The amplitude, or tallness, of a wave stands for the loudness of a sound. A taller wave stands for a louder sound.

✓ **What part of a wave diagram models a low pressure part of a sound wave?**

E73

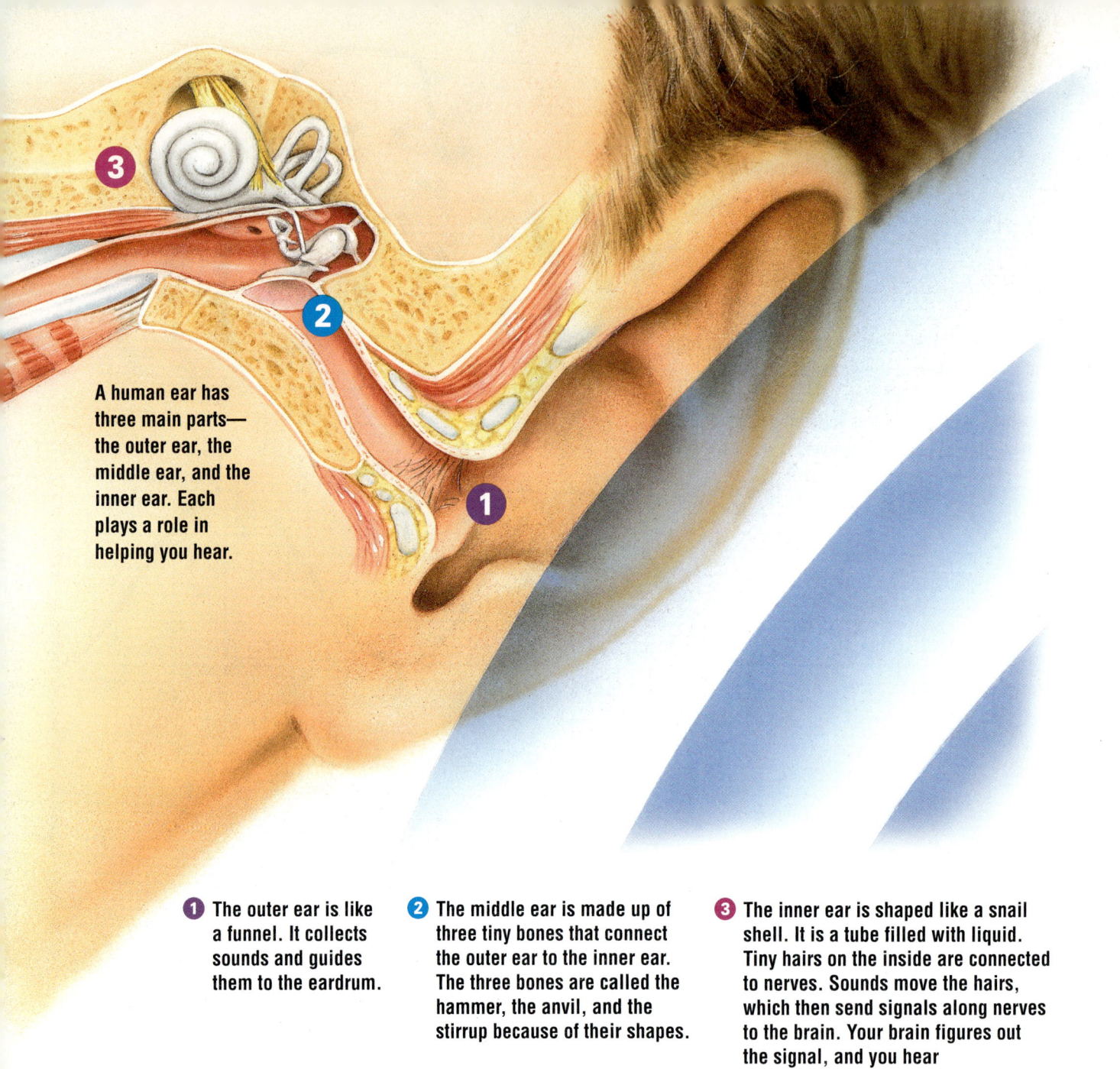

A human ear has three main parts—the outer ear, the middle ear, and the inner ear. Each plays a role in helping you hear.

1 The outer ear is like a funnel. It collects sounds and guides them to the eardrum.

2 The middle ear is made up of three tiny bones that connect the outer ear to the inner ear. The three bones are called the hammer, the anvil, and the stirrup because of their shapes.

3 The inner ear is shaped like a snail shell. It is a tube filled with liquid. Tiny hairs on the inside are connected to nerves. Sounds move the hairs, which then send signals along nerves to the brain. Your brain figures out the signal, and you hear a sound.

Hearing Sounds

We hear sound when sound waves reach our ears. Our ears take in the sound waves and turn them into signals that go to our brains. Our brains figure out these signals and tell us what the sound is.

The first part of the ear that a sound wave hits is the outer ear. The outer ear is like a funnel that collects sound waves and guides them to the eardrum.

The eardrum is made of thin material that bends easily. It is about 1 centimeter ($\frac{1}{2}$ in.) across. It works like the top of a drum. The eardrum vibrates when sound waves hit it. As the eardrum moves back and forth, it moves a tiny bone at the outside end of the middle ear.

The middle ear is about the size of the tip of your little finger. In it, vibrations pass through three tiny bones. The bones connect the eardrum to the inner ear.

E74

The inner ear is shaped like a snail shell. It is filled with liquid. The walls of the inner ear are lined with tiny hairs. These hairs are connected to nerves.

The third bone of the middle ear vibrates one end of the inner ear. These vibrations cause waves in the liquid. The waves move the tiny hairs. This causes nerve cells to send signals to your brain. Your brain interprets the signals as sounds.

✓ **Which part of the ear connects it to the outside world?**

Summary

Sound is made by vibrating objects. The vibrations travel through matter as areas of high and low pressure called sound waves. A wave diagram is a way to model the amplitude and wavelength of a sound wave. Sound waves move through the three parts of the ear. You sense the vibrations as sound.

Review

1. What is sound?
2. What are sound waves?
3. Which part of the ear is connected to nerves that send signals to the brain?
4. **Critical Thinking** Sometimes you can hear and feel the rumble of a passing truck. What are you feeling?
5. **Test Prep** The middle ear contains —
   A liquid
   B the eardrum
   C three bones
   D hairs

LINKS

MATH LINK

Find a Rule Some music scale notes can be found by shortening the length of a string to a fraction. For example, if the base pitch is played on a length of 1, an *octave* (AHK•tiv) higher would be played on a length of $\frac{1}{2}$. What would be the length of the second octave higher? The third octave?

WRITING LINK

Informative Writing—Description
Suppose that you are a sound wave traveling through someone's ear. Write a description for your classmates of what happens to you as you move from the outer ear to the inner ear.

SOCIAL STUDIES LINK

Flutes and Drums In many countries traditional music is played on flutelike and drumlike instruments. Choose a country. Find pictures of these types of musical instruments from that country. Make a map showing the location of the country. Add labeled pictures of the instruments.

GO ONLINE TECHNOLOGY LINK

Learn more about early recorders by visiting the Jerome and Dorothy Lemelson Center for Invention and Innovation Internet site.
www.si.edu/harcourt/science

Smithsonian Institution®

LESSON 2

Why Do Sounds Differ?

In this lesson, you can...

INVESTIGATE making different sounds.

LEARN ABOUT differences in sounds.

LINK to math, writing, music, and technology.

INVESTIGATE

Making Different Sounds

Activity Purpose If you pluck a guitar string, you hear a sound. If you pluck another guitar string, you hear a different sound. How are the sounds different? What causes the difference? In this activity you will **observe** sounds made by a vibrating rubber band. You will **compare** observations and **infer** what causes differences in sounds.

Materials
- safety goggles
- foam cup
- long rubber band
- paper clip
- ruler
- masking tape

Activity Procedure

1. **CAUTION** **Put on the safety goggles.** With a pencil, punch a small hole in the bottom of the cup. Thread the rubber band through the paper clip. Put the paper clip inside the cup, and pull the rubber band through the hole. (Picture A)

2. Turn the cup upside down on a table. Stand the ruler on the table next to it, with the 1-cm mark at the top. Tape one side of the cup to the ruler. Pull the rubber band over the top of the ruler, and tape it to the back. (Picture B)

3. Pull the rubber band to one side and let it go. **Observe** the sound. **Record** your observations.

◀ The word *piano* is short for *pianoforte* (pee•ah•noh•FOR•tay). *Piano* is the Italian word for "soft." *Forte* is the Italian word for "loud." Why do you think this instrument is called a pianoforte?

E76

Picture A

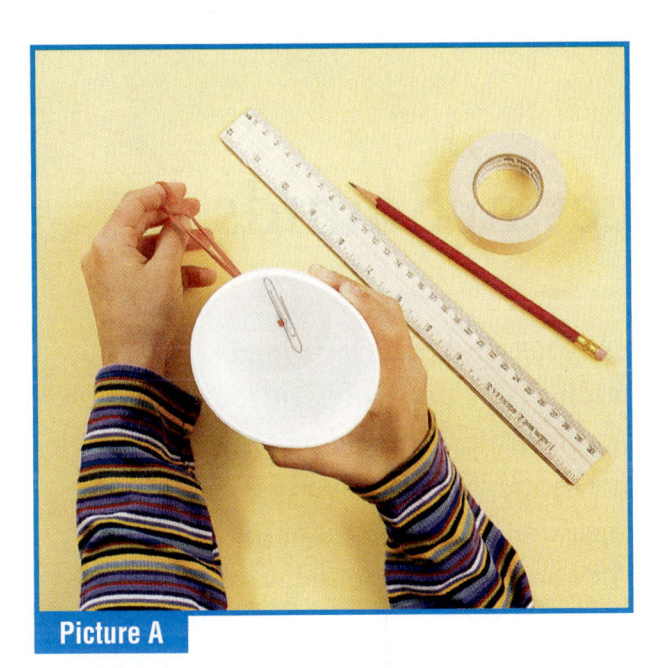

Picture B

4. Repeat Step 3, but this time pull the rubber band farther. **Observe** the sound. **Record** your observations.

5. With one finger, hold the rubber band down to the ruler at the 4-cm mark. Pluck the rubber band. **Observe** the sound. **Record** your observations.

6. Repeat Step 5, but this time hold the rubber band down at the 6-cm mark. Then do this at the 8-cm mark. **Observe** the sounds. **Record** your observations.

Draw Conclusions

1. **Compare** the sounds you observed in Steps 3 and 4.
2. **Compare** the sounds you observed in Steps 5 and 6.
3. When was the vibrating part of the rubber band the shortest?
4. **Scientists at Work** Scientists use their observations to help them **infer** the causes of different things. Use your observations from Steps 5 and 6 to infer what caused the differences in the sounds.

Investigate Further Try moving your finger up and down the ruler as you pull on the rubber band. Can you play a scale? Can you play a tune? What cause and effect relationship do you **observe? Form a hypothesis** to explain that relationship. **Plan and conduct an experiment** to test the hypothesis.

Process Skill Tip

Scientists use their observations to **infer** the causes of their results. In this investigation your observations helped you infer the causes of different sounds.

LEARN ABOUT

FIND OUT

- the difference between loud and soft sounds
- the difference between high and low sounds

VOCABULARY

loudness
pitch

Differences in Sounds

Loudness

You can whisper and you can shout. One sound is soft, and the other is loud. You can close a door softly, or you can bang it shut so hard that everyone inside the building can hear. You can hear how loud or soft a sound is. This property is called loudness. **Loudness** is a measure of the amount of sound energy reaching your ears. The amplitude of a sound wave shows how loud the sound is.

The loudness of a sound depends on how far the vibrating object is moving as it goes back and forth. In the investigation the sound was louder when you pulled the rubber band farther. You added more energy to the rubber band by stretching it more. In the same way, if you hit a drum harder or slam a door harder, you make a louder sound.

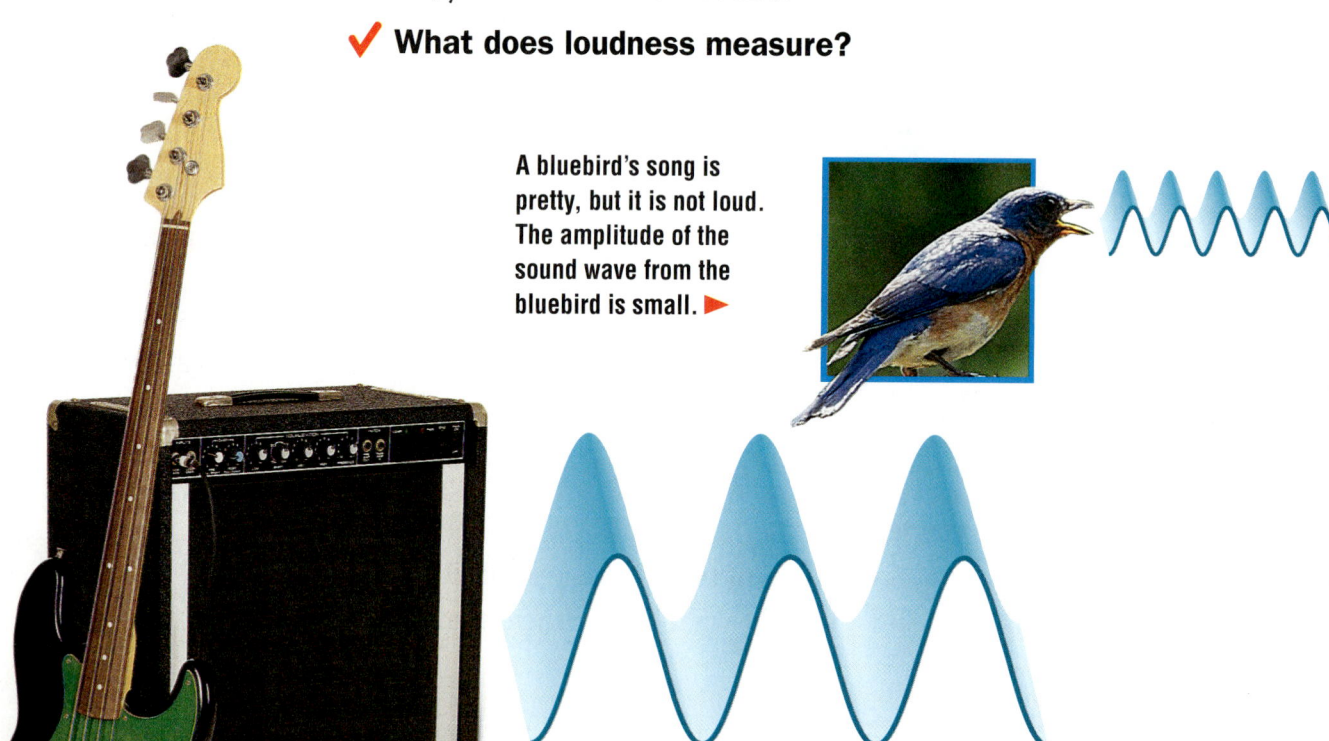

✓ **What does loudness measure?**

A bluebird's song is pretty, but it is not loud. The amplitude of the sound wave from the bluebird is small. ▶

◀ Noise from an amplified bass guitar is much louder than a bluebird's song. It's so loud that it can injure your ears if you don't protect them. The amplitude of the sound wave from the bass guitar amplifier is large.

E78

A tuba makes low sounds. The compressions of a tuba's sound wave are far apart. It has a long wavelength. ▼

◀ Piccolo music reminds some people of the high sounds of singing birds. A piccolo makes fast vibrations. The compressions of a piccolo's sound wave are close together. It has a short wavelength.

Pitch

You can make loud sounds and soft sounds. You can also make high sounds and low sounds. When you growl like a dog, you are making a low sound. When you squeak like a mouse, you are making a high sound.

A sound's **pitch** is a measure of how high or low it is. Pitch depends on how fast the source of the sound is vibrating. The faster the vibrations, the higher the pitch. Pitch is related to wavelength. The longer the wavelength, the lower the sound you hear.

You can change how fast a string or rubber band vibrates by changing its length. In the investigation, when you made the vibrating part of the rubber band shorter, it vibrated faster. The sound it made got higher in pitch.

✓ **What does the pitch of a sound depend on?**

The keys at the right-hand end of a piano make high sounds. The keys to the left make lower sounds. The lowest note on a modern piano vibrates about $27\frac{1}{2}$ times a second. The highest note on a piano vibrates about 4224 times a second. Humans can hear sounds from about 20 to about 20,000 vibrations a second. ▶

E79

Changing Pitch

Many musical instruments can be played at different pitches by changing the length of certain parts. A guitar or violin player puts his or her fingers down on the strings in different places. This changes the lengths of the vibrating strings. As a result, the violin or guitar plays different pitches.

Another way to make a different pitch is to change the thickness of the material that vibrates. A thin string vibrates faster than a thick string. Low-pitched guitar and piano strings have wire wrapped around them to make them thicker.

✓ **Name two ways you can change the pitch of a vibrating object.**

A trombone is a long tube. To play a note, a trombone player's lips vibrate. This makes the air inside the tube vibrate. ▼

When a trombone player pushes the slide out, the tube gets longer. This makes the pitch of the sound lower than before. Notice that the wavelength of the sound is longer. ▼

The cone-shaped object in the trombone is a mute (MYOOT). It makes a trombone note softer because the mute absorbs sound energy. With the mute the sound wave made by the trombone has less energy. Notice that the amplitude of the wave is smaller than the first wave, above, but the wavelength is the same. ▼

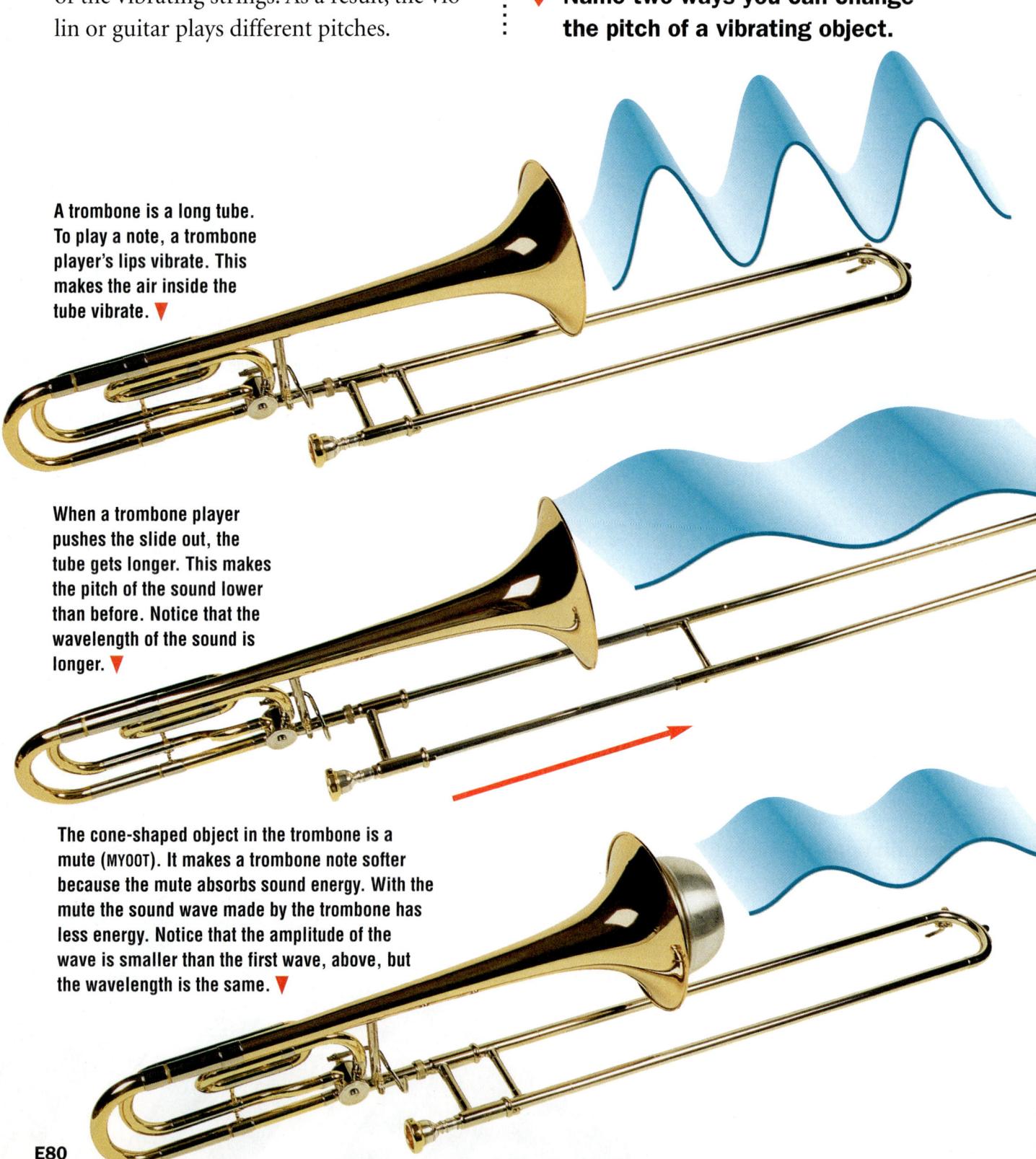

A voiceprint is an electronic "picture" of a voice. It shows the changing pitch and loudness of the voice as a person speaks. ▼

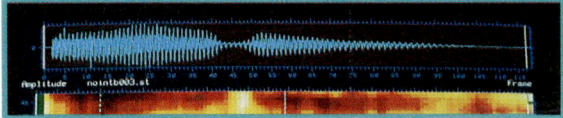

Summary

Loudness is a measure of the sound energy reaching your ears. It depends on the size of the vibrations. Pitch is a measure of how high or low a sound is. Pitch depends on how fast an object vibrates. You can change pitch by changing the length or the thickness of a vibrating object.

Review

1. What is the loudness of a sound?
2. What is the pitch of a sound?
3. What happens to sound as it gets farther away from the object making the sound?
4. **Critical Thinking** How do you think the finger holes on the side of a piccolo control the pitch of its sound?
5. **Test Prep** If you put your finger down on a guitar string to make the string shorter, the sound the string makes will get —
   - A lower
   - B higher
   - C louder
   - D softer

LINKS

MATH LINK

Calculate a Difference The highest note on a piano vibrates 4224 times a second. The lowest note on a piano vibrates $27\frac{1}{2}$ times a second. What is the difference between these two pitches?

WRITING LINK

Informative Writing—Description Sit still and listen for one minute. Time yourself. As you're listening, make a list of every sound you hear. Then write a paragraph for your teacher describing all the sounds. Be sure to include loudness and pitch in your descriptions.

MUSIC LINK

High and Low Two of the families of instruments in an orchestra are the brass instruments and the woodwind instruments. Find out the names of the instruments in each of these families. Then find out the highest and lowest pitches each instrument family can play.

TECHNOLOGY LINK

Learn more about how scientists and engineers are using sound energy by viewing *Sound Wave Energy* on the **Harcourt Science Newsroom Video.**

E81

LESSON 3

How Do Sound Waves Travel?

In this lesson, you can . . .

INVESTIGATE ways sound is reflected.

LEARN ABOUT how sound waves travel.

LINK to math, writing, health, and technology.

INVESTIGATE

Hearing Sounds

Activity Purpose Have you ever made a sound and heard it come back to you? In this investigation you will **gather and record data** while making a sound and listening to find out if it comes back to you.

Materials
- large metal spoon
- metal pot
- red crayon

Activity Procedure

1. Find a playing field with a scoreboard or building at one end. Use a pencil to make a drawing of the playing field.

2. Walk out onto the playing field. Use a pencil to record on your drawing where on the playing field you are standing and which way you are facing.

3. Bang the spoon against the pot once. Wait and observe whether or not the sound comes back to you. If the sound comes back to you, use a red crayon to mark that place. (Picture A)

◀ When the space shuttle reenters the atmosphere and coasts toward a landing, it is traveling much faster than the speed of sound.

E82

4 Move to another location on the playing field. Again, use a pencil to record where on the playing field you are standing and which way you are facing.

5 Repeat Step 3. If the sound comes back to you, be sure to use a red crayon to mark the spot on your drawing.

6 Move forward and back. Move from side to side. Each time you move, mark your position on your drawing, bang the pot once, and wait to see whether or not the sound comes back to you. Each time use the crayon to mark the places where the sound came back to you.

7 Keep moving to different places on the playing field until you have gathered information from 20 locations.

Picture A

Picture B

Draw Conclusions

1. Look at your drawing. How many different positions did you show? At how many different places did the sound come back to you?

2. Look at all the places marked in red on your drawing. Do they have anything in common?

3. **Scientists at Work** Each mark that you made on your drawing was a piece of data. When scientists do investigations, they **gather and record** as much **data** as they can. All the data helps them draw conclusions. How could you gather more data in an organized way?

Investigate Further Move to each of the places on the field where you heard the sound come back to you. Blow a whistle loudly in each place. Does the sound come back to you? Describe a simple **experiment** to test this **hypothesis**: Only short, loud sounds come back to you.

Process Skill Tip

Scientists often use drawings when they **gather and record data**. Their drawings help them see patterns in the information they gather. They use the patterns to help them draw conclusions.

LEARN ABOUT

How Sound Travels

FIND OUT

- how quickly sound travels
- the cause of echoes
- what happens when you go faster than sound

VOCABULARY

speed of sound
echo
sonic boom

Speed

Have you ever been to a baseball game and watched a batter hit a home run? If you were sitting all the way across the ballpark, you saw the batter hit the ball a split second before you heard the crack of the bat. This is because sound waves take more time to move through the air than light does. Even so, it took less than a second for the sound wave to travel from the bat to your ears.

The speed at which a sound wave travels is called the **speed of sound**. Sound waves move at different speeds through different materials. In dry, cool air, sound waves travel 340 meters (about 1115 ft) per second. The speed of sound traveling through steel is 5200 meters (about 17,060 ft) per second.

In hard, solid materials, sound waves move very fast. This is because the particles in solids are close together and bump into each other often. The particles in liquids don't bump into each other as often as particles in solids do. So vibrations take longer to move through liquids. Sound moves more slowly through liquids than through most solids.

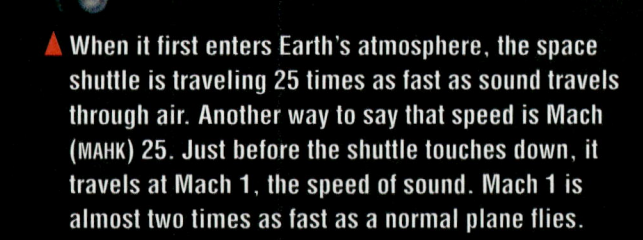

▲ When it first enters Earth's atmosphere, the space shuttle is traveling 25 times as fast as sound travels through air. Another way to say that speed is Mach (MAHK) 25. Just before the shuttle touches down, it travels at Mach 1, the speed of sound. Mach 1 is almost two times as fast as a normal plane flies.

E84

Sound moves even more slowly in gases. The particles in gases are far apart. They don't bump into each other as often as particles in liquids, so vibrations take longer to move through gases. But what if there were no particles at all, or very few particles? In that case, there would be no sound at all. This is very much like the conditions in space. Suppose you are in a spacesuit outside a space shuttle. No matter how loudly you shouted, no one in the shuttle would hear you. You could talk back and forth only by using a radio.

✔ **What does the speed of sound measure?**

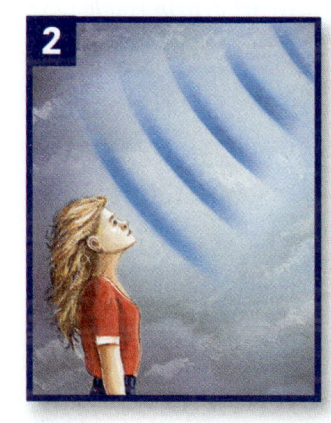

1 In air, sound travels about 1 mile in 5 seconds. You can use this to find the distance to a thunderstorm. Light travels so fast that you see a lightning bolt almost as it happens. Start the stopwatch when you see the flash, and wait to hear the thunder.

2 When you hear the thunder, you stop the stopwatch. It reads 10 seconds.
10 sec ÷ 5 sec/1 mi = 2 mi
The storm is about 2 miles away.

Sound waves travel at different speeds in different materials. The arrangement of particles in materials affects how the waves move. ▼

Speeds of Sound Through Different Materials

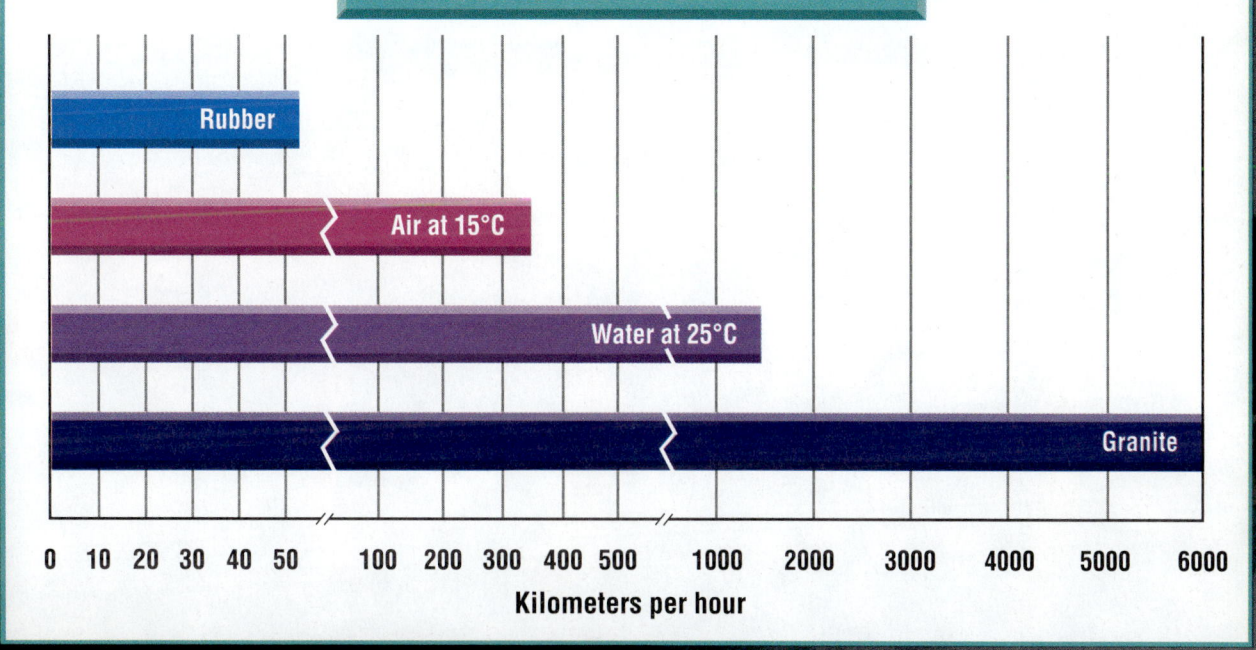

- Rubber
- Air at 15°C
- Water at 25°C
- Granite

Kilometers per hour: 0 10 20 30 40 50 100 200 300 400 500 1000 2000 3000 4000 5000 6000

E85

Reflection

As sound waves travel through the air, an object such as a wall may be in their path. In this case, the sound waves hit the object and bounce, or reflect, off it. A sound reflection is called an **echo**. In the investigation, you heard an echo when you faced the scoreboard or building, hit the pot with the spoon, and heard the sound come back to you.

Not all echoes are clear or easy to recognize. A line of trees, for example, doesn't reflect a clear echo. That is because the surfaces of the trees are uneven. Each sound wave hits a different surface and is reflected in a different direction.

It is very much like what happens to your reflection in a pool of water. If the water is smooth and still, you can see yourself clearly. But if the surface of the pond ripples, your reflection gets broken up. Rough or uneven surfaces do the same thing to sound waves.

✓ **What is an echo?**

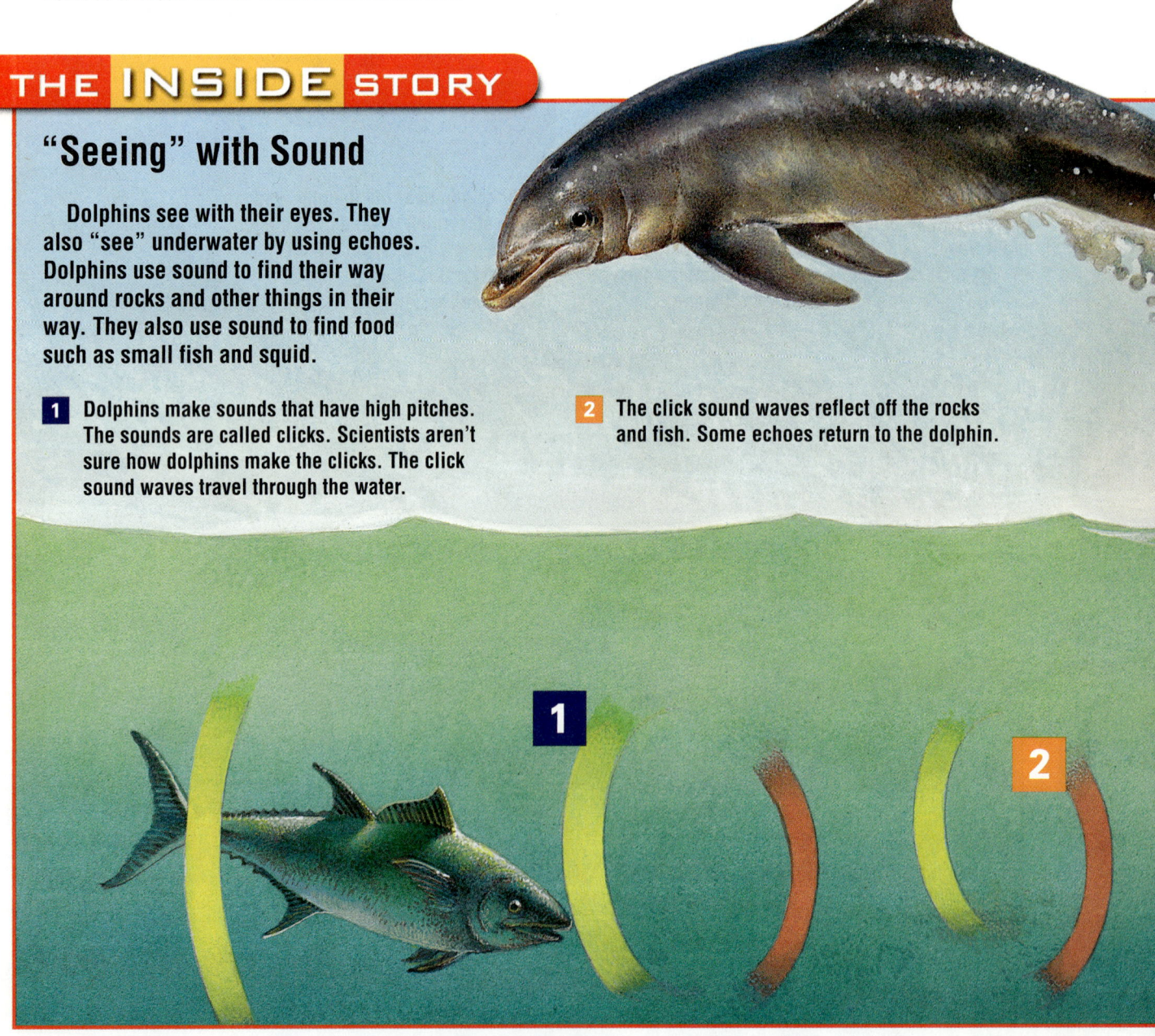

THE INSIDE STORY

"Seeing" with Sound

Dolphins see with their eyes. They also "see" underwater by using echoes. Dolphins use sound to find their way around rocks and other things in their way. They also use sound to find food such as small fish and squid.

1 Dolphins make sounds that have high pitches. The sounds are called clicks. Scientists aren't sure how dolphins make the clicks. The click sound waves travel through the water.

2 The click sound waves reflect off the rocks and fish. Some echoes return to the dolphin.

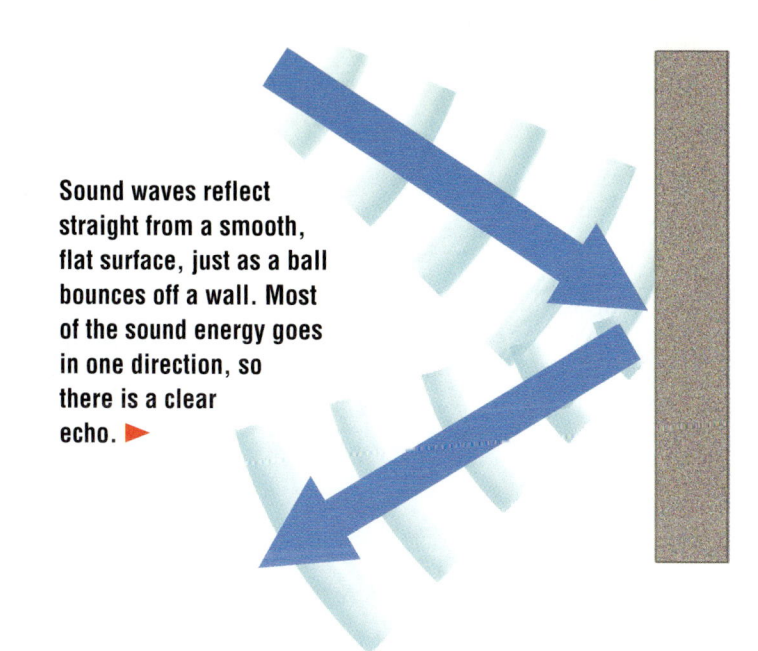

Sound waves reflect straight from a smooth, flat surface, just as a ball bounces off a wall. Most of the sound energy goes in one direction, so there is a clear echo. ▶

When sound waves hit a rough, uneven surface, they are reflected in many different directions. The sound energy is spread out, so there is no clear echo. ▶

3 Dolphins have an organ called a melon on the tops of their heads. It senses the echoes of the clicks. The melon absorbs the sound and helps the dolphin avoid rocks and find its food.

E87

Sonic Booms

Some jet airplanes can fly faster than sound. Their powerful engines produce loud sounds. What happens to these sounds when the plane is moving faster than they are?

An airplane traveling faster than sound makes sound waves that move away in all directions. But the airplane is moving faster than the sound waves moving away in front of it. When the plane catches up to these sound waves, they are squeezed closer together. All the energy of the sound waves becomes one strong wave. This strong wave is called a shock wave. You can hear this shock wave as a loud "boom-boom." People call the double boom a **sonic boom**. Any object moving faster than sound makes such a shock wave. You hear the "crack" of a rifle shot because the bullet is moving faster than sound.

A plane is always making sound waves. So if it is flying faster than sound, its sonic boom travels with it, much like the plane's shadow does.

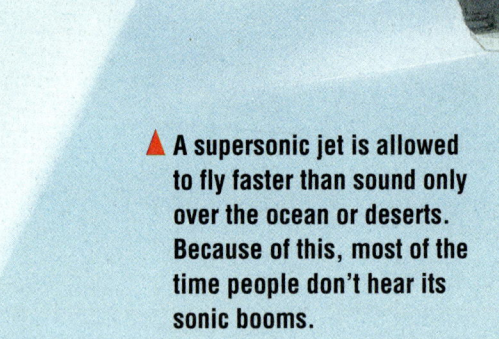

▲ A supersonic jet is allowed to fly faster than sound only over the ocean or deserts. Because of this, most of the time people don't hear its sonic booms.

Suppose you and 20 of your friends were to stand in a line down the length of a football field. You stand on a goal line. Each of your friends stands on a different yard line. Coming from the direction nearest you, an airplane flies down the field going faster than sound. You will be the first to hear its sonic boom. Then, one by one, each of your friends will hear it. Finally, the person standing on the far goal line will hear it.

✓ **What is a sonic boom?**

A sonic boom is a large, quick air pressure increase followed by a large quick decrease. Then the pressure returns to normal. ▶

Summary

Sound waves travel at different speeds through different materials. They travel fastest through hard, solid materials. Sound waves reflect off objects in their paths. An echo is a sound reflection off a smooth, hard surface. Objects traveling faster than the speed of sound cause shock waves that we hear as sonic booms.

Review

1. What does the speed of sound measure?
2. Why is there no sound in outer space?
3. Where does the energy of a sonic boom come from?
4. **Critical Thinking** Why don't you hear echoes in a forest?
5. **Test Prep** In which material would sound waves probably travel the fastest?
   A cotton
   B milk
   C iron
   D oxygen

LINKS

MATH LINK

Compare Whole Numbers The speed of sound in air is 340 meters per second. In water it is 1497 meters per second. About how many times as fast is the speed of sound in water as in air?

WRITING LINK

Informative Writing—Narration Suppose you are at home and a thunderstorm is going on outside. By watching the lightning and listening to the thunder, you track the storm. Write a story for a younger child telling what you see and hear, and where the storm is going.

HEALTH LINK

Ultrasound Doctors use ultrasound in medical tests. Find out what ultrasound is and how it works. Then find out about some of the tests it's used for. Make a poster or display to show what you learned.

TECHNOLOGY LINK

Learn more about sound wave differences by exploring *Waves of Music* on **Harcourt Science Explorations CD-ROM.**

SCIENCE AND TECHNOLOGY

Active NOISE CONTROL

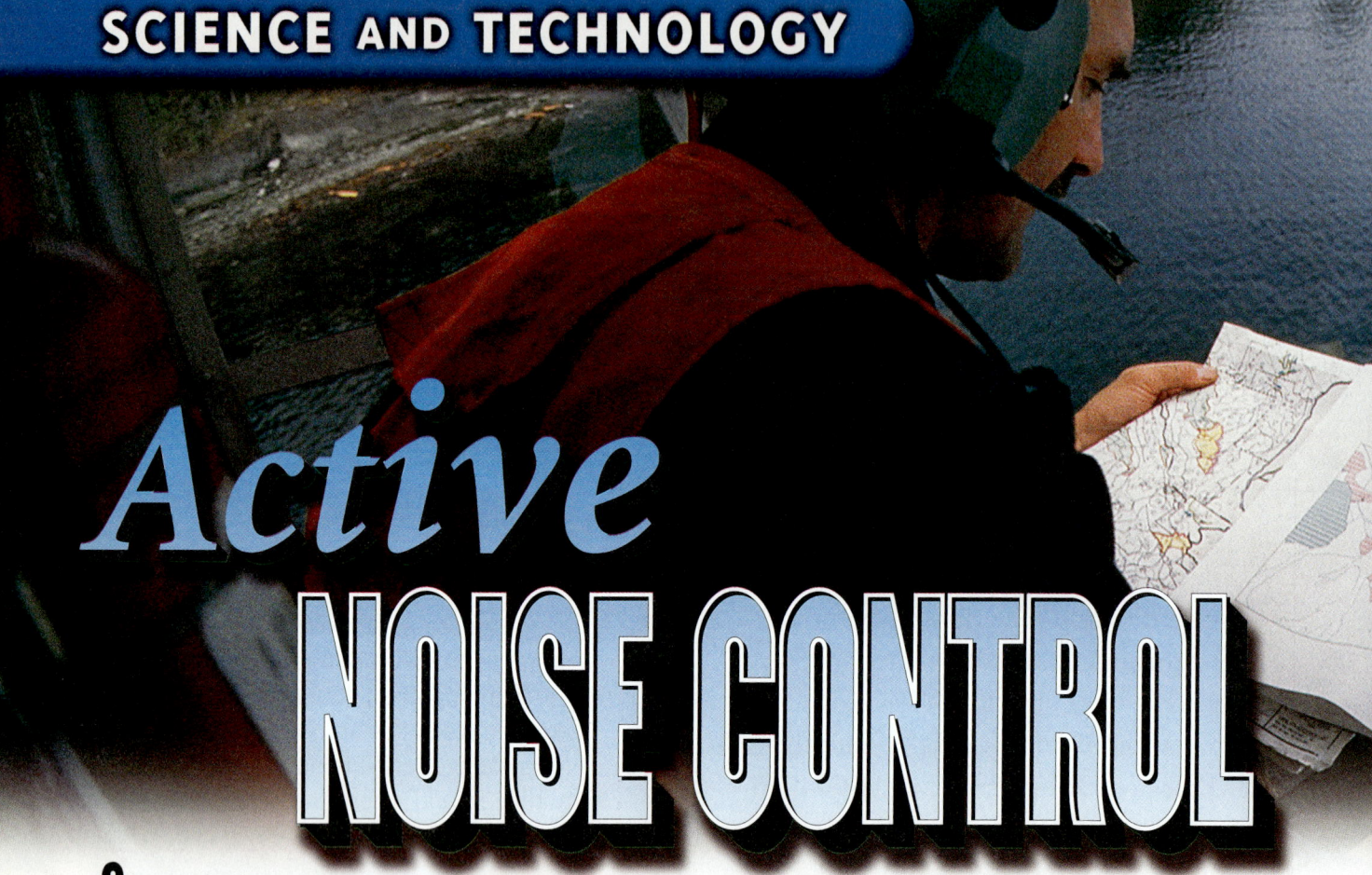

Sound can be beautiful, as some music is. Sound can give information, as in the case of warning bells or someone speaking to tell you how to fix your bicycle. But sometimes sound is just noise.

Noise

Some noise is unwanted sound. It upsets people and makes them angry. Think of how listening to a jackhammer or a chainsaw outside your window all day long would make you feel. A sound that one person thinks is pleasantly loud may be an unwanted noise to another person. Still, any loud sound, whether or not you like it, can cause permanent damage to your ears.

Noise Reduction

Most ways of reducing noise involve absorbing sound or spreading out sound energy. For example, inside a car muffler, sound waves bounce off many walls and dividers. Each bounce takes a little energy out of the sound wave. As a result, the car makes less noise. Rugs, curtains, and ceiling tiles work in much the same way. All these ways of reducing noise are *passive*—they don't need energy to make them work.

For several years now, scientists have been working on a process called active noise control (ANC). ANC makes sounds to cancel out noise. It does this by making sound waves that are the exact opposite of the noise waves. Where a noise wave has a compression, the ANC wave doesn't. When the two waves meet, their areas of high and low pressure cancel each other out.

Another way ANC ideas could be used is to reduce vibrations while making lenses for cameras and telescopes. For example, it's important that lenses be as smooth as possible to give a clear image. Most lenses now are ground by a robot using a grinding tool. The tool vibrates, so the surface of the lens isn't completely smooth. A person must do the final polishing. This adds time and cost. If the grinder did not vibrate, no human polisher would be needed. This would lower the cost of lenses.

THINK ABOUT IT

1. Why do you think ANC works best indoors?
2. Do you think ANC could be used to block out noise from your neighbor's stereo?

An ANC system is made up of microphones to pick up the noise, a computer to analyze the noise, and speakers to make the sound waves that cancel other sounds.

ANC works best indoors on noise that repeats, for example inside airplanes and cars, where you might hear the sound of tires on the road or propellers turning. ANC headphones for use in helicopters are one success story. They allow the person wearing them to hear people talking and sounds of warning sirens, but they cancel out the low-pitched sounds from the rotor blades.

Other Uses for ANC

What works for noise may also work for other unwanted vibrations. ANC technology might help prevent or lessen earthquake damage. When a building begins to shake, opposing vibrations made by an ANC system could help stop the shaking.

CAREERS
ACOUSTICAL ENGINEER

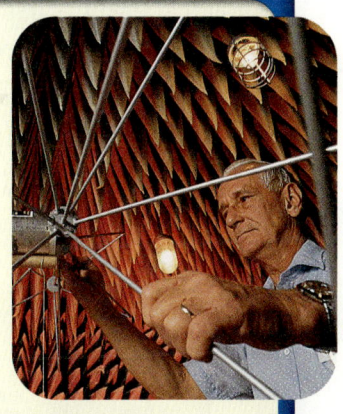

What They Do *Acoustics* (uh·KOOS·tiks) is the science of sound. Acoustical engineers analyze sounds and design ways to control sound. They work with industries to control noise, and they help design buildings such as hospitals that need quiet. They also help design buildings that have special sound needs, such as concert halls.

Education and Training To be an acoustical engineer, you must have at least a bachelor's degree in engineering. Some acoustical engineers study physics and then engineering. Engineers who have the letters *PE* after their names have passed state tests to prove they have the knowledge needed to be professional engineers.

WEB LINK
For Science and Technology updates, visit the Harcourt Internet site.
www.harcourtschool.com

PEOPLE IN SCIENCE

Amar Gopal Bose
SOUND ENGINEER

To celebrate finishing his college research, Amar Bose treated himself to a new sound system. But he didn't like the way the speakers sounded. He began to study acoustics (uh•KOOS•tiks), the science of sound, so he could build better speakers.

The speaker in a stereo system changes electric signals to vibrations. The vibrations create sound waves. Most sound systems need two speakers to play sounds correctly. One speaker makes high sounds, and one makes low sounds. Each speaker is usually put into a wooden box. The size and shape of the box affect how the speaker sounds.

Bose graduated from the Massachusetts Institute of Technology (MIT) and went to Delhi, India, to teach at the National Physics Laboratory. He later returned to teach at MIT. During this time, he continued experimenting with sound. Starting in 1959, Bose received a number of patents for designs of sound systems, including loudspeakers. Five years later, Bose started his own company with a former student.

At the beginning, Bose wasn't paid a salary and he worked at night after teaching classes at MIT. Now, his company is successful and has more than 2,500 workers.

Bose still listens to music. He took violin lessons when he was younger but decided to study science instead. When he has time, he listens to classical music, including classical music of India.

THINK ABOUT IT

1. The speaker that handles low-pitched sounds is called a woofer. The speaker that handles high-pitched sounds is called a tweeter. Why might this be so?
2. With an adult's permission, look at a sound system in your school, home, or family car. What size and shape are the speakers? How do they sound?

ACTIVITIES FOR HOME OR SCHOOL

SOUNDS OF WATER GLASSES

How do water glasses make sounds with different pitches?

Materials
- 4 or 5 identical water glasses
- water
- metal spoon

Procedure
1. Put a different amount of water in each glass.
2. Predict which glass will have the highest pitch and which will have the lowest pitch.
3. Tap each glass lightly with the back of the spoon and listen.

Draw Conclusions
Were your predictions correct? What relationship did you observe between pitch and water level?

SOUNDS AND MATTER

Can you hear sounds through a solid, a liquid, and a gas?

Materials
- tuning fork
- board eraser
- metric ruler
- balloon
- water

Procedure
1. **Listen to a sound through a gas.** Hold the tuning fork about 20 cm from one ear. Strike the fork with the eraser. 
2. **Listen to a sound through a solid.** Place one ear on a desk. Cover your other ear with your hand. Have a partner strike the tuning fork with the eraser and hold the base of the tuning fork against the desktop about 20 cm from your ear.
3. **Listen to a sound through a liquid.** Fill the balloon with water until it is about 20 cm long. Place one end of the balloon against your ear. Cover your other ear with your hand. Have your partner strike the tuning fork and hold its base against the opposite end of the balloon.

Draw Conclusions
Was the tuning fork loudest when you heard it through the air, through the water, or through the desk? Explain.

CHAPTER 3 Review and Test Preparation

Vocabulary Review

Use the terms below to complete the sentences. The numbers in ( ) tell you where to look in the chapter if you need help.

sounds (E70)
sound waves (E71)
compression (E71)
amplitude (E72)
wavelength (E72)
loudness (E78)
pitch (E79)
speed of sound (E84)
echo (E86)
sonic boom (E88)

1. The ____ of a sound describes how high or low a sound is.
2. Moving areas of high and low pressure that carry sound are ____.
3. Vibrations that you hear are ____.
4. The amount of sound energy reaching your ears is ____.
5. A reflection of sound is an ____.
6. How fast sound moves is the ____.
7. The sound of a shock wave produced by an object moving faster than the speed of sound is a ____.
8. A ____ is a place where particles are squeezed closer together by a sound wave.
9. The height of a wave above rest position is its ____.
10. The distance from one point on a wave ripple to the same point on the next ripple is its ____.

Connect Concepts

Use the terms in the Word Bank to complete the diagram.

pitch   **sound wave**   **sound**   **echo**
loudness   **vibrates**   **reflect**

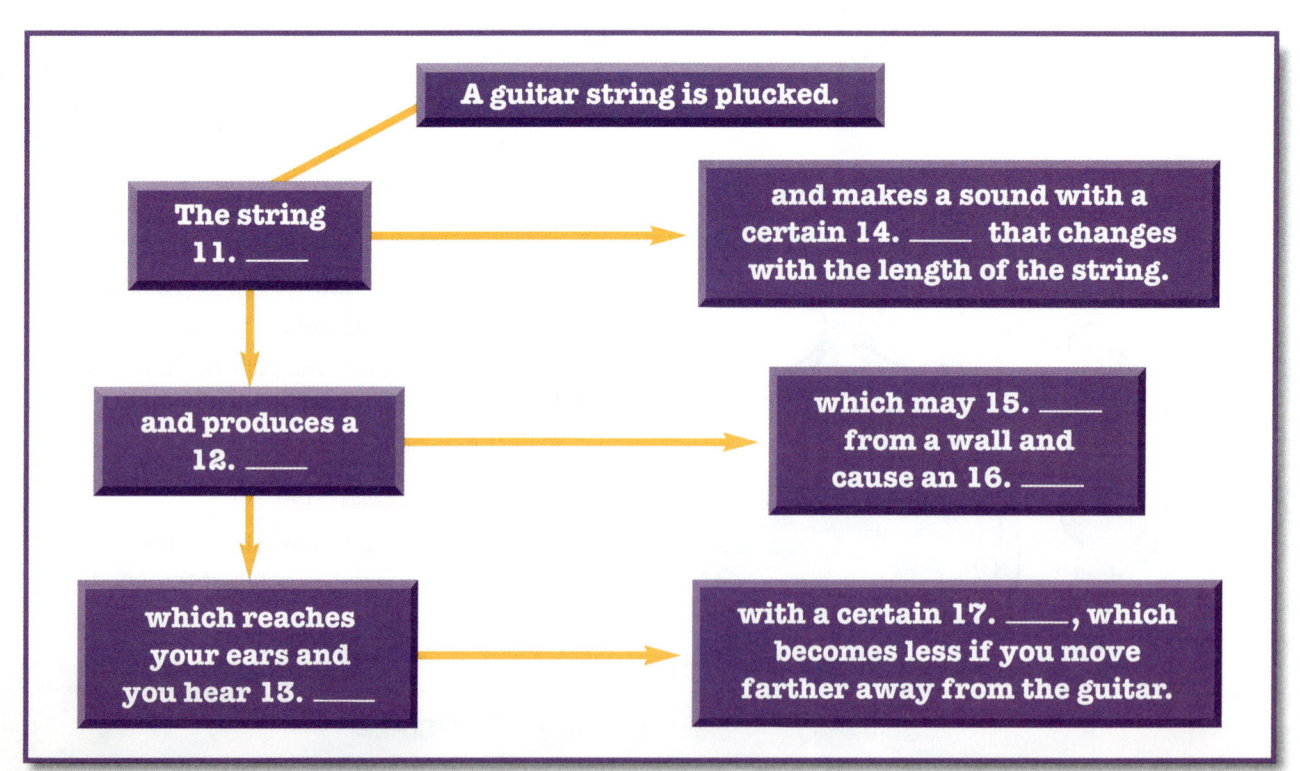

A guitar string is plucked.

The string 11. ____

and produces a 12. ____

which reaches your ears and you hear 13. ____

and makes a sound with a certain 14. ____ that changes with the length of the string.

which may 15. ____ from a wall and cause an 16. ____

with a certain 17. ____, which becomes less if you move farther away from the guitar.

E94

Check Understanding

Write the letter of the best choice.

18. Sound waves cannot travel through —
    A a solid
    B gases
    C empty space
    D liquids

19. What we hear as pitch is related mostly to —
    F reflection
    G how far away the source of the sound is
    H the speed of sound
    J how fast the source of the sound is moving back and forth

20. You can make the sound louder if you pluck a guitar string by —
    A moving the string farther before letting go
    B stopping the string when it starts to move
    C shortening the string
    D lengthening the string

21. A sound wave has areas called ____ where particles are squeezed together.
    F echoes
    G compressions
    H sonic booms
    J pitches

22. If the ____ of a wave changes, you will hear a softer sound because less energy is reaching your ears.
    A pitch
    B wavelength
    C amplitude
    D echo

23. You are more likely to hear an echo when standing —
    F close to a short wall
    G facing a tall, smooth wall
    H in a large, open field
    J in a very small room

24. A ____ is the sound you hear when something is moving faster than the speed of sound.
    A vibration
    B pitch wave
    C high pitch
    D sonic boom

Critical Thinking

25. Explain how the vibrations you cause by hitting a drum move from the drum to your brain, where they are interpreted as sound.

26. How does a sonic boom form?

Process Skills Review

27. What features would you use to describe a sound that you **observed**?

28. What is the difference between **observing** a vibration and **inferring** how the vibration affects air particles?

29. Why do scientists sometimes use drawings to **record** the **data** they **gather**?

Performance Assessment

Sound Vibrations

Strike a tuning fork. After you hear the sound of the fork, place its base on a tabletop. Observe and report what happens. Explain your observations in terms of vibrations and sound waves. You may use a drawing as part of your explanation.

E95

CHAPTER 4

Light

Flick! Bounce, reflect, bounce! That's what happens to the light from a flashlight if you turn it on and shine it at your image in a mirror. The light goes so fast it seems to hit the mirror and you at the same instant you turn the flashlight on!

Vocabulary Preview

reflection
refraction
absorption
opaque
translucent
transparent
prism
visible spectrum

Fast Fact

We see stars as they were when their light left them. This table shows how long it takes the light from some space objects to reach us.

The Speed of Light

Object in Space	Distance from Earth	Light Reaches Us In
Moon	384,462 km	$1\frac{1}{3}$ seconds
Venus	41.2 million km	$2\frac{1}{3}$ minutes
Sun	149.7 million km	$8\frac{1}{2}$ minutes
Alpha Centauri	40.2 trillion km	$4\frac{1}{3}$ years
Sirius	81.7 trillion km	$8\frac{1}{2}$ years
Andromeda Galaxy	21.2 billion billion km	$2\frac{1}{4}$ million years

Andromeda Galaxy

Fast Fact

Have you ever seen your reflection in a pool of water? This three-meter mirror is a pool of mercury, a liquid metal. It is part of a telescope. The whole pool is spun to give the mirror a smooth curve like a saucer.

Fast Fact

Light travels at the speed of 299,330 kilometers per second (186,000 mi per sec). If you could run that fast, you would be able to circle the Earth more than seven times in just one second!

LESSON 1

How Does Light Behave?

In this lesson, you can . . .

INVESTIGATE how light travels.

LEARN ABOUT things light can do.

LINK to math, writing, drama, and technology.

INVESTIGATE

How Light Travels

Activity Purpose Have you ever noticed how the shadow of a tree changes during the day? It's long in the morning, short at noon, and long again in the late afternoon. These changes happen because the tree blocks the light and the position of the sun in the sky changes. In this investigation, you will change the position of index cards and use a light bulb to **observe** how light travels.

Materials
- 3 index cards
- ruler
- pencil
- clay
- small, short lamp without a lampshade

Activity Procedure

1. Make a large X on each card. To draw each line, lay the ruler from one corner of the card to the opposite corner. (Picture A)

2. On each card, make a hole at the place where the lines of the X cross. Use the pencil to make the holes.

3. Use the clay to make a stand for each card. Make sure the holes in the cards are the same height. Stack the cards on top of each other. Line up the edges. Then, hold them tightly together and use a pencil to make sure the holes are the same size and at the same height. (Picture B)

◀ Late in the day, the position of the sun causes long shadows.

E98

4. Turn on the light. Look through the holes in the cards. Move the cards around on the table until you can see the light bulb through all three cards at once. You may have to pull down the blinds or dim the room lights to help you see the light bulb. Draw a picture showing where the light is and where the cards are.

5. Move the cards around to new places on the table. Each time you move the cards, draw a picture showing where the cards are. Do not move the light! **Observe** the light through the holes each time.

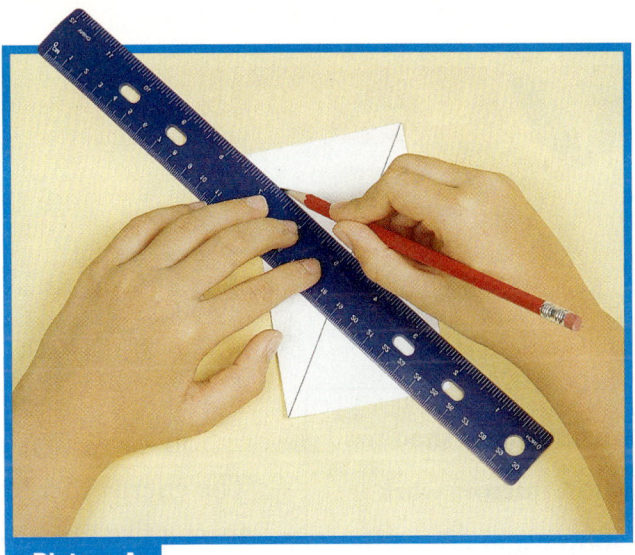

Picture A

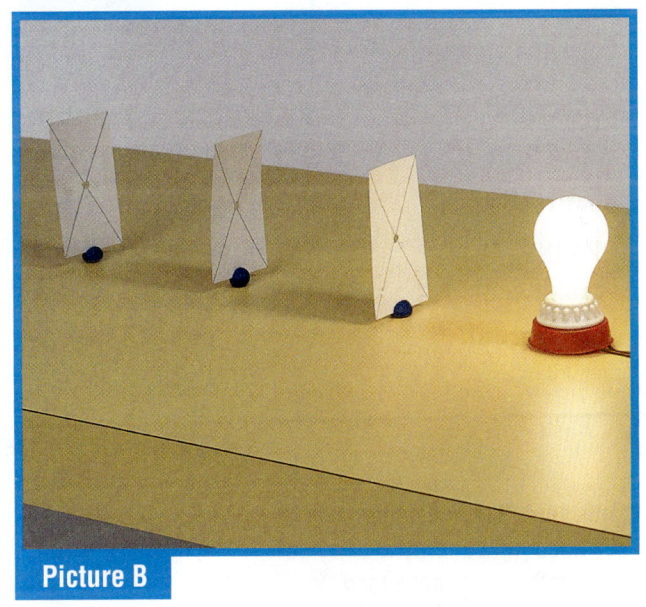

Picture B

Draw Conclusions

1. Where were the cards when you were able to see the light?

2. Were there times you couldn't see the light? Where were the cards then?

3. **Scientists at Work** Scientists **observe** carefully and then **record** what they observe. Often they draw pictures to **communicate** what they observe. Did drawing pictures help you describe what you saw? Explain.

Investigate Further Do you **predict** you will get the same results if the cards are at an angle to the lamp? Use the clay to attach the cards to a meterstick. Put a stack of books near the light. Rest the meterstick on books and hold it at an angle to the table. Test your prediction.

Process Skill Tip

Scientists can learn many things about the world just by **observing**. Then they **record** what they see. After they observe the same thing many times, they **communicate** by telling other scientists what they have observed.

LEARN ABOUT

Light

FIND OUT

- what makes shadows
- how mirrors work
- how water affects the path of light.

VOCABULARY

reflection
refraction
absorption
opaque
translucent
transparent

Light Energy

You know that energy is the ability to cause things to change. The energy in a fire changes a sheet of paper into ashes. The heat from a fire can change your hands from cold to warm. Bacteria use energy to change a dead log into soil for plants.

Light is also a kind of energy. Light energy can make many changes. Without light energy, you could not see anything. Light energy gives things colors. The sun shines on the soil, and plants grow. Doctors use the light energy of lasers to perform some operations. Light energy can make cars move. In space, satellites and the space station use solar cells to change light energy into electricity. If all satellites depended on batteries instead, the added weight would make them too expensive to launch into orbit.

✓ What are three changes light energy can cause?

Plants can't live in complete darkness. They need light energy to carry out photosynthesis to make food. ▼

▲ Scientists are finding new ways to use light. The solar panels on the rear of the roof change light energy from the sun into electricity. Some of the energy is used right away. The rest is stored in batteries to be used later.

◀ The sun provides energy to Earth.

Shadows

When you put your hand in front of a lamp, you make a shadow on the wall. The shadows move and change shape as you move your hand. Shadows move and change because of the way light travels.

Light travels in straight lines. When you put your hand in front of a lamp, some of the straight lines of light hit your hand. The shadow on the wall shows where the light is blocked by your hand. When you move your hand, the shadow moves because your hand blocks different lines of light.

In the investigation you could see the light bulb only when the holes in the three cards were in a straight line. When one of the holes wasn't in line with the others, it blocked the line of light. How did this show that light travels in a straight line?

When you stand in the sun, you block some of the lines of sunlight. As the sun moves in the sky, you block different lines of light. When the sun is low in the sky, in the morning and in the afternoon, your shadow is long. When the sun is high overhead, your shadow is short.

Long ago, people figured out that they could predict the pattern of changing shadows during a day. They used that pattern to tell time. A device used to do so is called a sundial. It is made up of a triangular pointer called a *gnomon* (NOH•mahn) and a circular dial marking the hours of the day. As the sun moves across the sky, the shadow of the gnomon moves from left to right and points to the hours of the day.

✓ **How does light travel?**

▲ Early in the morning, the sun is rising in the east. The shadow of the gnomon on this sundial points to eight o'clock on the far left side of the dial.

▲ Later in the day, the sun is in the west. The shadow of the gnomon has moved to point to two o'clock on the dial.

E101

Bouncing Light

Look in a mirror. What do you see? You probably see yourself and some of the things around you. You are looking in front of you at the mirror. But the things you see in the mirror are next to you or even behind you. How is this possible?

Hold a lamp in front of a mirror, and you will see the lamp in the mirror. The light from the lamp moves in a straight line to the mirror. When it hits the mirror, it bounces off. It is still traveling in a straight line. But now it's going in a new direction. It is coming straight back to you. The bouncing of light off an object is called **reflection** (rih•FLEK•shuhn). You see objects in a mirror because their light is reflected straight back to you.

Light bounces from a mirror like a ball bounces from a wall. If you roll a ball straight at a wall, it bounces straight back to you. If you roll a ball toward a wall at an angle, it bounces away from the wall at an angle. This is why you can use a mirror to look around a corner. The light strikes the mirror at an angle and bounces to your eyes.

◀ When light bounces off a mirror, the light changes direction. The letters on the sign are backward. This is because a mirror reverses an image from left to right.

Light travels in straight lines. Even if it bounces off many mirrors, you can still see the object. If the mirrors are lined up exactly right, you can see many reflections of the object. ▼

Light bouncing off a smooth surface gives an image you can see. A mirror is very smooth. So are shiny metal and still water. You can see yourself in these things. But most things aren't as smooth as mirrors. Most things are bumpy. When light hits a bumpy surface, each straight line of light goes off in a different direction. Then you don't see any image.

A mirror can also have a smooth, curved surface. Mirrors like this make your reflection seem bigger or smaller than you really are. Carnival fun-houses and science museums often have such mirrors on display.

✓ **What is reflection?**

◀ If the water is rippling, each wave reflects light in a different direction. Since the light is traveling in so many directions, it is hard to see a clear picture on the surface of the water.

The water on the lake is so still that it acts like a mirror. ▼

Bending Light

Light doesn't bounce off every surface. There are some things light goes through. That's why you can see through air, water, and glass.

Light travels at different speeds in air, water, and glass. So when light goes from one thing to another, such as from air to glass, it changes speed. Any time light goes from one kind of matter to another, it changes speed. If light hits the new matter straight on, it keeps going straight. But if light hits the new matter at a slant, the light bends. The bending of light when it moves from one kind of matter to another is called **refraction** (rih•FRAK•shuhn).

Light moving from air to glass is like an in-line skater moving from a sidewalk to the grass. If the skater is going straight into the grass, both front wheels hit the grass at the same time. The skater slows down because grass is softer than concrete. But he or she continues to go straight. If the skater does not go straight into the grass, one wheel hits the grass first. The other is still on the sidewalk. The wheel that hits the grass first slows down first. This makes the skater turn toward the grass. If the skater were moving at an angle from the grass onto concrete, his or her path would bend closer to the grass for the same reason.

Scientists use refraction to study objects and to fix problems. The thick hand lenses that you use to observe small objects use refraction to make an object seem larger than it really is. Eye doctors make lenses to correct people's eyesight. Both eyeglasses and contact lenses are designed to control refraction.

✓ **What is refraction?**

Half of this toy diver is in the water. You see the bottom half through the water. The light bends when it hits the water. You see the top half through air. This light isn't bending. So the toy diver looks as if it is broken in two. ▼

▲ Here the light hits the glass at an angle. This time the light bends and changes direction.

Light travels through air and glass. This light hits the glass straight on and keeps going straight. ▶

Here the light is refracted three times. So the pencil looks as if it is broken into four pieces. ▶

E105

Stopping Light

You have learned that you can see through air, water, and glass. Light travels through these forms of matter. But most matter doesn't let light pass. When light hits a wall, the wall stops, or absorbs, the light. Stopping light is called **absorption** (ab•SAWRP•shuhn). Have you ever watched rain falling on grass? The soil absorbs the water. Most matter absorbs light in the same way.

When light hits most objects, some of the light bounces off and the rest is absorbed. Smooth, shiny objects reflect almost all the light that hits them. Other objects absorb most of the light that hits them and reflect the rest. If an object doesn't produce its own light, what you see when you look at it is the light that bounces off it.

There are three ways an object can interact with light. Scientists have a name for each of them. An **opaque** (oh•PAYK) object reflects or absorbs all light. If you try to look through an opaque object, you see only light reflecting from the object. A wood door is opaque.

A **translucent** (trans•LOO•suhnt) object reflects and absorbs some light. You can see a blurry or fuzzy image when you look through a translucent object. Some light is reflected from the object and some goes through. A fogged-over window is translucent.

A **transparent** (trans•PAIR•uhnt) object does not reflect or absorb much light. You can see a clear image when you look through a transparent object. Windows and plastic wrap are transparent. Colored, clear glass is also transparent.

✓ **What is absorption?**

▲ You can't see through this opaque, blue plate.

▲ The boy's hand and face are blurred behind this translucent plate.

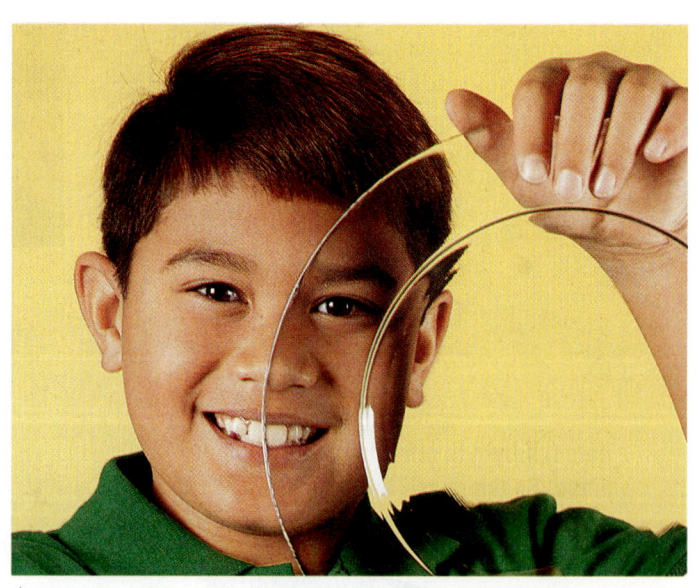

▲ You can see a clear image through this transparent plate.

Summary

Light energy can cause things to change. Plants require light to make food. Some machines use energy from light to generate electricity. Light travels in a straight line unless it is reflected, refracted, or absorbed. Mirrors produce clear images because their surfaces are smooth. Bumpy surfaces don't produce clear images. Objects can be classified as opaque, translucent, or transparent based on how they interact with light.

Review

1. What does a mirror do?
2. Your shadow is shorter than you at 10:00 in the morning. How do you predict its length will change over the next two hours?
3. Give one example each of an object that is opaque, translucent, and transparent. Then use *reflection* and *absorption* to explain why each object matches its description.
4. **Critical Thinking** You stick your hand into an aquarium to get something out. Why does your hand look as if it is cut off from your arm?
5. **Test Prep** Which is an example of light energy being used?
   A water boiling
   B a plant growing
   C a ball bouncing
   D a girl lifting a chair

LINKS

MATH LINK

Elapsed Time How many hours of daylight are there if the sun rises at 6:15 A.M. and sets at 7:15 P.M.? If it rises at 7:00 A.M. and sets at 5:30 P.M.?

WRITING LINK

Informative Writing—Description Write a short story for your classmates that describes a building reflected in a puddle. Include one description each for when the water is smooth and when it is rippling.

DRAMA LINK

Shadow Puppets Make a screen out of a cloth sheet. Shine a light behind it. Make shadow animals on the sheet. Use them to tell a story to the class.

ART LINK

Stained Glass Stained glass art uses properties of light and materials. Use library resources to find an example of stained glass art such as a window, lamp, or sculpture. Explain for your classmates how the artist used properties of light.

TECHNOLOGY LINK

Learn more about how light can be used by watching *Using Natural Light* on the **Harcourt Science Newsroom Video.**

LESSON 2

How Are Light and Color Related?

In this lesson, you can . . .

INVESTIGATE rainbows.

LEARN ABOUT light and color.

LINK to math, writing, art, and technology.

INVESTIGATE

Making a Rainbow

Activity Purpose Grass and leaves from trees appear in many colors of green when you see them in daylight. At night under moonlight, you see them only in shades of gray. The daytime world is a colorful place. You know that you can see colors only when the light is shining. In the dark you can't see color. So is color in the objects or in the light? In this investigation you can **observe** where colors come from.

Materials
- small mirror
- clear glass
- water
- flashlight

Activity Procedure

1. Gently place the mirror into the glass. Slant it up against the side.
2. Fill the glass with water. (Picture A)
3. Set the glass on a table. Turn out the lights. Make the room as dark as possible.

◀ You can see many, many more than twelve colors. But, the colors of these twelve pencils can be mixed to draw much of the colorful world around you.

Picture A

Picture B

4. Shine the flashlight into the glass of water. Aim for the mirror. Adjust your aim until the light hits the mirror. If necessary, adjust the mirror in the water. Make sure the mirror is slanted.

5. **Observe** what happens to the light in the glass. Look at the light where it hits the ceiling or the wall. **Record** what you observe. (Picture B)

Draw Conclusions

1. What did the light look like as it went into the glass?
2. What did the light look like after it came out of the glass?
3. **Scientists at Work** Scientists **draw conclusions** based on what they **observe**. What conclusions can you draw about where color comes from?

Investigate Further Change the angles of the mirror and the flashlight. Which setup gives the best result? Draw a picture of the best arrangement.

Process Skill Tip

You **draw conclusions** when you have gathered data by observing, measuring, and using numbers. Conclusions tell what you have learned.

LEARN ABOUT

FIND OUT
- how many colors are in light
- what makes a rainbow

VOCABULARY

prism
visible spectrum

Light and Color

Prisms

Have you ever drawn a picture of the sun? Did you color it yellow? People often do. But sunlight is really made of many different colors. Yellow is only one of them. The sunlight you see is really white light. White is the color of all the sun's colors mixed together.

Different colors of light travel at different speeds in water and in glass. So when white light moves from air to glass or from air to water, the different colors of light bend at different angles. They separate into each individual color.

In the investigation you used water and a mirror to break white light into different colors. Scientists use glass triangle prisms to experiment with light. A **prism** (PRIZ•uhm) is a solid object that bends light. When white light hits the prism, each color of light bends at a different angle. Red light is bent the least. Blue light is bent the most. Light that passes through a prism separates into a rainbow. The colors of a rainbow make up the visible spectrum. The **visible spectrum** (SPEHK•truhm) is made up of all the colors of light that people can see.

✓ What is a prism?

◀ White light is made up of many different colors of light. When a beam of white light passes through a prism, it is refracted twice—once when it passes from air into glass and again when it passes from glass into air. The colors of light are refracted different amounts each time, so the beam spreads out into rainbow bands of color.

THE INSIDE STORY
How Rainbows Form

You can sometimes see a rainbow in the sky during a summer rain when the sun is out. Because of the way raindrops refract and reflect white sunlight, you can see a rainbow only when the sun is behind you. ▶

Each drop of falling water in a rainstorm is like a tiny prism and mirror. Sunlight enters a drop, is reflected from the back wall, and then passes out through the front. So, it is refracted twice, just as it is in a prism.

There are more colors in a rainbow than anyone could count. However, most people use just six colors to remember the order in which the bands always appear: red, orange, yellow, green, blue, and violet.

Adding Colors

A prism breaks white light into colors. You can also add colors together. When you add different colored lights together, they form other colors. Shining a red light and a green light onto the same spot will make a yellow light. Shining a blue light and a red light onto the same spot will make a purple light. You can add red light, blue light, and green light in different ways to make all other colors.

Televisions and computer monitors add light colors. The inside of a TV screen is coated with millions of tiny dots of red, green, and blue. Dots that are near each other are made to glow in different patterns and brightnesses. Your eyes combine the colors to make the pictures you see.

✓ **What is one method for making colors?**

Seeing Colors

All the colors of light, called white light, hit every object you see. Most objects absorb most of the light, but not all of it. The light that is not absorbed is reflected and is the color you see. For example, green grass absorbs all of the white light except the green part. The green part reflects back to your eyes, and you see green grass.

Mixing paint colors is a way of controlling absorption and reflection. Yellow paint reflects yellows and absorbs other colors. Blue paint reflects blues and absorbs other colors. When you mix yellow and blue, all the colors are absorbed, or subtracted out, except greens. So, you see shades of green when you mix blue and yellow paint. When you mix all paint colors, almost all light is absorbed. So you see very dark brown or black.

✓ **Why do you see color?**

Three basic light colors are red, blue, and green. They will form all other colors. Adding all three of these colors will give white light.

◄ The red rose absorbs all parts of white light except red. Red light is reflected, and we see a red flower.

Summary

White light is made up of many colors mixed together. A prism separates the colors. Raindrops act like prisms to form rainbows. You can make colors by adding different colored lights. The colors of objects you see are the colors of light that the objects reflect.

Review

1. Describe how a prism works.
2. Name the colors that make up white light.
3. What happens if you add different colors of light?
4. **Critical Thinking** Why don't you see a rainbow during most rainstorms?
5. **Test Prep** Which light colors are absorbed and which are reflected by a yellow tulip? (HINT: Look at the lights on page E112.)
   A Absorbed—red, reflected—blue and green
   B Absorbed—blue, reflected—red and green
   C Absorbed—green, reflected—red and blue
   D Absorbed—red, reflected—red and green

LINKS

MATH LINK

Identify Solid Figures The bases of a triangular prism are triangles. What are the bases of a rectangular prism?

WRITING LINK

Informative Writing — Narration Find five different words that describe colors of red. Write a paragraph for your teacher, describing a scene that includes each of these colors.

ART LINK

Color Wheel Find out what a color wheel is and how an artist might use one. Draw one, and explain it to a classmate.

SOCIAL STUDIES LINK

Sources of Dyes Before artificial dyes were invented, people used natural materials to dye cloth. Colors made by such dyes were often named after the source of the dye. Use library resources to find out the sources of these colors: tyrean purple, cochineal red, and indigo. Make a poster to share what you learned.

TECHNOLOGY LINK

Visit the Harcourt Learning Site for related links, activities, and resources.
www.harcourtschool.com

SCIENCE THROUGH TIME

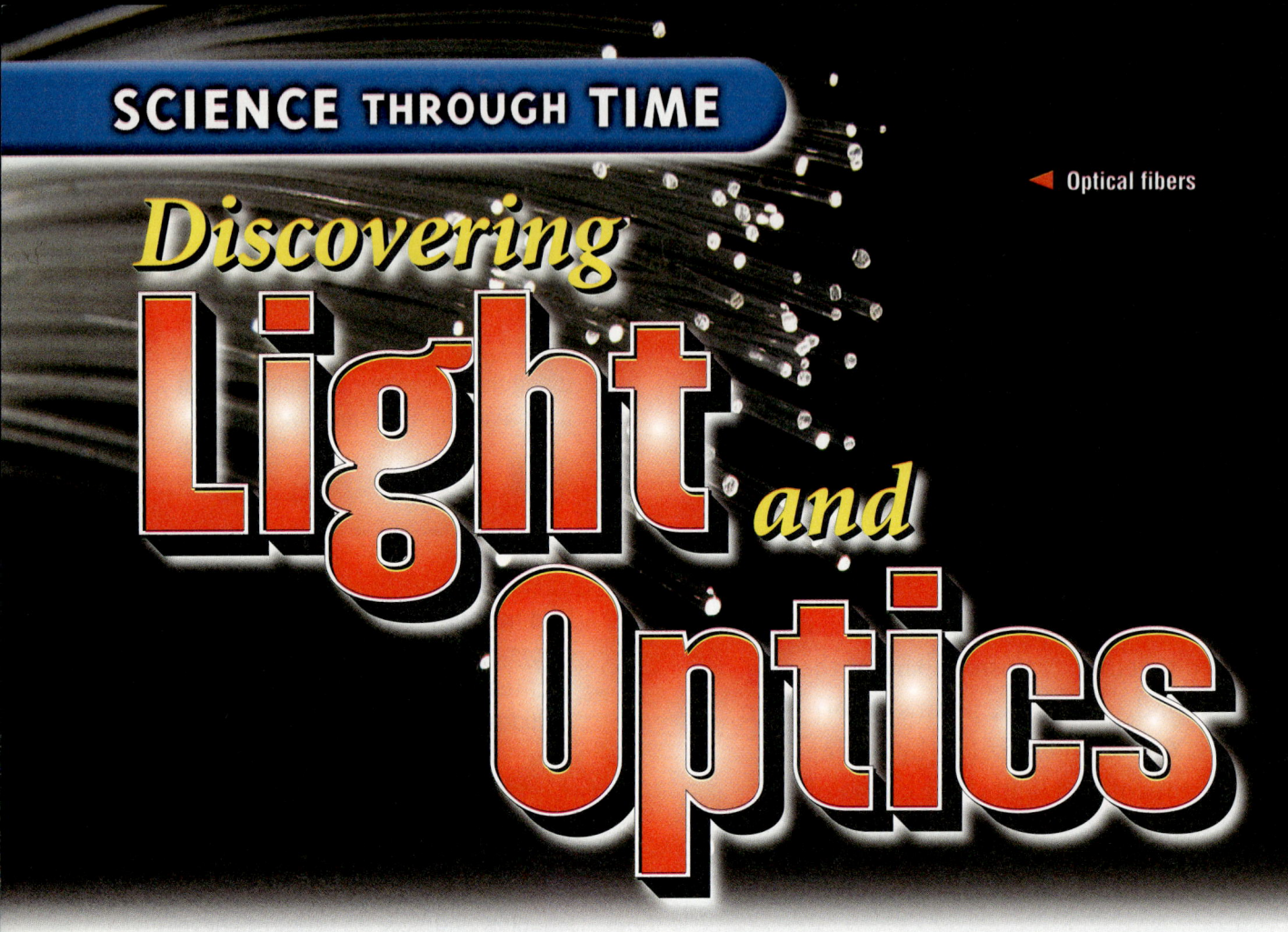

◀ Optical fibers

Discovering Light and Optics

We use our eyes to see. A curved lens inside the eye bends light, focusing an image on the retina. This image is sent to the brain, which interprets the image.

Using Lenses

Lenses in tools such as microscopes, telescopes, and even eyeglasses work the same way. All lenses have at least one curved surface. The curve of the lens bends and focuses the light. The image formed by the lens might be smaller than, larger than, or the same size as the original object.

People have worn eyeglasses for hundreds of years. The Italian explorer Marco Polo saw people in China wearing glasses around 1275. After books became common in the late 1400s, glasses became common for reading. During the 1600s, people discovered that using lenses would correct nearsightedness. Nearsighted people have difficulty seeing objects far away. More than 125 million people in the United States now have corrected vision.

Today, many people correct their eyesight with contact lenses. The first glass contact lenses were made in the 1930s. They were expensive, uncomfortable, and hard to make. In 1961, a Czechoslovakian scientist patented a flexible plastic lens that absorbed water. His soft contact lenses were first sold in 1970. They have become more and more popular ever since then.

Lasers—Light in a Straight Line

If you've ever shone a flashlight into a dark room, you've seen a property of most light beams. In most cases, a beam spreads apart as it leaves its source. Lasers turn a regular beam of light into a narrow, straight beam of bright light. Laser light is very focused and has only one color.

The History of Optics

1450 Concave lenses are used in eyeglasses.

1590 Microscope is invented.

1609 Galileo builds a telescope and observes the moons of Jupiter.

1666 Sir Isaac Newton discovers that white light is made up of all colors.

1784 Benjamin Franklin invents bifocals, for people who need correction of both close-up and distance vision.

1960 T. H. Maiman builds the first laser.

1988 First transatlantic optical fiber carries telephone message.

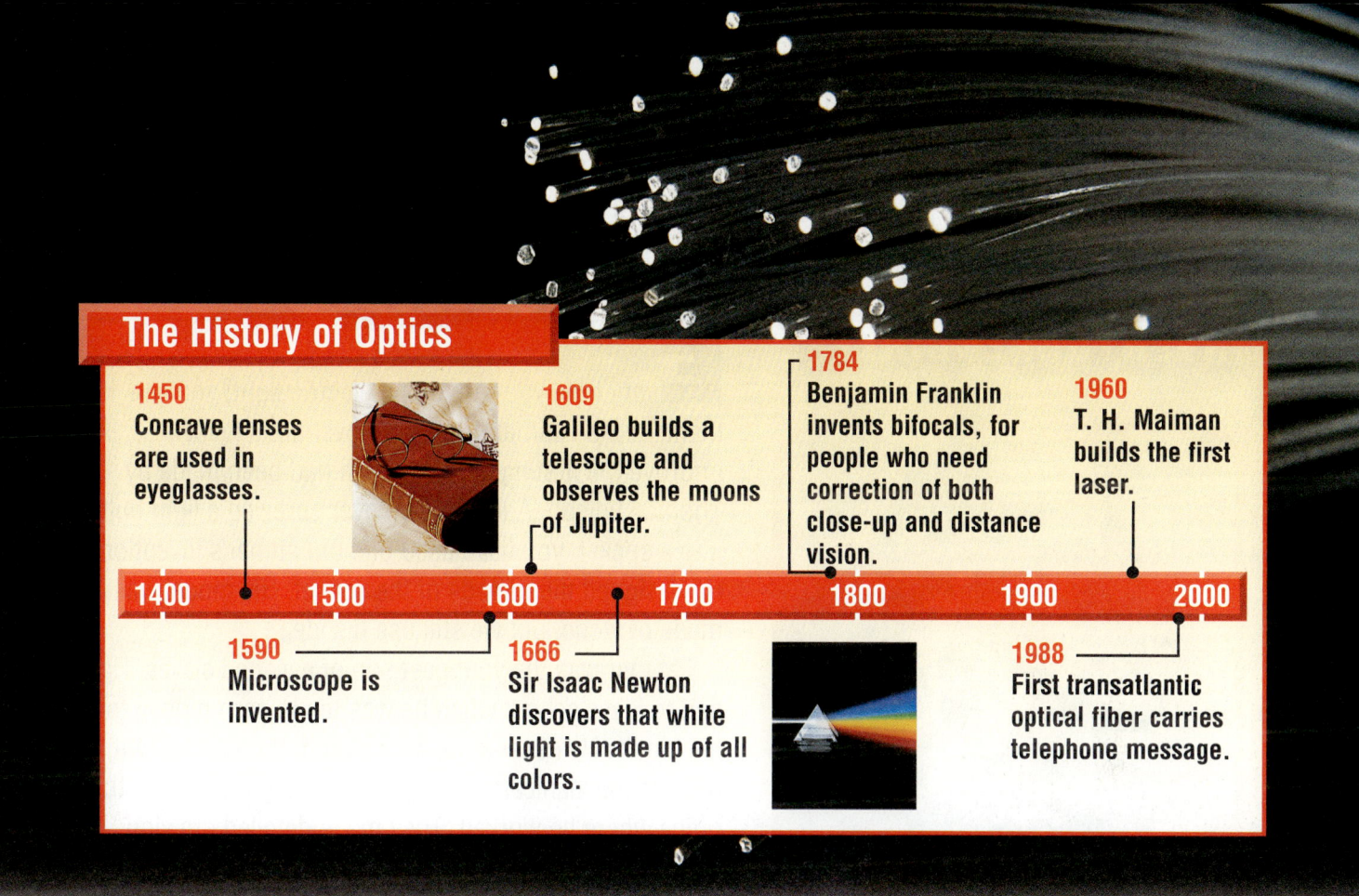

The word *LASER* stands for *l*ight *a*mplification by *s*timulated *e*mission of *r*adiation. This phrase describes how a laser works. Energy is added to a material. Adding energy stimulates, or causes, light radiation. The light that results is amplified, or made stronger, by the shape of the laser.

Laser light is used in many ways. Lasers are used to scan bar codes on products. Laser light has been bounced off the moon to accurately measure its distance from Earth. Physicians use lasers to do surgery. The most common use of lasers is in compact disc (CD) and digital video disc (DVD) players. A laser beam cuts information onto the discs. The narrow beam allows a disc to hold more information than a tape. Lasers are then used to read and play back the recorded information. Besides music, entire encyclopedias have been put on CDs.

Telephones have long used electric current and copper wire to carry messages. Flashes of light can be used to send messages, too. Laser beams can carry many different messages along very thin glass fibers called optical fibers. Many fibers, each carrying a different message, can be squeezed into a single cable. Fiber-optic telephone lines are now used between many cities. Lines were laid across the Atlantic and Pacific Oceans in the late 1980s.

Fiber optics are also used in medicine to make surgery easier. Doctors can use the fibers to see inside the body while making only small cuts—or no cuts at all.

THINK ABOUT IT

1. How can lenses change an image?
2. What are two uses of optical fibers?

PEOPLE IN SCIENCE
Lewis Howard Latimer
INVENTOR, ENGINEER

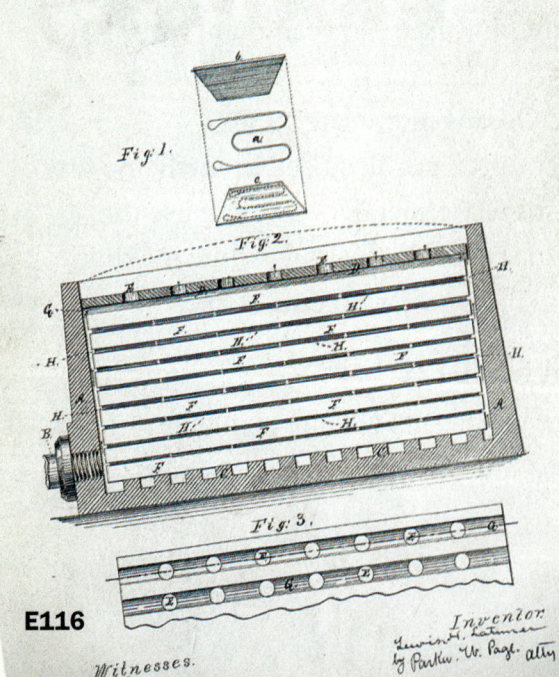

Every time you turn on an electric light, you can thank Lewis Latimer. His many inventions helped improve the first light bulb, which had been made by Thomas Edison. And if you've ever screwed a light bulb into a socket, you have used one of Latimer's inventions. He designed the threads of the socket. His model was made of wood, but we still use his idea.

Latimer was the youngest son of escaped slaves. He had to leave school when he was ten to earn money for his family. He never stopped learning, though. He taught himself mechanical drawing by watching the men in the office where he worked. They made detailed drawings of inventions for patent applications. (Having a patent means the inventor "owns" the idea and the invention.) Latimer's office was near the office of Alexander Graham Bell, who invented the telephone. When Bell applied for a patent, he asked Latimer to make the drawing.

Later Latimer worked with the Edison Pioneers, a group of 80 inventors. He was the only African American in the group. He helped install lighting systems in New York, Philadelphia, Montreal, and even London.

THINK ABOUT IT

1. What do inventing and writing poetry have in common?
2. How is teaching yourself something, perhaps by watching others, different from learning in a classroom?

ACTIVITIES FOR HOME OR SCHOOL

COLORS

What colors are reflected off different colors of paper?

Materials
- glue
- strips of colored construction paper
- prism

Procedure

1. Glue strips of construction paper together in the order of the colors of the rainbow: red, orange, yellow, green, blue, and violet.

2. Use a prism to separate the colors in sunlight. Aim the colors from the prism at the different colors of construction paper.

3. Observe how the light from the prism is reflected by the different colors of construction paper.

Draw Conclusions

What colors from the prism are reflected from the green strip of construction paper? Explain.

MAKE A PERISCOPE

How can you see around a corner?

Materials
- glue
- aluminum foil
- 2 index cards
- shoe box
- black construction paper
- flashlight

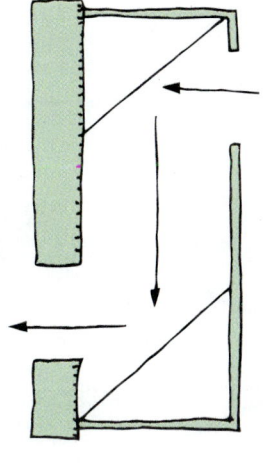

Procedure

1. Glue aluminum foil, shiny side out, to the index cards to make mirrors. Make the foil as smooth as possible.

2. Line the inside of the box with black paper. Cut out a hole in the bottom of the box, about 3 cm from one end. Cut out a hole in the lid about 3 cm from one end.

3. Fold the ends of the aluminum foil mirrors to make tabs. Then glue the aluminum-foil mirrors to the inside of the box as shown.

4. While the glue is still damp, shine a flashlight straight into one of the openings. Look into the second opening and adjust one of the mirrors so that you can clearly see the flashlight. Let the glue dry.

5. Put the lid back on the box, and look through your periscope.

Draw Conclusions

How could you use a periscope to see around a corner?

E117

CHAPTER 4 Review and Test Preparation

Vocabulary Review

Use the terms below to complete the sentences 1 through 8. The page numbers in ( ) tell you where to look in the chapter if you need help.

reflection (E102)   **translucent** (E106)
refraction (E104)   **transparent** (E106)
absorption (E106)   **prism** (E110)
opaque (E106)   **visible spectrum** (E110)

1. The bending of light is called ____.
2. A ____ breaks white light into colors.
3. All the colors that you can see make up the ____.
4. You can't see through aluminum foil at all, so it is ____.
5. The bouncing of light off objects is called ____.
6. A window is ____ because you can see a clear image through it.
7. Stopping light and holding it in is ____.
8. A fogged-over window is ____. You see a blurry image through it.

Check Understanding

Write the letter of the best choice.

13. Suppose you drop a penny into a shallow pool of water. You try to grab it but cannot seem to get your fingers in the right place. This happens because of —
    A reflection
    B absorption
    C refraction
    D light energy

14. Suppose you are standing at a pond. Your friend tries to sneak up on you, but you see him coming. You see him in the pond because of —
    F refraction
    G reflection
    H noise in the grass
    J absorption

15. White light is really —
    A all colors of light mixed
    B a mixture of yellow and white light
    C bright in the morning
    D a mixture of red and green light

Connect Concepts

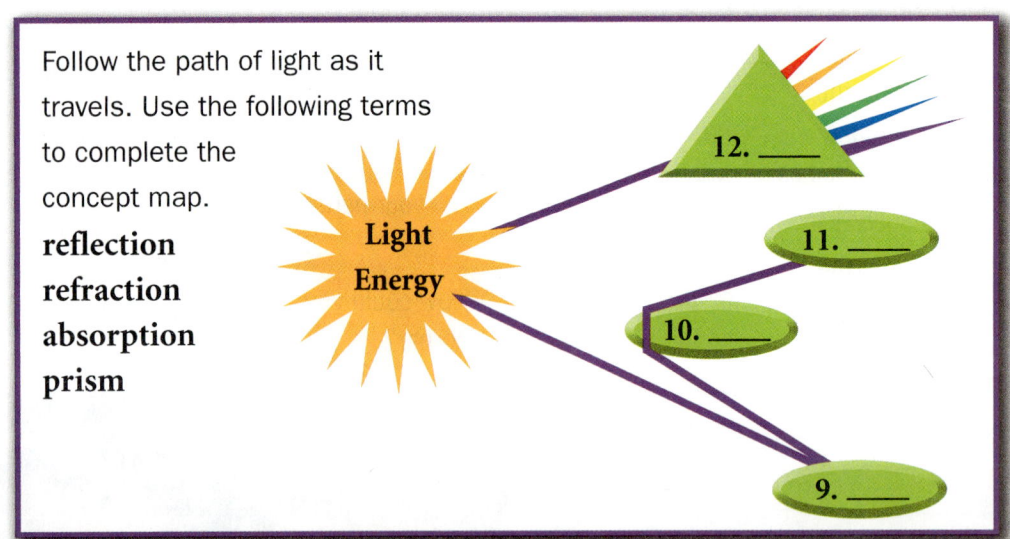

Follow the path of light as it travels. Use the following terms to complete the concept map.

reflection
refraction
absorption
prism

12. ____
11. ____
10. ____
9. ____

E118

16. Light travels —
    F through walls
    G around objects
    H in straight lines
    J in a curvy pattern

17. Most light bulbs have a coating inside the glass that makes them look white. Light still passes through the coating, so it is —
    A opaque
    B transparent
    C translucent
    D a prism

18. A bright, yellow raincoat looks yellow because —
    F it absorbs yellow light and reflects all other colors
    G it reflects a mix of blue and red light
    H it absorbs blue light and reflects a mix of red and green light
    J it refracts yellow light differently than other colors

Critical Thinking

19. A skylight has water drops on it from a rainstorm. The sun comes out, and you see a rainbow on the wall. What is happening?

20. Describe how you could use a mirror to signal your friend in the house across the street.

21. You go to see a play. The light on the stage is yellow. You look up at the lights. They are red and green. Explain.

22. For art class, your teacher has you draw a bowl of fruit. The bowl contains a red apple, an orange, and a banana. After you have finished, your teacher puts a green spotlight on the fruit and asks you to draw it again. Why do you need to draw a new picture?

Process Skills Review

Write *True* or *False*. If the statement is false, correct it to make it true.

23. When you **observe** what is happening in an experiment, you use only your eyes.

24. Scientists sometimes draw pictures to help them **draw conclusions** about their experiments.

Performance Assessment

Make a Model Prism

With a partner, use construction paper to make a large model of a prism breaking a ray of white light into its colors. Be sure to show the colors in the right order. Label each color. Make a hole in the model and add some string so it can be hung up in the classroom. You will need construction paper, glue, scissors, string, and a pencil.

UNIT E EXPEDITIONS

There are many places where you can learn about matter and energy. By visiting the places below, you can learn more about how matter changes and how heat affects matter. You'll also have fun while you learn.

The Discovery Center of Science & Technology

WHAT A learning center with exhibits and hands-on activities

WHERE Bethlehem, Pennsylvania

WHAT CAN YOU DO THERE? Visit the learning center, see the exhibits, and find out more about science through the many activities they offer.

The United States Mint

WHAT A facility where all kinds of United States coins are made

WHERE Denver, Colorado

WHAT CAN YOU DO THERE? Tour the mint and learn what properties a metal must have before it can become a coin.

GO ONLINE Plan Your Own Expeditions

If you can't visit the Discovery Center of Science & Technology or the United States Mint, visit a science center or a mint near you. Or log on to The Learning Site at www.harcourtschool.com to visit these science sites and see what more you can learn about energy and changes in matter.

References

Science Handbook

Using Science Tools — **R2**
   Using a Hand Lens — R2
   Using a Thermometer — R2
   Caring for and Using a Microscope — R3
   Using a Balance — R4
   Using a Spring Scale — R4
   Measuring Liquids — R5
   Using a Ruler or Meterstick — R5
   Using a Timing Device — R5

Glossary — R6

Index — R16

Using Science Tools

Using a Hand Lens

A hand lens magnifies objects, or makes them look larger than they are.

1. Hold the hand lens about 12 centimeters (5 in.) from your eye.
2. Bring the object toward you until it comes into focus.

Using a Thermometer

A thermometer measures the temperature of air and most liquids.

1. Place the thermometer in the liquid. Don't touch the thermometer any more than you need to. Never stir the liquid with the thermometer. If you are measuring the temperature of the air, make sure that the thermometer is not in line with a direct light source.
2. Move so that your eyes are even with the liquid in the thermometer.
3. If you are measuring a material that is not being heated or cooled, wait about two minutes for the reading to become stable, or stay the same. Find the scale line that meets the top of the liquid in the thermometer, and read the temperature.
4. If the material you are measuring is being heated or cooled, you will not be able to wait before taking your measurements. Measure as quickly as you can.

SCIENCE HANDBOOK

Caring for and Using a Microscope

A microscope is another tool that magnifies objects. A microscope can increase the detail you see by increasing the number of times an object is magnified.

Caring for a Microscope

- Always use two hands when you carry a microscope.
- Never touch any of the lenses of a microscope with your fingers.

Using a Microscope

1. Raise the eyepiece as far as you can by using the coarse-adjustment knob. Place your slide on the stage.
2. Always start by using the lowest power. The lowest-power lens is usually the shortest. Start with the lens in the lowest position it can go without touching the slide.
3. Look through the eyepiece, and begin adjusting it upward with the coarse-adjustment knob. When the slide is close to being in focus, use the fine-adjustment knob.
4. When you want to use a higher-power lens, first focus the slide under low power. Then, watching carefully to make sure that the lens will not hit the slide, turn the higher-power lens into place. Use only the fine-adjustment knob when looking through the higher-power lens.

You may use a Brock microscope. This is a sturdy microscope that has only one lens.

1. Place the object to be viewed on the stage.
2. Look through the eyepiece, and begin raising the tube until the object comes into focus.

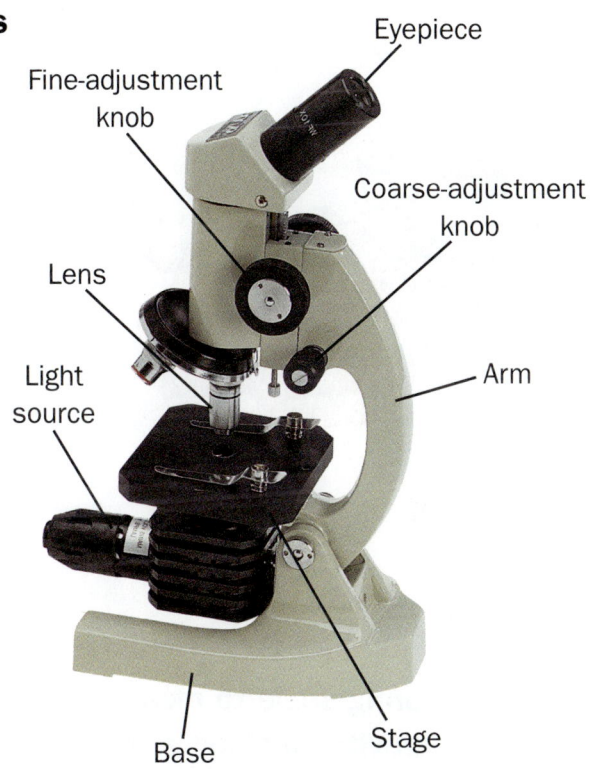

A Light Microscope

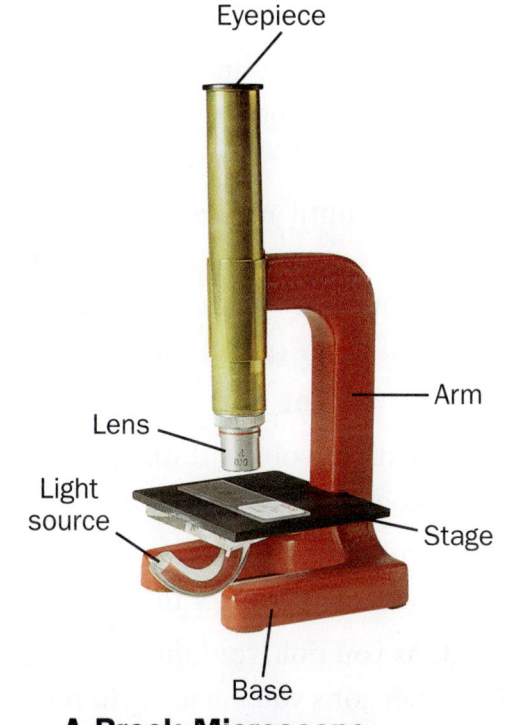

A Brock Microscope

R3

Pans

Middle mark

Standard masses

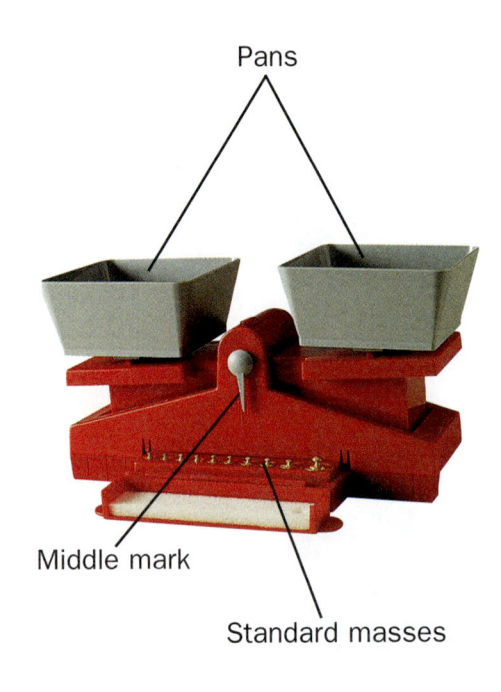

Using a Balance

Use a balance to measure an object's mass. Mass is the amount of matter an object has.

1. Look at the pointer on the base to make sure the empty pans are balanced.
2. Place the object you wish to measure in the left-hand pan.
3. Add the standard masses to the other pan. As you add masses, you should see the pointer move. When the pointer is at the middle mark, the pans are balanced.
4. Add the numbers on the masses you used. The total is the mass in grams of the object you measured.

Using a Spring Scale

Use a spring scale to measure forces such as the pull of gravity on objects. You measure weight and other forces in units called newtons (N).

Measuring the Weight of an Object

1. Hook the spring scale to the object.
2. Lift the scale and object with a smooth motion. Do not jerk them upward.
3. Wait until any motion of the spring comes to a stop. Then read the number of newtons from the scale.

Measuring the Force to Move an Object

1. With the object resting on a table, hook the spring scale to it.
2. Pull the object smoothly across the table. Do not jerk the object.
3. As you pull, read the number of newtons you are using to pull the object.

SCIENCE HANDBOOK

Measuring Liquids

Use a beaker, a measuring cup, or a graduate to measure liquids accurately.

1. Pour the liquid you want to measure into a measuring container. Put your measuring container on a flat surface, with the measuring scale facing you.
2. Look at the liquid through the container. Move so that your eyes are even with the surface of the liquid in the container.
3. To read the volume of the liquid, find the scale line that is even with the surface of the liquid.
4. If the surface of the liquid is not exactly even with a line, estimate the volume of the liquid. Decide which line the liquid is closer to, and use that number.

Beaker   **Graduate**

Using a Ruler or Meterstick

Use a ruler or meterstick to measure distances and to find lengths of objects.

1. Place the zero mark or end of the ruler or meterstick next to one end of the distance or object you want to measure.
2. On the ruler or meterstick, find the place next to the other end of the distance or object.
3. Look at the scale on the ruler or meterstick. This will show the distance you want or the length of the object.

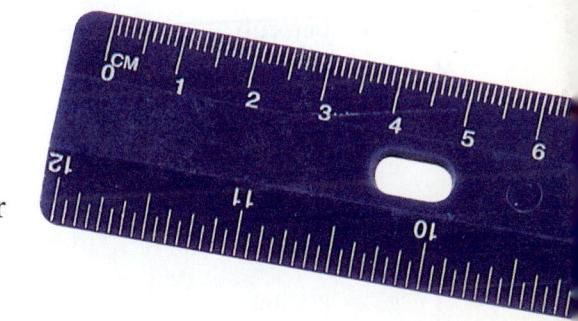

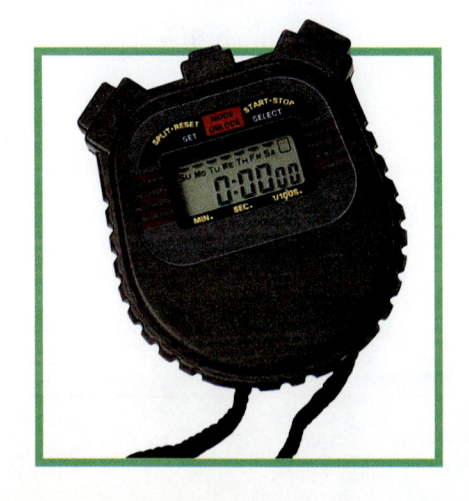

Using a Timing Device

Use a timing device such as a stopwatch to measure time.

1. Reset the stopwatch to zero.
2. When you are ready to begin timing, press *Start*.
3. As soon as you are ready to stop timing, press *Stop*.
4. The numbers on the dial or display show how many minutes, seconds, and parts of seconds have passed.

R5

Visit the Multimedia Science Glossary to see illustrations of these words and to hear them pronounced.
www.harcourtschool.com/science

Glossary

As you read your science book, you will see words that may be new to you. The words have phonetic respellings to help you quickly know how to say them. In this Glossary you will see a different kind of respelling. Here, diacritical marks are used, as they are used in dictionaries. *Diacritical respellings* can show more exactly how words should sound.

When you see the ′ mark after a syllable, say that syllable more strongly than the other syllables. The page number after the meaning tells where to find the word in your book. The boldfaced letters in the Pronunciation Key show how each respelling symbol sounds.

PRONUNCIATION KEY

a	**a**dd, m**a**p	m	**m**ove, see**m**	u	**u**p, d**o**ne
ā	**a**ce, r**a**te	n	**n**ice, ti**n**	û(r)	b**ur**n, t**er**m
â(r)	c**a**re, **air**	ng	ri**ng**, so**ng**	yo͞o	f**u**se, f**ew**
ä	p**al**m, f**a**ther	o	**o**dd, h**o**t	v	**v**ain, e**v**e
b	**b**at, ru**b**	ō	**o**pen, s**o**	w	**w**in, a**w**ay
ch	**ch**eck, cat**ch**	ô	**or**der, j**aw**	y	**y**et, **y**earn
d	**d**og, ro**d**	oi	**oi**l, b**oy**	z	**z**est, mu**s**e
e	**e**nd, p**e**t	ou	p**ou**t, n**ow**	zh	vi**s**ion, plea**s**ure
ē	**e**qual, tr**ee**	o͝o	t**oo**k, f**u**ll	ə	the schwa, an unstressed vowel representing the sound spelled
f	**f**it, hal**f**	o͞o	p**oo**l, f**oo**d		
g	**g**o, lo**g**	p	**p**it, sto**p**		
h	**h**ope, **h**ate	r	**r**un, poo**r**		
i	**i**t, g**i**ve	s	**s**ee, pa**ss**		*a* in *above*
ī	**i**ce, wr**i**te	sh	**s**ure, ru**sh**		*e* in *sicken*
j	**j**oy, le**dge**	t	**t**alk, si**t**		*i* in *possible*
k	**c**ool, ta**k**e	th	**th**in, bo**th**		*o* in *melon*
l	**l**ook, ru**l**e	th	**th**is, ba**th**e		*u* in *circus*

Other symbols:
- • separates words into syllables
- ′ indicates heavier stress on a syllable
- ′ indicates light stress on a syllable

R6

GLOSSARY

Multimedia Science Glossary: www.harcourtschool.com/science

A

absorption [ab•sôrp′shən] The stopping of light when it hits a wall or other opaque object **(E106)**

abyssal plains [ə•bis′əl plānz′] Huge flat areas of ocean floor that are covered with thick layers of sediment **(D50)**

acceleration [ak•sel′ər•ā′shən] A change in the speed or direction of an object's motion **(F48)**

adaptation [ad′əp•tā′shən] A body part or behavior that helps an organism meet its needs in its environment **(A48)**

air mass [âr′mas′] A huge body of air which all has similar temperature and moisture **(D13)**

air pressure [âr′presh′ər] Particles of air pressing down on the Earth's surface **(D7)**

amplitude [am′plə•tōōd′] A measure of the strength of a sound wave; shown by height on a wave diagram **(E72)**

anthracite [an′thrə•sīt′] A hard, black rock; fourth stage of coal formation **(C55)**

artery [är′tər•ē] A blood vessel that carries blood away from the heart **(A105)**

arthropod [är′thrə•pod] An invertebrate with legs that have several joints **(A16)**

asteroid [as′tə•roid] A small rocky object that moves around the sun **(D71)**

atmosphere [at′məs•fir] The layer of air that surrounds our planet **(D6)**

axis [ak′sis] An imaginary line which runs through both poles of a planet **(D65)**

B

barometer [bə•rom′ət•ər] An instrument that measures air pressure **(D20)**

bituminous coal [bi•tōō′mə•nəs kōl′] A fairly hard, dark brown or black rock; third stage of coal formation **(C55)**

brain [brān] The control center of your nervous system **(A110)**

buoyancy [boi′ən•sē] The ability of matter to float in a liquid or gas **(E20)**

C

camouflage [kam′ə•fläzh′] An animal's color or pattern that helps it blend in with its surroundings **(A52)**

capillary [kap′ə•ler′ē] A tiny blood vessel that allows gases and nutrients to pass from blood to cells **(A104)**

carbon dioxide [kär′bən dī•ok′sīd′] A gas breathed out by animals **(A72)**

cardiac muscle [kär′dē•ak mus′əl] A type of muscle that works the heart **(A99)**

cast [kast] A fossil formed when sediments or minerals fill a mold; it takes on the same outside shape as the living thing that shaped the mold **(C38)**

cell [sel] The basic building block of life **(A6)**

cell membrane [sel′ mem′brān] The thin layer that encloses and gives shape to a cell **(A7)**

cell wall [sel′ wôl′] A structure that keeps a cell rigid and provides support to an entire plant **(A8)**

R7

charge [chärj] A measure of the extra positive or negative particles that an object has **(F6)**

chemical change [kem′i•kəl chānj′] A change that produces one or more new substances and may release energy **(E28)**

chemical reaction [kem′i•kəl rē•ak′shən] Another term for chemical change **(E28)**

chloroplast [klôr′ə•plast′] A part of a plant cell that contains chlorophyll, the green pigment plants need to make their food **(A8)**

circuit [sûr′kit] A path that is made for an electric current **(F12)**

cirrus [sir′əs] Wispy, high-altitude clouds that are made up of ice crystals **(D15)**

climate [klī′mit] The average temperature and rainfall of an area over many years **(A41, B28)**

comet [kom′it] A small mass of dust and ice that orbits the sun in a long, oval-shaped path **(D71)**

community [kə•myoō′nə•tē] All the populations that live in the same area **(B14)**

compression [kəm•presh′ən] The part of a sound wave in which air is pushed together **(E71)**

condensation [kon′dən•sā′shən] The process by which water vapor changes from a gas to liquid **(D34)**

conduction [kən•duk′shən] The transfer of thermal energy caused by particles of matter bumping into each other **(E49)**

conductor [kən•duk′tər] A material that electric current can pass through easily **(F13)**

conservation [kon′sər•vā′shən] The careful management and wise use of natural resources **(B68)**

consumer [kən•soō′mər] A living thing that eats other living things for energy **(B21)**

continental shelf [kon′tə•nen′təl shelf′] The ocean floor of the shore zone **(D49)**

convection [kən•vek′shən] The transfer of thermal energy by particles of a liquid or gas moving from one place to another **(E50)**

core [kôr] The dense center of Earth; a ball made mostly of two metals, iron and nickel **(C6)**

crater [krā′tər] A large basin formed at the top of a volcano when the top falls in on itself **(C22)**

crust [krust] Earth's outer layer; includes the rock of the ocean floor and large areas of land **(C6)**

cumulonimbus [kyoō′myoō•lō•nim′bəs] Towering, dark rain clouds with a nimbus, or halo, of gray-white **(D15)**

cumulus [kyoōm′yə•ləs] Puffy cotton-ball clouds that begin to form when water droplets condense at middle altitudes **(D15)**

cytoplasm [sīt′ō•plaz′əm] A jellylike substance that fills most of the space in a cell **(A7)**

D

decomposer [dē′kəm•pōz′ər] A living thing that feeds on the wastes of plants and animals or on their remains after they die **(B21)**

deep ocean current [dēp′ ō′shən kûr′ənt] An

GLOSSARY

Multimedia Science Glossary: www.harcourtschool.com/science

ocean current formed when cold water flows underneath warm water **(D44)**

density [den′sə•tē] The property of matter that compares the amount of matter to the space it takes up **(E14)**

dissolve [di•zolv′] To form a solution with another material **(E19)**

diversity [di•vûr′sə•tē] Variety **(B29)**

dormancy [dôr′mən•sē] State of much lower activity that some plants enter to survive colder weather **(A78)**

E

earthquake [ûrth′kwāk′] A vibration, or shaking, of Earth's crust **(C14)**

echo [ek′ō] A sound reflection **(E86)**

ecosystem [ek′ō•sis′təm] Groups of living things and the environment they live in **(B12)**

efficiency [i•fish′ən•sē] How well a machine changes effort into useful work **(F85)**

effort force [ef′ərt fôrs′] The force put on one part of a simple machine, for example, when you push or pull on a lever **(F70)**

electric cell [i•lek′trik sel′] A device that supplies energy to move charges through a circuit **(F12)**

electric current [i•lek′trik kûr′ənt] A flow of electric charges **(F12)**

electric field [i•lek′trik fēld′] The space around an object in which electric forces occur **(F8)**

electromagnet [i•lek′trō•mag′nit] An arrangement of wire wrapped around a core, producing a temporary magnet **(F25)**

embryo [em′brē•ō] A young plant **(A20)**

energy [en′ər•jē] The ability to cause a change **(E42)**

energy pyramid [en′ər•jē pir′ə•mid] A diagram that shows how much food energy is passed from one organism to another along a food chain **(B22)**

environment [in•vī′rən•mənt] Everything that surrounds and affects an animal, including living and nonliving things **(A40)**

epicenter [ep′i•sent′ər] The point on the surface of Earth that is right above the focus of an earthquake **(C15)**

esophagus [i•sof′ə•gəs] The tube that connects your mouth with your stomach **(A112)**

evaporation [ē•vap′ə•rā′shən] The process in which a liquid changes to a gas **(D34)**

F

fault [fôlt] A break in Earth's crust along which rocks move **(C14)**

fibrous roots [fī′brəs rōōts′] Long roots that grow near the surface **(A79)**

flowers [flou′ərz] Reproductive structures in flowering plants **(A22)**

focus [fō′kəs] The point underground where the movement of an earthquake first takes place **(C15)**

food web [fōōd′ web′] A diagram that shows how food chains connect and overlap **(B23)**

force [fôrs] A push or pull **(F46)**

fossil [fos′əl] A preserved clue to life on Earth long ago **(C36)**

R9

fossil fuel [fos′əl fyoo′əl] Fuel formed from the remains of organisms that lived long ago **(C52)**

frame of reference [frām′ uv ref′ər•əns] The things around you that you can sense and use to describe motion **(F41)**

friction [frik′shən] A force that keeps objects that are touching each other from sliding past each other easily **(F58)**

front [frunt] The border where two air masses meet **(D14)**

fruit [froot] The part of a flowering plant that surrounds and protects the seeds **(A22)**

fuel [fyoo′əl] A material that can burn **(E56)**

fulcrum [fool′krəm] The fixed point, or point that doesn't move, on a lever **(F70)**

fungi [fun′jī′] Living things that look like plants but cannot make their own food; for example, mushrooms **(A26)**

G

gas [gas] The state of matter that has no definite shape and takes up no definite amount of space **(E8)**

gas giants [gas′ jī′ənts] Planets which are large spheres made up mostly of gases—for example, Jupiter, Saturn, Uranus, and Neptune **(D78)**

germinate [jûr′mə•nāt′] To sprout; said of a seed **(A84)**

gravity [grav′ə•tē] A force that pulls all objects toward each other **(F56)**

greenhouse effect [grēn′hous′ i•fekt′] The warming of Earth caused by the atmosphere trapping thermal energy from the sun **(D12)**

H

habitat [hab′ə•tat′] An environment that meets the needs of an organism **(B20)**

heart [härt] The muscle that pumps blood through blood vessels to all parts of the body **(A105)**

heat [hēt] The transfer of thermal energy from one piece of matter to another **(E48)**

hibernation [hī′bər•nā′shən] A period when an animal goes into a long, deep "sleep" **(A59)**

humidity [hyoo•mid′ə•tē] The amount of water vapor in the air **(D21)**

hygrometer [hī•grom′ə•tər] A tool to measure moisture in the air **(D21)**

hyphae [hī′fē] Densely packed threadlike parts of a fungus **(A27)**

I

inclined plane [in′klīnd plān′] A flat surface with one end higher than the other **(F84)**

infrared radiation [in′frə•red′ rā′dē•ā′shən] The bundles of light energy that transfer heat **(E52)**

inner planets [in′ər plan′its] The planets closest to the sun; Mercury, Venus, Earth, and Mars **(D76)**

instinct [in′stingkt] A behavior that an animal begins life with **(A56)**

insulator [in′sə•lāt′ər] A material that current cannot pass through easily **(F13)**

intertidal zone [in′tər•tīd′əl zōn′] A narrow strip, along the shore, that is covered with water during high tide and exposed during low tide **(B36)**

invertebrate [in•vûr′tə•brit] An animal without a backbone **(A16)**

K – L

kinetic energy [ki•net′ik en′ər•jē] Energy of motion **(E42)**

large intestine [lärj′ in•tes′tən] The last part of the digestive system where water is removed from food **(A113)**

lava [lä′və] Melted rock that reaches Earth's surface **(C20)**

lever [lev′ər] A simple machine made up of a bar that turns on a fixed point **(F70)**

lignite [lig′nīt] A soft, brown rock; the second stage of coal formation **(C55)**

liquid [lik′wid] The state of matter that takes the shape of its container and takes up a definite amount of space **(E7)**

loudness [loud′nes] Your perception of the amount of sound energy reaching your ear **(E78)**

lungs [lungz] The main organs of the respiratory system **(A104)**

M

magma [mag′mə] Melted rock inside Earth **(C20)**

magma chamber [mag′mə chām′bər] An underground pool that holds magma, below a volcano **(C21)**

magnet [mag′nit] An object that attracts certain materials, such as iron or steel **(F18)**

magnetic field [mag•net′ik fēld′] The space all around a magnet where the force of the magnet can act **(F19)**

magnetic pole [mag•net′ik pōl′] The end of a magnet **(F18)**

mantle [man′təl] The thickest layer of Earth; found just below the crust **(C6)**

mass [mas] The amount of matter something contains **(E6)**

matter [mat′ər] Everything in the universe that has mass and takes up space **(E6)**

metamorphosis [met′ə•môr′fə•sis] The process of change; for example, from an egg to an adult butterfly **(A44)**

microorganisms [mī′krō•ôr′gən•iz′əmz] Organisms that are so small they can only be seen with a microscope; many have only one cell **(A9)**

mid-ocean ridge [mid′ō•shən rij′] A vast chain of mountains that runs along the centers of Earth's oceans **(D50)**

migration [mī•grā′shən] The movement of a group of one type of animal from one region to another and back again **(A57)**

mimicry [mim′ik•rē] An adaptation in which an animal looks very much like another animal or an object **(A52)**

mold [mōld] A common type of fungi that often look cottony or woolly **(A28)**

mold [mōld] A fossil imprint made by the outside of a dead plant or animal **(C38)**

motion [mō′shən] A change of position **(F40)**

N

natural gas [nach′ər•əl gas′] A gas, mostly methane, usually found with petroleum **(C53)**

near-shore zone [nir′shôr′ zōn′] Ocean zone that starts at the low-tide mark and goes out into the ocean **(B36)**

nerve [nûrv] A group of neurons that carries signals from the brain to the body and from the body to the brain **(A110)**

neuron [noor′on′] A nerve cell **(A110)**

newton [noo′tən] The metric, or Système International (SI), unit of force **(F51)**

niche [nich] The role or part played by an organism in its habitat **(B21)**

nucleus [noo′klē•əs] A cell's control center **(A7)**

nutrient [noo′trē•ənt] A substance, such as a mineral, which all living things need in order to grow **(A72)**

O

opaque [ō•pāk′] Reflecting or absorbing all light; no image can be seen **(E106)**

open-ocean zones [ō′pən•ō′shən zōnz′] The deep parts of the oceans, located far from shore **(B36)**

orbit [ôr′bit] The path that an object such as a planet makes as it revolves around a second object **(D64)**

organ [ôr′gən] A group of tissues of different kinds working together to perform a task **(A98)**

outer planets [ou′tər plan′its] The planets farthest from the sun; Jupiter, Saturn, Uranus, Neptune, and Pluto **(D78)**

oxygen [ok′si•jən] One of the many gases in air **(A41)**

P

parallel circuit [par′ə•lel sûr′kit] A circuit that has more than one path along which current can travel **(F14)**

peat [pēt] A soft, brown material made up of partly decayed plants; first stage of coal formation **(C55)**

petroleum [pə•trō′lē•əm] A thick brown or black liquid fossil fuel; crude oil **(C53)**

phase [fāz] One of the different shapes the moon seems to have as it orbits around Earth **(D64)**

photosynthesis [fōt′ō•sin′thə•sis] The process by which a plant makes its own food **(A73)**

physical change [fiz′i•kəl chānj′] Any change in the size, shape, or state of a substance **(E26)**

pistil [pis′təl] A flower part that collects pollen **(A85)**

pitch [pich] A measure of how high or low a sound is **(E79)**

planet [plan′it] A large object that moves around a star **(D71)**

plate [plāt] Continent-sized slab of Earth's crust and upper mantle **(C8)**

pollination [pol′ə•na′shən] Transfer of pollen from a stamen to a pistil by wind or animals **(A85)**

population [pop′yoo•lā′shən] A group of the same species living in the same place at the same time **(B13)**

position [pə•zish′ən] A certain place **(F40)**

precipitation [prē·sip′ə·tā′shən] Water that falls to Earth as rain, snow, sleet, or hail **(D35)**

preservation [prez′ər·vā′shən] The protection of an area **(B72)**

prism [priz′əm] A solid object that bends light; not a lens **(E110)**

producer [prə·dōōs′ər] A living thing, such as a plant, that makes its own food **(B21)**

pulley [pŏŏl′ē] A simple machine made up of a rope or chain and a wheel around which the rope or chain fits **(F78)**

R

radiation [rā′dē·ā′shən] The bundles of energy that move through matter and through empty space **(E52)**

reclamation [rek′lə·mā′shən] The repairing of some of the damage done to an ecosystem **(B63)**

redesign [rē′di·zīn′] Changing the design of packaging or products in order to use fewer resources **(B71)**

reflection [ri·flek′shən] The bouncing of light off an object **(E102)**

refraction [ri·frak′shən] The bending of the path of light when it moves from one kind of matter to another **(E104)**

relative motion [rel′ə·tiv mō′shən] A motion that is described based on a frame of reference **(F41)**

resistor [ri·zis′tər] A material that resists the flow of current but doesn't stop it **(F13)**

revolution [rev′ə·lōō′shən] The movement of any object in an orbit, such as Earth moving around the sun **(D65)**

rotation [rō·tā′shən] The motion of a planet or other object as it turns on its axis **(D65)**

S

salinity [sə·lin′ə·tē] The amount of salt in water **(B30)**

satellite [sat′ə·līt′] An object that moves around another object in space; the moon is a satellite of Earth **(D64)**

screw [skrōō] An inclined plane wrapped around a pole **(F86)**

seismograph [sīz′mə·graf′] An instrument that records earthquake waves **(C16)**

series circuit [sir′ēz sûr′kit] A circuit that has only one path for current **(F14)**

shelter [shel′tər] A place where an animal is protected from other animals or from the weather **(A43)**

shore zone [shôr′ zōn′] The place where land and ocean meet **(D49)**

simple machine [sim′pəl mə·shēn′] One of the basic machines that make up other machines **(F70)**

small intestine [smôl′ in·tes′tən] A long tube of muscle where most food is digested **(A112)**

smooth muscle [smōōth′ mus′əl] A type of muscle found in the walls of some organs such as the stomach, intestines, blood vessels, and bladder **(A99)**

solar energy [sō′lər en′ər·jē] The energy given off by the sun **(E57)**

solar system [sō′lər sis′təm] A group of objects in space that move around a central star **(D70)**

R13

solid [sol′id] The state of matter that has a definite shape and takes up a definite amount of space **(E6)**

solubility [sol′yōō•bil′ə•tē] A measure of the amount of a material that will dissolve in another material **(E19)**

solution [sə•lōō′shən] A mixture in which the particles of different kinds of matter are mixed evenly with each other and particles do not settle out **(E18)**

sonic boom [son′ik bōōm′] A shock wave of compressed sound waves produced by an object moving faster than sound **(E88)**

sound [sound] A series of vibrations that you can hear **(E70)**

sound wave [sound′ wāv′] A moving pattern of high and low pressure that you can hear **(E71)**

space probe [spās′ prōb′] An uncrewed space vehicle that carries cameras, instruments, and other research tools **(D88)**

speed [spēd] A measure of an object's change in position during a unit of time; for example, 10 meters per second **(F42)**

speed of sound [spēd′ uv sound′] The speed at which a sound wave travels through a given material **(E84)**

spinal cord [spī′nəl kôrd′] The tube of nerves that runs through your spine, or backbone **(A110)**

spore [spôr] A tiny cell that ferns and fungi use to reproduce **(A27, A85)**

stability [stə•bil′ə•tē] The condition that exists when the changes in a system over time cancel each other out **(B8)**

stamen [stā′mən] A flower part that makes pollen **(A85)**

star [stär] A huge, burning sphere of gases; for example, the sun **(D70)**

static electricity [stat′ik ē′lek•tris′i•tē] An electric charge that stays on an object **(F6)**

stomach [stum′ək] A bag made up of smooth muscles that mixes food with digestive juices **(A112)**

storm surge [stôrm′ sûrj′] A very large series of waves caused by high winds over a large area of ocean **(D41)**

stratosphere [strat′ə•sfir′] The layer of atmosphere that contains ozone and is located above the troposphere **(D8)**

stratus [strā′təs] Dark gray clouds that form a low layer and sometimes bring light rain or snow showers **(D15)**

striated muscle [strī′āt•ed mus′əl] A muscle with light and dark stripes; a muscle you can control by thinking **(A100)**

succession [sək•sesh′ən] The process that gradually changes an existing ecosystem into another ecosystem **(B52)**

surface current [sûr′fis kûr′ənt] An ocean current formed when steady winds blow over the surface of the ocean **(D44)**

system [sis′təm] A group of parts that work together as a unit **(B6)**

T

taproot [tap′rōōt′] A plant's single main root that goes deep into the soil **(A79)**

telescope [tel′ə•skōp′] A device people use to observe distant objects with their eyes **(D84)**

GLOSSARY

Multimedia Science Glossary: www.harcourtschool.com/science

temperature [tem′pər•ə•chər] A measure of the average energy of motion of the particles in matter **(E43)**

thermal energy [thûr′məl en′ər•jē] The energy of the random motion of particles in matter **(E42)**

tide [tīd] The daily changes in the local water level of the ocean **(D42)**

tissue [tish′ōō] A group of cells of the same type **(A98)**

trace fossil [trās′ fos′əl] A fossil that shows changes that long-dead animals made in their surroundings **(C37)**

translucent [trans•lōō′sənt] Allowing some light to pass through; blurry image can be seen **(E106)**

transparent [trans•pâr′ənt] Allows most light to pass through; clear image can be seen **(E106)**

transpiration [tran′spə•rā′shən] The giving off of water vapor by plants **(A78)**

trenches [trench′əz] Valleys that form on the ocean floor where two plates come together; the deepest places in the oceans **(D50)**

troposphere [trō′pə•sfir′] The layer of atmosphere closest to Earth **(D8)**

tuber [tōō′bər] A swollen underground stem **(A87)**

V

vein [vān] A large blood vessel that returns blood to the heart **(A105)**

vent [vent] In a volcano, the rocky opening through which magma rises toward the surface **(C20)**

vertebrate [vûr′tə•brit] An animal with a backbone **(A16)**

visible spectrum [viz′ə•bəl spek′trəm] The range of light energy that people can see **(E110)**

volcano [vol•kā′nō] A mountain that forms when red-hot melted rock flows through a crack onto Earth's surface **(C20)**

volume [vol′yōōm] The amount of space that matter takes up **(E13)**

W

water cycle [wôt′ər sī′kəl] The constant recycling of water on Earth **(D34)**

wave [wāv] An up-and-down movement of water **(D40)**

wavelength [wāv′length] The distance from one compression to the next in a sound wave **(E72)**

wedge [wej] A machine made up of two inclined planes placed back-to-back **(F88)**

weight [wāt] A measure of the force of gravity upon an object **(F57)**

wheel and axle [hwēl′ and ak′səl] A simple machine made up of a large wheel attached to a smaller wheel or rod **(F80)**

work [wûrk] That which is done on an object when a force moves the object through a distance **(F74)**

A

Abdominal muscles, R28
Absorption, E106
Abyssal plains, D50
Acceleration, F48
　pushing and, F49
Activity pyramid, R12
Adams, John C., D91
Adaptations, A48
　animal, A48–53, A56–61
　plant, A74, A80
Agricola, Georgius, C58
Air
　in atmosphere, D6
　property of, D4–5
　sun and, D12
Air masses, D13
　meeting of, D14
　over water, D21
Airplane, inventors of, F92
Air pressure, D7, D18–20
Aldabra tortoises, A37
Aldrin, Edwin, D87
Algae
　in food chain, B21
　green, A4
　as one-celled organisms, A9
　polyps and, B30
Aluminum
　density of, E3
　recycling, B69
American bison, A51
American cockroach, A62
American holly, A22
Ammonoids, C33–34
Amoeba, A9
Ampere, F12
Amplitude, E72–73
Anaconda, B29
Anemometer, D21
Anemone, B31, D42
Animal adaptations
　behaviors, A56–61
　body parts, A48–53
Animal behaviorist, A64
Animal cells, A7
Animals
　body coverings, A50
　body supports, A16
　body types, A14–15
　color and shape, A52
　fast, A36
　hibernation of, A59
　largest, A3
　learned behaviors of, A60–61
　migration of, A57
　needs of, A40–45
　tracks, C40
　and their young, A44
　in tropical rain forests, B32
Animal tracks, C40
Animatronic dinosaur, C45
Anthracite, C55
Antiquities Act, B74–75
Ants, A16, A68
　robot, A62–63
Apollo 11, D87
Appalachian Trail, B75
Archaeopteryx, C42
Archer, F46
Archimedes' screw, F82–83
Arctic fox, A43
Arms
　bones and muscles in, A99
　movement, A100
Armstrong, Neil, D87
Arteries, A105–106, R32
Arthropods, A16
Ascension Island, A57
Asteroids, D71
Astronauts, F62
　Apollo mission, D87
　space shuttle, D87
　using moon rover, D82
Atlantic green turtle, A57
Atlantic Ocean, D31
Atlas statue, E3
Atmosphere, D6
　greenhouse effect, D12
　layers of, D8
　mass of 1-m×1-m column, D7
　telescopes and, D85
Atmospheric scientist, D26
Auger, F87
Axis, D65
　Earth's, D72

B

Babbage, Charles, F67
Backbone, A99
Bacteria
　as decomposers, B21
　fighting, R10
　in soil, A2
Balance, using, R4
Barometer, D20
Barrel cactus, A75
Bathyscaph, D54
Bats
　echoes and, E66
　North American, A59
　skeleton of, A17
　sound and hearing of, E67
Bay of Fundy, D42
Beaker, R5
Bears
　brown, A42
　in food chain, B21
　polar, A50
Behaviors
　adaptive, A56–61
　instinctual, A56
　learned, A60–61
Berson, Dr. Solomon, A116
BetaSweet carrots, A88–89
Biceps, A99–100, R28–29
Bicycle
　friction and, F58–59
　helmet, R17
　safety, R16–17
　Ultimate Bike, F61
Bicycle mechanic, F61
Birds
　adaptations, A49
　beaks, A46–48
　carrying seeds, A84
　migration of, A58
Bituminous coal, C55
Black-footed ferrets, B48
Blizzard safety, R19
Blood, A105–107
Blood cells, R33
Blood vessels, R32
Blue jets, D25
Blue-ringed octopus, A12
Blue whale, A3
Boats, F90–91
Bobsled, accelerating, F49
Boiling points (chart) E38
Bones
　dinosaur, C44
　human, A98–99

INDEX

Botanist, A90
Bracket fungi, A28
Brain, human, A110, R36–37
Brain coral, B31
Bread mold, A28
Breastbone, A99
Breathing, A104–106, R35
   rates, A102–103
Bridges, B3
Bristlecone pine, A69
British soldier lichen, A29
Brock microscope, R3
Bronchi, R35
Brown bears, A42
Bulbs
   light, E39
   tulip, A86
Bullhorn acacia, A68
Bunsen burner, E29
Buoyancy, E20
Buoys, D32
Burning
   as chemical change, E29–30
   fuel, E56
Butterfly
   metamorphosis, A44
   monarch, A54–57
   morpho, B29
   viceroy, A52

C

Cactus
   adaptations of, A74
   barrel, A75
   need for water, A70
   saguaro, A69
Caiman, B29
Calf muscle, A99
California condor, B49
Callisto, D88
Camouflage, A52
Capillaries, A104–105
Capuchin, B29
Capybara, B29
Carbon dioxide, A72
   in atmosphere, D6
   forming a mixture, E29
   greenhouse effect and, E56
   heart, lungs, and, A106–107

   human respiratory system and, A104
   photosynthesis and, A73, D7
   polyps and, B30
Car braking (chart), F37
Cardiac muscle, A99, A100–101
Caribou, B2-3
Carson, Rachel, D56
Cast, fossil, C38
Caterpillar, A44, B25
Cell membrane, A7–8
Cell(s), A6
   animal, A7
   blood, A95, R33
   bone, A98
   model of, A4–5
   plant, A8
   replacement of human, A94
Cell wall, A8
Centipede, A16
Chameleon, A42, A52
Chanterelle, A27
Charge, F6
Chase, Mary Agnes Meara, A90
Cheetah, A36, A60
Chemical changes, E28, E30
Chemical energy, E28
Chemical reaction, E28
Chemicals
   and ecosystem damage, B60
   testing water for, B73
Chimpanzee, A60, A64
Chlorophyll, A73
Chloroplasts, A8
Chrysalis, A44
Cinder cone volcanoes, C21
Circuit, F12
   parallel, F14
   series, F14
Circulatory system, A105, R32-33
Cirrus cloud, D15
Clavicle, R26
Cleaner wrasse, B31
Cliff swallows, B3
Climate, A41, B28
Closterium, A4
Cloud(s)
   formation of, D34
   types, D15
Clownfish, B31

Coal
   burning, E56
   formation of, C54
   types, C55
Cold front, D14–15
Collarbone, A99, R26
Colors
   adding, E112
   basic, E112
   light and, E110–113
   seeing, E112
Colo volcano, C24
Comets, D71
Community, B14
Compass, F30
Composite volcanoes, C21
Compression, E71
Computer models of ecosystems, B42–43
Computer programmer, B43
Computers
   cooling systems for, E59
   first, F67
   safe use, R14
Concave lenses, E115
Condensation, in water cycle, D34
Conduction, E49
Conductor, F13
Cone-bearing plants, A20–21
Cones, A18–19
Conservation, B68
   in national parks, B75
   of resources, B68–73
Consumers, B21
Continental shelf, D49
Continents, C6
Convection, E50
Copper, density of, E3
Coprolites, C37
Coral, B30–31, B64
Coral reef, B26–27
   ecosystem, B30
   map of, B28
   water temperatures in, B30
Core, Earth's, C6–7
Cork tree, A6
Cowles, Dr. Henry Chandler, B44

R17

Crabs, D42
Crater, C22
Crater Lake, OR, C22–23
Craters, moon's, D61, D84
Crewed missions, D87
Crinoid, B31
Crocodile, saltwater, A3
Crust, Earth's, C6–7
Cumulonimbus, D15
Cumulus, D15
Curare, B33
Curveball, F38
Customary measures, R6
Cuvier, Georges, C58–59
Cycad, A20
Cytoplasm
  in animal cells, A7
  in plant cells, A8

D

Dante, C26–27
Dante II, C26–27
Darwin's finch, A48
Dead Sea, D36
Decomposers, B21, B28
Decorator crab, B31
Deep Flight II, D54–55
Deep-ocean currents, D44
Deimos, D80
Deltoid, A99, R28
Density, E14
  of common materials (chart), E3
Deposition, D41
Desert, A40
Desert fox, A43
Dial spring scale, F52
Diaphragm, R34
Diatoms, B31
Digestive system
  in humans, A111–112, R30–31
  in snails, A15
Dinosaurs
  animatronic, C45
  bones of, C36, C44
  duckbill, C58
  footprints of, C33
  fossils of, C32, C40
Diorama, B27

Disease, species endangerment and, B48
Dissolve, E19, E27
Diversity, B29
Dodder, A69
Dogs, sound and hearing of, E67
Dolphins
  hair on, A51
  sound and hearing of, E67
  speed of, A36
Dormancy, A78
Drawbridge, F67
Dromaeosaurs, C32
Duckbill dinosaur, C58

E

Earle, Sylvia, D54
Ears, caring for, R24
Earth
  atmosphere of, D6–9
  axis of, D65
  comparative size of, D70
  distance from moon, D62
  distance from sun, D60, D69
  gravity between sun and, F56
  as inner planet, D76–77
  layers of, C4–5, C7–8
  mass of, E2
  orbit of, D64–65
  planet year of, D72
  revolution of, D65
  rotation of, D65
  seasons and, D66
  structure of, C6–7
  tilt of, D61
  weight on (chart), F57
Earthquake(s), C14
  in California, C14
  destruction from, C12, C28
  epicenter of, C15
  focus of, C15
  measuring, C14–17
  New Madrid, Missouri, C3
  safety, R19
  Tokyo, Japan, C28
Earthworms, A15
Echo, E86
Eastern hemlock, A78
Ecologist, B44

Ecosystem(s), B12
  adding to, B64–65
  change in, B24
  communities in, B14
  computer models of, B42–43
  conservation of, B75
  damage to, B60–61
  forest, B63
  humans and, B60–65
  living parts of, B12
  living things in, B20–25
  populations in, B13
  protected, B72
  rapid changes in, B54–57
  repair of, B62–63
  roles in, B21
  seashore, B43
  tropical, B28–33
  water, B61
  yard as, B10–11
Edison, Thomas A., F31
Efficiency, F85
Effort force
  with inclined plane, F85
  with lever, F70–71, F74
  with pulley, F78–79
  with screw, F86
  with wedges, F88
  with wheel and axle, F80
Eggs, insect, A44
Egrets, B13
Electric
  cell, F12
  current, F12
  field, F8
Electricity
  history of, F30–31
  origin of word, F30
  static, F30
  use (chart), F3
  U.S. production of, E56
Electromagnet, F25
Electromagnetism, F30–31
Electron, F30
Electronic scale, F52
Elephants
  African, A3, A43
  changes over time, C43
Elliptical orbit, D72
El Niño, D26
ELVES, D25

INDEX

Embryo, plant, A20
Emergencies, safety in, R18–21
Endangered species, B48–49
Energy, E42
  chemical, E28
  kinetic, E42
  light, E100
  potential, E28
  released by earthquake, C15
  thermal, E56–57
Energy pyramid, B22
Entomologist, A63
Environmental Protection Agency (EPA), B72–73
Environments, A40
  plant adaptations for, A74
Epicenter, C15
Equator, B28
Erosion, waves and, D41
Eruptions, C18–19, C22–25
Esophagus, A111–112, R30
Estuary, B12
Euglena, A9
Europa, D74
European goldfinch, A48
Evacuation, B56
Evaporation, D34, E27
  humidity and, D21
  in water cycle, D34
Eyelid, R29
Eyes
  caring for, R24
  corrective lenses for, E114

F

Faraday, Michael, F31
Fastball, F38
Fault, C14
Feathers, bird, A49
Femur, A99, R26
Ferrets, black-footed, B48
Fiber optics, E115
Fibrous roots, A79
Fibula, A99, R26
Field geology technician, C27
Filtering, R35
Finches, A48
Fire
  brush, B57
  forest, B50, B55–56
  safety, R18
Fireworks, E24
First aid
  for bleeding, R21
  for burns, R22
  for choking, R20
  for insect bites and stings, R23
  for nosebleeds, R22
  for skin rashes from plants, R23
Fish
  fossil of, C49
  gray snapper, B13
  largest, A3
  porcupine, A50
  scales of, B3
Fish ladders, B62
Fixed pulley, F78
Flexors, R28
Flooding, B54, D3
Florida
  natural wetlands in, B65
Flowers, A22
  healthy, A72
  seeds in, A84
Focus, earthquake, C15
Food
  animals' need for, A42
  bird beaks and, A46–47
  safe preparation of, R10–11
  serving size, R9
Food chains, B21
Food Guide Pyramid, R8
Food web, B23
Footprints, dinosaur, C33
Force(s), F46
  adding, F50
  changing motion, F48
  changing speed, F49
  effort, F70–71, F74, F78–79, F85, F88
  friction as, F58
  gravity as, F56
  levers and, F72
  measuring, F51–52
  pushes and pulls, F46
  resulting, F70–71, F74, F78–79, F85, F88
  on sliding box, F54–55
  starting motion, F47
  weight, F57
  work and, F74

Forest, pine, B20
Forest ecosystem, replanting trees in, B63
Forest edge ecosystem, food chain in, B21
Forest fires, B50, B55–56
Fossil fuel, C52
Fossils, C36
  animal tracks, C40–41
  dinosaur, C32, C40, C44, C58–59
  formation of, C36–39
  history of, C58
  importance of, C44
  making, C34–35
  shell, C36
  trace, C37
  track, C37
Foxes, A43
Frame of reference, F41
Franklin, Benjamin, E115, F30
Freezing points (chart), E38
Fresh water, from salt water, D32–33
Freshwater ecosystem, food chain in, B21
Friction, F47, F58
  bicycle and, F58–59
  car brakes and, F37
  gecko feet and, F37
  inclined plane and, F85
  in-line skating and, F58
  snowboarder and, F54
Frogs, B10
Front, D14
Fruit-bearing plants, A22–23
Fruits, A18–19, A22
Fuel, E56
  burning, E56
Fulcrum, F70–71, F74
Fulton, Robert, F90
Fungi, A26
  lichens, A28–29
  molds, A28
  mushrooms, A26–27
  in soil, A2
  structure of, A26–27

R19

G

Gagarin, Yuri, D87
Galápagos Islands, A48
Galileo (Galilei), D90–91, E115
Galileo, D88
Galle, Johann, D91
Gas, E8
Gas giants, D78
Gastrocnemius, R29
Geckos, F37
Genetic engineer, A89
Germinate, A84
Gesner, Konrad von, C58
Giant clam, B30
Giant river otter, B29
Giant sequoia, A69
Ginkgoes, C43
Giraffes, A42
Glaciers, C43
Gnomon, E101
Gold, density of, E3
Gombe Stream Game Preserve, A64
Gomphotherium, C42
Goodall, Jane, A64
Graduate, R5
Grafting, A86
Grand Canyon, B75
Grant, Ulysses S., B75
Grass, growth of, B8
Gravity, D42
  as force, F56
  snowboarder and, F54
Gray fox, A43
Gray snapper, B13
Gray whales, A58
Great blue heron, B12
Great Red Spot, D78
Greenhouse effect, D12, E56
Ground squirrel, A59
Grouper, B31
Gypsy moth caterpillars, B25

H

Habitats, B20
  coral reef, B30–32
  loss of, B48
Hale-Bopp comet, D71
Half Dome, B72
Hamstring, A99, R29
Hand lens, R2
Hawai'i
  Keck Observatory in, D85
  volcanoes in, C24
Hawk, A49
Hawkes, Graham, D54–55
Heart, human, A99, A105–106, R32
Heart muscle, A96, A99, R29
Heat, E48
Hedgehog, A51
Herschel, Caroline, D90
Herschel, William, D90
Hertz, Heinrich, F31
Hibernation, A59
Himalayas, C4
Honey mushroom, A3
House finch, A48
Hubble Space Telescope (HST), D86
Human-powered vehicles (HPVs), high-speed, F60–61
Humans
  body structures, A98
  cell replacement in, A94
  circulatory system in, A105
  ecosystems and, B56, B60–65
  intestines of, A95
  respiratory system in, A104
  sound and hearing of, E67
Humerus, A99, R26
Humidity, D21
Hummingbird, A36
Humpback whale, A60–61
Hunting, B48
Hurricane(s), B54, B56
  rating scale, D3
  safety, R19
  storm surges during, D41
Hygrometer, D21
Hyphae, A27

I

Ice
  density of, E3
  melting of all world's, E3
  skating on, F36
Ice Age, C43
Iceland, C3
Igneous rocks, C48
Iguana, A51
Inclined planes, F82, F84–85
Indiana Dunes, B44
Indian Ocean, D31
Indonesian volcanoes
  Colo, C24
  Krakatau, E66
Infrared radiation, E52
Inner core, Earth's C7
Inner planets, D76–77
Inputs, B7
Insects, A16
Instincts, A56
Insulator, F13
Internet safety, R15
Intertidal zone, B36
Intestines, A95, A111–113, R30–31
Inventors, E62, F92
Invertebrates, A16
Involuntary muscles, R29
Io, D80
Iron
  density of, E3
  freezing and boiling point of, E38
  molten, E39

J

Jackrabbit, A36
Jackson, Shirley Ann, E34
Japan
  Mount Fuji volcano, C21, C23
  Tokyo earthquake, C28
  Unzen volcano, C24
Jones, Frederick McKinley, E62
Juniper, A21
Jupiter
  discovery of moons, D90
  distance from sun, D69, D71
  moons of, D74, D80, D88
  as outer planet, D78
  in solar system, D70
  tilt of, D61
  weight on (chart), F57

INDEX

K–L

Kanamori, Hiroo, C28
Kangaroo rat, A40
Kayaks, F90-91
Keck telescope, D85
Kinetic energy, E42
Koala, A44–45
Krakatau volcano, E66
Lambeosaur, C32
Large intestine, A111, A113, R30–31
Lasers, E114–115
Lava, C20–21
Lead, density of, E3
Leaves, function of, A78
Legs, bones and muscles in, A99
Lenses, E114
Leverrier, Urbain, D91
Levers, F70
  boat oar, F68
  broom, F71
  experimenting with, F68–69
  forces and, F72
  lengths of (chart), F66
  parts of, F70–72
  in piano, F73
  in pliers, F73
  seesaw, F72
  in tools, F73
  wheelbarrow, F71
Liana, B33
Lichens, A28–29, B24
Life cycle, plant, A84
Light
  bending, E104
  bouncing, E102–103
  color and, E110–113
  as energy, E100
  laser, E114–115
  optics and, E114–115
  plants and, A70–71
  shadows and, E101
  stopping, E106
  travel of, E98–99
  using, E100
  white, E110
Light bulb, temperature inside, E39
Light microscope, R3

Lightning
  blue jets, D25
  forest fires and, B54
  frequency of, D2
  temperature of, E39
Lignite, C55
Limestone, C36
  fern fossil in, C48
Liquids, E7
  measuring, R5
Liver, R30
Living things
  cells in, A6
  distances traveled by, B2
  in ecosystems, B20–25
  fossils and changes of, C42–43
  homes and roles of, B18–19
  See also Animals; Plants
Lodestone, F30
Loma Prieta earthquake, C15
Loudness, E78
Lungs, A104–106, R34–35

M

Machines. *See* Simple machines
Mag-lev train, F31
Magma, C20
  chamber, C21
Magnet, F18
  electromagnet, F25
  lodestone as, F30
  poles of, F18
  temporary, F25
Magnetic field, F19
Magnetic pole, F18
Magnetism, history of, F30–31
Magnolia pod fossil, C48
Maiman, T. H., E115
Mammals
  caring for young, A44
  ocean, A41
Mangrove swamps, B14–15
Mangrove trees, B12–13
Mantle, C6
Manual of Grasses, The (Chase), A90
Mariana Trench, D31, D54
Marine biologist, D56
Mars
  Deimos, D80
  distance from sun, D69, D71
  as inner planet, D76–77
  Olympus Mons volcano, D77
  Phobos, D81
  Sojourner probe, D88
  tilt of, D61
  weight on (chart), F57
Martinique
  Mount Pelée volcano on, C21
Mass, E6
Matter, E6
Maxwell, James Clerk, F31
Mealworms, A38–39
Measurement systems, R6
Medical physicist, A116
Medicines from rain forest, B32–33
Mercalli scale, C16–17
Mercury (element)
  density of, E3
  freezing and boiling point of, E38
Mercury (planet)
  distance from sun, D69, D71
  as inner planet, D76–77
  planet year of, D72
  tilt of, D61
  weight on (chart), F57
Mesosphere, D8
Metamorphosis, A44
Meteorologist, D20, D25
Meterstick, R5
Metric measures, R6
Microbiologist, A32
Microorganisms, A9–10
Microrobots, A63
Microscope
  invention of, E115
  light, R3
  using, R3
  viewing cells with, A7–8
Mid-ocean ridge, D50
Migration, A57
Mildew, A28
Mimicry, A52
Minerva Terrace hot springs, B74
Mir, D87

R21

Mirror, E102–103
Mitochondria, A7–8
Mold
  fossil, C38
  fungus, A28
Molting, A44
Monarch butterfly
  instincts of, A56
  migration of, A57
  travel of, A54–55
Moody, Pliny, C33
Moon (of Earth)
  craters on, D61, D84
  distance from Earth, D62
  orbit of, D64–65
  phases of, D64–65
  tides and, D42, D43 (chart)
  weight on, F57
Moon rover, D82
Moray eel, B26
Morel, A27
Morpho butterfly, B29
Motion, F40
  changing, F48
  relative, F41
  speed and, F42–43
  starting, F47
Motor nerves, R36
Mount Everest, D31
Mount Fuji, C21, C23
Mount Mazama, C22
Mount Pelée volcano, C21, C24
Mount Pinatubo volcano, C24
Mount St. Helens volcano, C24–25
Mount Spurr, C26–27
Mount Vesuvius, C21, C23
Mouse, B2
Mouth, R30, R34
Movable pulley, F78
MRI machine, F2, F31
Mulberry trees, A78
Muscle(s)
  cardiac, A100–101
  smooth, A99–100
  striated, A100
  tissues, A96–97
Muscular system, A99, R28–29
Mushroom
  cells of, A26
  chanterelle, A27
  honey, A3
  life cycle of, A27
  morel, A27
  poisonous, A24

N

National Aeronautics and Space Administration (NASA), D26, F62
National forests, B72
National Oceanic and Atmospheric Administration (NOAA), D26
National parks
  history of, B74–75
  list of, B72
  Petrified Forest, C39
  using, B66–67
National Parks Service (NPS), B44, B74–75
National Trails System Act, B75
Natural gas, C53
Neap tides, D43
Near-shore zone, B36
Neptune
  discovery of, D91
  distance from sun, D69, D71
  as outer planet, D78–79
  tilt of, D61
  weight on (chart), F57
Nerves, A111
Nervous system, A110–111, R36-37
Neuron, A110
New Madrid earthquake, C3
Newton, Sir Isaac, E115
Newton (N), F51, R4
Niche, B21
Nitrogen, freezing and boiling point of, E38
North African ostrich, A3
North American bats, A59
Northern Hemisphere, D66–67
North Pole
  Earth's axis and, D65
  ocean water near, D37
Nose, R25, R34
Nuclear reactor, E34
Nucleus, cell, A7–8
Nutrients, A72

Nutrition, R8

O

Observatory, D85
Ocean(s)
  currents, D44–45
  depth of, D30–31
  exploring, D54–55
  floor, features of, D50–51
  size of, D31
  tides, D42
  waves, D40–41
Ocean water, D34–37
  content of (chart), D36
Ochoa, Ellen, F62
Octopus, A12, B31
Oersted, Hans, F31
Olympus Mons, D77
Onnes, Heike, F31
Opaque, E106
Open-ocean zone, B36
Optical telescopes, D84
Optics
  history of, E115
  light and, E114–115
Orbit, D65
  elliptical, D72
Organs, A98
Osprey, A49, B64
Ostriches, A3, A36
Outer core, Earth's, C7
Outer planets, D78–79
Owen, Richard, C58
Oxygen
  animals' need for, A41
  in atmosphere, D6
  freezing and boiling point of, E38
  heart, lungs, and, A106–107
  human respiratory system and, A104–105
  mountain climbers and, D4–5
  photosynthesis and, A73, D7

P

Pacific Ocean
  Mariana Trench, D31, D54
  size of, D31
Palissy, Bernard, C59

R22

INDEX

Parallel circuit, F14
Paramecium, A9
Parashant National Monument, AZ, B75
Paricutín, C2
Parrotfish, B30
Pathfinder, D88
Peach tree, A22
Peat, C55
Pelvis, A99, R26–27
Penguins, A44, A49
Penicillium, A28
Penny, changes in, E4
Peregrine falcon, A36
Petrified Forest National Park, C39
Petroleum, C53
Phases, of moon, D64
Phobos, D81
Photocopiers, F3
Photosynthesis, A73, D7, E100
Physical activity, R12
Physical changes, E26–27, E30
Physicist, E34
Piano, levers in, F73
Pike, Dr. Leonard M., A89
Pine forest, organisms in, B20
Pine trees, A21
   bristlecone, A69
   fire and, B55
   white, A21
Piranha, B29
Pistil, A85
Pitch, E79
Planets, D71
   discovering, D90–91
   distances between, D74–75
   distances from sun (chart), D69
   inner, D76–77
   movement of, D68–69
   order from sun (chart), D76
   outer, D78–79
   tilts of (chart), D61
   weight on (chart), F57
Planet years (chart), D72
Plant cells, A8
Plants
   adaptations of, A74, A80
   basic needs of, A72
   "breathing" of, A76–77
   cone-bearing, A20–21
   food for, A73
   fruit-bearing, A22–23
   leaves of, A78
   life cycles of, A84–87
   light and, A70–71
   light energy and, E100
   new from old, A86
   with seeds, A20–23
   skin rashes from, R23
   in tropical rain forests, B32
Platelets, R33
Plates, Earth's, C8, C20
Pliers, levers in, F73
Pluto
   discovery of, D91
   distance from sun, D69, D71
   first detailed photos of, D91
   as outer planet, D78–79
   planet year of, D72
   tilt of, D61
   weight on (chart), F57
Polar bears, A50
Pollination, A85
Pollutants, microbes and, A32
Pollution, B48, B57–58
Polo, Marco, E114
Polyps, B30
Pond
   changes in, B50–51
   pollution of, B57–58
   waves in, E72
Population, B13
Porcupine fish, A50
Position, F40
Posture, at computer, R14
Potato tubers, A87
Potential energy, E28
Prairie dogs, B24
Precipitation, D35
Preservation, B72
Prisms, E110–112
Producers, B21
Prominences, D70
Propellers, F90
Protoceratops, C40
Pull, F46, F51
Pulley, F76–79
Pumpkin seeds, A23
Pupa, A44
Push, F46, F49–50

Q – R

Quadriceps, A99, R28
Queen Mary, F91
Radiation, E52
   infrared, E53
Radioactivity in fossils, C59
Radioimmunoassay (RIA) test, A116
Radio telescopes, D84–85
Radius, A99, R26
Rain, D18
Rainbow, E108–109
Raindrops, as prisms, E111
Rain-forest orchid, B29
Rain forests
   destruction of, B61
   tropical, B28–29
   See also Tropical rain forests
Ramp, F84. *See also* Inclined planes
Raspberry bushes, A82
Reclamation, B63
   strip-mine, B62–63
Recycling
   to reduce trash, B69
   symbol for, B69
   tires, B49
Red blood cells, A95, R33
Redesign, B71
Red fire sponge, A14
Red mangrove tree, B12
Red sprite, D24
Reflecting telescope, D84
Reflection, E102–103
Refracting telescope, D84
Refraction, E104–105
Relative motion, F41
Resistor, F13
Resources
   conservation of, B68–73
   from tropical rain forests, B32
Respiratory system, A104–105, R34–35
Resulting force
   with inclined plane, F85
   with lever, F70–71, F74
   with pulley, F78–79

R23

with screw, F86
with wedges, F88
with wheel and axle, F80
Revolution, Earth's, D65
Rib cage, A99, R26
Richter scale, C16
Ride, Sally, F62
River turtle, B29
Roaches, robot, A62–63
Robins, sound and hearing of, E67
Robot ants and roaches, A62–63
Robot volcano explorer, C26–27
Rocks, age of, C48
Roots, underwater mangrove, B15
Rose hip, A22
Rotating-drum barometer, D20
Rotation, Earth's, D65, D72
Rotifers, A10
Ruler, using, R5
Rust, E29

S

Safety
bicycle, R16–17
earthquake, R19
fire, R18
Internet, R15
storm, R19
Saffir-Simpson Hurricane Scale, D3
Saguaro cactus, A69
Salinity, B30
Salmon, B62
bear catching, A42
migration of, A58
Salt water
fresh water from, D32–33
ocean water as, D36–37
Saltwater crocodile, A3
San Andreas fault, C14
Sandstone, C36
Satellite, D64, F56
Satellite photograph, D22
Saturn
distance from sun, D69, D71
as outer planet, D78
rings around, D80
tilt of, D61

Titan, D80
weight on (chart), F57
Sayler, Gary, A32
Scale
dial spring, F52
electronic, F52
large, F53
spring, F51–52, R4
Science tools, using, R2–5
Screws, F86–87
Scuba support crew, D55
Sea Around Us, The **(Carson),** D56
Sea fan, B31
Seahorse, A37
Seashore ecosystem, B43
Seasons, D66
Sea urchin, B30
Sedimentary rocks, C36, C44
Seedlings
growth of, A82–83
in mangrove swamp, B14
Seeds
plants with, A20–23, A84
watermelon, A18
Seesaw, F72
Seismograph, C16
Seismologist, C28
Sense organs, caring for, R24–25
Sensors, A63
Sensory nerves, R36
Series circuit, F14
Serving size, R9
Shadows, light and, E101
Shale, C36
Sharks, whale, A3
Shelter, animals' need for, A43
Shield volcanoes, C21
Shore zone, D49
Shoulder muscles, A99
Shrimp, B12
Silent Spring **(Carson),** D56
Silver, tarnishing of, E28
Simple machines, F70
inclined planes, F84–85
lever, F68–74
pulley, F76–79
screw, F86–87
water transportation and, F90–91
wedges, F88

wheel and axle, F76, F80
Skeletal muscle, A96
Skeletal system, A98–99
bones in, R26
caring for, R27
Skeleton
bat, A17
coral polyp, B30–31
human. *See also* Skeletal system
Skin, caring for, R25
Skin adhesive, A114–115
Skull, R26–27
Small intestine, A111–112, R30–31
Smooth muscle, A96, A100
Snails, A15, B21
Snowshoe hare, A52
Sodium chloride, D36
Soil
bacteria in, A2, B21
fungi in, A2
nutrients in, A72
Sojourner **probe,** D88
Solar energy, E57
Solar system, D70
asteroids, D71
comets, D71
planets, D71
sun, D70
Solid, E6
Solubility, E19
Solution, E18
Sonic boom, E88
Sound
ranges of (chart), E67
speed of, E84
wave, defined, E71
wave diagram, E73
waves, E72–73
Southern Hemisphere, D66
South Pole
Earth's axis and, D65
ocean water near, D37
Space exploration
crewed missions, D87
space probes, D88–89
space station, D87
telescopes and, D84–86
Species
competition among, B48
endangered, B48–49

INDEX

Speed, F42–43
  acceleration and, F48
  of activities (chart), F42
  changing, F49
  of sound, E84
Spider, A16
Spider plant, A86
Spider web, B18
Spinal cord, A111, R36
Spine, A99, R26–27
Spiral staircase, F87
Sponges
  cells of, A14
  living and harvested, B32
  real versus artificial, A12–13
  red fire, A14
  as simplest animals, A14
Spores
  fungi, A24–25, A27
  plants, A85
Spring scale, F51–52, R4
Spring tides, D43
Sprites, D25
Stability, B8
Staghorn coral, B31
Stamen, A85
Star, D70
Starfish, D42
Static electricity, F30
Stationary front, D14
Steel, making, E30
Stems, vine, A74
Stephenson-Hawk, Denise, D26
Stomach
  human, A111–112, R30
  whale, A95
Stonehenge, D68
Stopwatch, F42, R5
Storms
  ecosystems and, B54
  safety in, R19
Storm surge, D41
Stratosphere, D8
Stratus cloud, D15
Striated muscles, A100
Strip-mine reclamation, B62–63
Succession, B52
Sugar, forms of, E27
Sun
  air and, D12
  distance from Earth, D60
  gravity between Earth and, F56
  infrared radiation of, E53
  planets' distance from (chart), D69
  planets in order from (chart), D76
  planets' paths around, D72
  shadows and, E101
  in solar system, D70
Sunspots, D70
Superconductors, F31
Superveggies, A88–89
Surface current, D44
Surgical nurse, A115
Swamp, B13
System(s), B6
  characteristics of, B6–9
  fishbowl as, B4
  human, A98
  interaction in, B4–5, B7
  parts of, B6
  stability and change in, B8
Système International (SI) measures, F51, R6

T

Taproot, A79
Telescopes, D82–86
Temperatures
  in atmosphere, D8
  daily (chart), D22
  land versus water, D20
  of light bulb, E39
  of lightning, E39
  of water in coral reef, B30
Texas, Glen Rose, C37
Thales, F30
Theophrastus, C58
Thermal energy, E56
Thermometer, using, R2
Thermosphere, D8
Thunderstorms
  along cold front, D14
  effect on ecosystems, B54
  frequency of, D2
  unusual flashes during, D24–25
  warning sirens for, B56
  See also Lightning
Tibia, A99, R26
Tide pool, D42
Tides, D42–43
Tiger centipede, B29
Tigers, A38, A60
Timing device, using, R5
Tissue, A98
Titan, D80
Tokyo, earthquake damage in, C28
Tombaugh, Clyde, D91
Tongue, caring for, R25
Tornadoes
  safety and, R19
  sirens for, B56
Tortoise, A37, A40
Toucan, B29
Touch, A108–109
Trace fossils, C37
Trachea, A104–105, R35
Tracks, fossilized, C37
Translucent, E106
Transparent, E106
Transpiration, A78
Trees
  American holly, A22
  cork, A6
  giant sequoia, A69
  peach, A22
  planting, B64
  replanting, B63
  tagged, B72
Trench, ocean, D50
Triceps, A99–100, R28–29
Trieste, D54
Tropical ecosystems, B28–33
Tropical rain forests, B28–29
  resources from, B32
  See also Rain forests
Troposphere, D8
Tubers, A87
Tulips, A86
Tyrannosaurus rex, C59
Tyrrell Museum, Alberta, C32

U

Ulna, A99, R26
Ultimate Bike, F61

Under the Sea-Wind (Carson), D56
Unzen volcano, C24
U.S. Bureau of Fisheries, D56
U.S. Department of Agriculture, A90
U.S. Nuclear Regulatory Commission (NRC), E34
Urania Observatory, D91
Uranus
  discovery of, D90–91
  distance from sun, D69, D71
  as outer planet, D78–79
  tilt of, D61
  weight on (chart), F57

V

Vacuoles, A7–8
Vegetables, A88–89
Veins, A105–106, R32
Vent, C20
Venus
  distance from sun, D69, D71
  as inner planet, D76
  tilt of, D61
  weight on (chart), F57
Venus' flytrap, A80–81
Vertebrates, A16
Viceroy butterfly, A52
Vinegar, E29
Vines, A74
  liana, B33
Vise, F86
Visible spectrum, E110
Volcanoes, C20
  Antarctic, C26–27
  building effects of, C22
  cinder cone, C21
  composite, C21
  destruction from, C24
  eruptions of, C18–19, C22–C25, E66
  eruption warnings, B56
  formation of, C20
  in Iceland, C3
  on Mars, D77
  rapid ecosystem changes and, B55
  shield, C21
  vent, C20

Volt, F12
Volta, Alessandro, F30–31
Voltaic pile, F30–31
Volume, E13
Voluntary muscles, R29
Volvox, A10
Voyager 2, D89, D91
Vulture, A40

W–Y

Walking stick, A52–53
Warm front, D14
Water
  animals' need for, A43
  conservation measures (chart), B68
  density of, E3
  evaporation, D21
  ocean, D34–37
  plants' need for, A70, A72
  temperatures in coral reef, B30
Water currents, D38–39
Water cycle, D34–35
  in a yard, B6–7
Water ecosystem, B12
  human wastes in, B61
Waterlily, A74
Watermelon, A18
Water transportation, F90–91
Water vapor
  in atmosphere, D6
  in water cycle, D34
Wavelength, E72
Waves
  ocean, D40–41
  pond, E72
  sound, E72–73
Weather
  air and, D12–17
  mapping and charting, D22–23
  measuring, D20–21
  predicting, D20–23
Weather map, D22–23
Wedges, F88
Weekly activities, planning, R12
Weight, F57
Wetlands
  in Florida, B65
  flow control device for, B65
Whale, A41

  blue, A3
  gray, A58
  humpback, A60–61
  stomach of, A95
Whale sharks, A3
Wheel and axle, F76, F80
Wheelbarrow, F67, F71
White blood cells, R33
White light, E110
White mulberry, A78
White pine, A21
Wild and Scenic Rivers Act, B75
Wild orchids, A76
Wilson, Woodrow (President), B75
Wind
  speed of, D10–11
  water waves from, D40
Wind pipe, R34
Wind scale (chart), D11
Windsock, D21
Winter storm safety, R19
Wizard Island, C22
Wolves, B2
Woolly mammoths, C43
Work, F74
Workout, guidelines for, R13
Worms, A15, C37
Wright, Orville, F92
Wright, Wilbur, F92
Yalow, Rosalyn Sussman, A116
Yard
  as ecosystem, B10–11
  season changes and, B8–9
  water cycle in, B6–7
Yeasts, A28
Yellowstone National Park, B54
  establishment of, B74
  Minerva Terrace hot springs, B74
Yosemite National Park, B72, B74–75

PHOTO CREDITS:

Page Placement Key: (t)-top (c)-center (b)-bottom (l)-left (r)-right (fg)-foreground (bg)-background

Cover and Title Pages

Gary Neil Corbett/Superstock

Contents

Page: iv (fg) Steinhart Aquarium/Tom McHugh/Photo Researchers; iv (bg) Mark Lewis/Liaison International; v (fg) Steve Kaufman/DRK Photos; v (bg) H. Richard Johnson/FPG International; vi (fg) Francois/Gohier/Photo Researchers; vii (fg) Dorling Kindersley; vii (bg) FPG International; viii (fg); Dennis Yankus/Superstock; vii (bg) Pierre-Yves Goavec/Image Bank; ix (fg) Steve Berman/Liaison International; ix (bg) Photone Disk #50.

Unit A

Unit A Opener (fg) Steinhart Aquarium/Tom McHugh/Photo Researchers; (bg) Mark Lewis/Liaison International; A2 (i) Dr. Jeremy Burgess/Science Photo Library/Photo Researchers; A2-A3 (bg) Jeffrey L. Rotman Photography; A3 (ti) Tom Volk/University of Wisconsin-La Crosse; A4 M.I. Walker/Photo Researchers; A6 (r) Leonard Lee Rue III/Photo Researchers; A6 (i) Ray Simons/Photo Researchers; A6 (l), A6 (li) Dave G. Houser/Corbis; A7 Dr. Gopal Murti/Phototake; A8 (b) Biophoto Associates/Science Source/Photo Researchers; A9 (bg) Jeff Lepore/Photo Researchers; A9 (t) Michael Abbey/Photo Researchers; A9 (cr) Dr. E. R. Degginger/Color-Pic; A9 (cl) Biophoto Associates/Photo Researchers; A10 Dwight R. Kuhn; A12 Alex Kerstitch/Bruce Coleman, Inc.; A14 Graeme Teague; A15 (t) Ed Reschke/Peter Arnold, Inc.; A15 (b) J.C. Carton/Bruce Coleman, Inc.; A16 (t) William E. Ferguson; A16 (c) Dr. E. R. Degginger/Color-Pic; A16 (bl) Larry Miller/Photo Researchers; A16 (br) Dwight R. Kuhn; A17 David Dennis/Animals Animals; A18 Bumann/StockFood America; A20 William H. Allen, Jr.; A20 (i) Biophoto Associates/Photo Researchers; A21 (t), A21 (ci) Dwight R. Kuhn; A21 (ti) Richard V. Procopio/PictureQuest; A21 (b), A21 (bi) William E. Ferguson; A22 (t) Richard Shiell; A22 (ti) Bill Johnson; A22 (bi) J&L Waldman/Bruce Coleman, Inc.; A22 (bl), A22 (br) Dr. E.R. Degginger/Color-Pic, Inc.; A22 (ci) Bill Beatty/Wild & Natural; A23 (t) David R. Frazier; A23 (ti) Lance Beeny; A23 (bi) Dwight R. Kuhn; A24 Fritz Polking/Peter Arnold, Inc.; A26 Dr. Jeremy Burgess/Science Photo Library/Photo Researchers; A27 (l) Dr. E. R. Degginger/Color-Pic; A27 (r) W. Wayne Lockwood, M.D./Corbis; A28 (t) Chris Hellier/Corbis; A28 (c) Dr. E. R. Degginter/Color-Pic; A28 (bl) Noble Proctor/Photo Researchers; A28 (bi) Robert and Linda Mitchell/Mitchell Photography; A29 Phil Degginger/Color-Pic; A30 (l) Kevin Collins/Visuals Unlimited; A30 (r) Alfred Pasieka/Peter Arnold, Inc.; A30 (bg) Dr. Dennis Kunkel/Phototake; A31 Barbara Wright/Animals Animals; A32 (i) The Center for Environmental Biotechnology; A32 Andre Jenny/Focus Group/PictureQuest; A36-A37 Manoj Shah/Stone; A37 (t) Rudy Kuiter/Innerspace Visions; A37 (b) Peter Weimann/Animals Animals; A38 Corel; A40 (b) John Cancalosi/DRK; A40 (tl) Larry Minden/Minden Pictures; A40 (bg) Rich Reid/Earth Scenes; A40 (tr) Renee Lynn/Photo Researchers; A41 Daniel J. Cox/ Natural Exposures; A42 (t) T. Kitchen/Natural Selection; A42 (bl) Daniel J. Cox/Natural Selection; A42-A43 (b) Bios/Peter Arnold, Inc.; A43 (t) David E. Myers/Stone; A43 (bl) Osolinski, S. OSF/Animals Animals; A43 (li) Stephen Krasemann/Stone; A43 (ri) E & P Bauer/Bruce Coleman, Inc.; A44 (l) Ralph Clevenger/Westlight; A44 (bg) B & C Alexander/Photo Researchers; A44 (i) Dan Suzio Photography; A45 (t) Ben Simmons/The Stock Market; A45 (i) D. Parer & E. Parer-Cook/Auscape; A46 (b) Joe McDonald/Bruce Coleman, Inc.; A48 (l) Robert Lankinen/The Wildlife Collection; A48 (r) Martin Harvey/The Wildlife Collection; A48 (c) Zefa Germany/The Stock Market; A49 (t) Fritz Polking/Dembinsky Photo Associates; A49 (b) Tui De Roy/Minden Pictures; A49 (i) Zig Leszczynski/Animals Animals; A50 (l) Tom and Pat Leeson; A50 (r) Zig Leszczynski/Animals Animals; A50 (c) Fred Bavendam/Peter Arnold, Inc.; A50-A51 (b) Stuart Westmorland/Stone; A51 (t) Bruce Wilson/Stone; A51 (c) Wolfgang Kaehler Photography; A51 (bl) Martin Harvey/The Wildlife Collection; A51 (br) Bruce Davidson/Animals Animals; A52 (ti) Bruce Wilson/Stone; A52 (t) Art Wolfe/Stone; A52 (bl) Stephen Krasemann/Stone; A52 (br) Stouffer Prod./Animals Animals; A53 (l) Lior Rubin/Peter Arnold, Inc.; A53 (r) John Shaw/Bruce Coleman, Inc.; A54 C. Bradley Simmons/Bruce Coleman, Inc.; A56-A57 Mike Severns/Stone; A58 (t) Grant Heilman Photography; A58-A59 (b) Daniel J. Cox/Stone; A59 (t) Joe McDonald/Animals Animals; A59 (bl) Darrell Gulin/Stone; A59 (br) J. Foott/Bruce Coleman, Inc.; A60 (t) Tom Brakefield/The Stock Market; A60 (b) Mark Petersen/Stone; A61 (t) Darryl Torckler/Stone; A62 Katsumi Kasahara/Associated Press; A63 Phil McCarten/PhotoEdit; A64 Michael K. Nichols/NGS Image Collection; A67 (l) Ralph Clevenger/Westlight; A67 (li) Dan Suzio Photography; A68-69 Bertram G. Murray, Jr./Animals Animals; A69 (l) Gilbert S. Grant/Photo Researchers; A69 (r) J.A. Kraulis/Masterfile; A70 Christi Carter/Grant Heilman Photography; A72 H. Mark Weidman; A73 Porterfield-Chickering/Photo Researchers; A73 (i) Dr. Jeremy Burgess/Science Photo Library/Photo Researchers; A74 (t) Frans Lanting/Minden Pictures; A74 (b) Patti Murray/Earth Scenes; A75 C.K. Lorenz/Photo Researchers; A76 Dr. E.R. Degginger/Color-Pic; A78 (tl), A78(bl) Runk/Schoenberger/Grant Heilman Photography; A78 (br) E.R. Degginger/Earth Scenes; A79 (t), A79 (ti) Runk/Schoenberger/Grant Heilman Photography; A79 (b) Jessie M. Harris; A79 (bi) Steve Solum/Bruce Coleman, Inc.; A80 (r) Bill Lea/Dembinsky Photo Associates; A80 (tl), A80 (bl) Kim Taylor/Bruce Coleman, Inc.; A82 Runk/Schoenberger/Grant Heilman Photography; A84 Gregory K. Scott/Photo Researchers; A86 Angel/Biofotos; A86 (l) Runk/Schoenberger/Grant Heilman Photography; A88 James Lyle/Texas A&M University; A89 Chris Rogers/The Stock Market; A90 Hunt Institute for Botanical Documentation/Carnegie Mellon University; A93 (t) Bruce Coleman, Inc.; A93 (b) Breck P. Kent/Animals Animals; A93 (b) Denise Tackett/Tom Stack & Associates; A96 (tr) Al Lamme/Len/Phototake; A96 (br) Astrid & Hanns-Frieder Michler/Science Photo Library/Photo Researchers; A96 (cr) M. Abbey/Photo Researchers; A98 Biophoto Associates/Science Source/Photo Researchers; A100 (tr) Al Lamme/Len/Phototake; A100 (br) Astrid & Hanns-Frieder Michler/Science Photo Library/Photo Researchers; A100 (cr) M. Abbey/Photo Researchers; A110 Biophoto Associates/Photo Researchers; A114 Produced with permission from ETHICON, INC., 2001 Somerville, NJ; A115 Owen Franken/Stone; A116 (t) UPI/Corbis; A116 (b) Will and Deni McIntyre/Photo Researchers; A120 (t) Keren Su/Corbis; A120 (b) Jan Butchofsky/Corbis.

Unit B

Unit B Opener (fg) Steve Kaufman/DRK Photos; (bg) H. Richard Johnson/FPG International; B2-B3 Kim Heacox/Peter Arnold, Inc.; B3 (l) G. Perkins/Visuals Unlimited; B3 (r) Herbert Schwind/Okapia/Photo Researchers; B4 Navaswan/FPG International; B6-B7 D. Logan/H. Armstrong Roberts, Inc.; B8 (t) Mark E. Gibson/Dembinsky Photo Associates; B8 (b) Larry Lefever/Grant Heilman Photography; B9 (t) Mark E. Gibson/Dembinsky Photo Associates; B10 Dr. E. R. Degginger/Color-Pic; B12 (bg) Doug Cheeseman/Peter Arnold, Inc.; B12 (li) Dr. E. R. Degginger/Color-Pic; B12 (ri) FarrellGrehan/Photo Researchers; B13 (bg) Luiz C. Marigo/Peter Arnold, Inc.; B13 (ri) M. Timothy O'Keefe/Bruce Coleman, Inc.; B13 (li) Bernard Boutrit/Woodfin Camp & Associates; B14 (bg) Jim Steinberg/Photo Researchers; B15 (t) M. Timothy O'Keefe/Bruce Coleman, Inc.; B16 (t) Tom Bean/The Stock Market; B16 (b) Grant Heilman Photography; B18 Ken M. Highfill/Photo Researchers; B20 (bg) Rob Lewine/The Stock Market; B20 (ci) Ken Brate/Photo Researchers; B20 (li) Art Wolfe/Stone; B20 (ri) Matt Meadows/Peter Arnold, Inc.; B21 (tl) David M. Phillips/Photo Researchers; B21 (tr) R & J Spurr/Bruce Coleman, Inc.; B21 (bl) Dwight R. Kuhn; B21 (br) Institut Pasteur/Phototake; B21 (cl) E. R. Degginger/Photo Researchers; B21 (cr) Lewis Kemper/Stone; B22-B23 (bg) Carr Clifton/Minden Pictures; B24 (t) David Carriere/Stone; B24 (b) E & P Bauer/Bruce Coleman, Inc.; B25 Roy Morsch/The Stock Market; B26 Stuart Westmorland/Stone; B29 (t) James Martin/Stone; B29 (c) Dr. E. R. Degginger/Color-Pic; B29 (b) Tom McHugh/Photo Researchers; B31 (t) Manfred Kage/Peter Arnold, Inc.; B31 (c) William Townsend, Jr./Photo Researchers; B31 (b) Norbert Wu/The Stock Market; B32 Dr. E. R. Degginger/Color-Pic; B33 Tom McHugh/Photo Researchers; B34 Francois Gohier; B36-B37 (bg) Jack McConnell; B37 (bli) Susie Leavines/Picture It!; B37 (bri) Jeff Foott/Bruce Coleman, Inc.; B37(tli) Gay Bumgarner; B37(tri) Dr. Charles Steinmetz, Jr.; B37 (ci) Gregory G. Dimijian/Photo Researchers; B38 (b) Fred Bavendam/Minden Pictures; B38 (t) Flip Nicklin/Minden Pictures; B39 (b) Dr. E. R. Degginger/Color-Pic; B39 (t) Flip Nicklin/Minden Pictures; B40 (b) University of Delaware Graduate School of Marine Studies; B42 Oakridge National Laboratory; B43 Norbert Wu; B43 (b) David Young-Wolff/PhotoEdit; B44 (b) David Muench/Stone; B44 (t) Courtesy of Indiana Dunes National Lakeshore/National Park Service; B48 Joel Sartore from Grant Heilman Photography; B48-B49 Jeff Foott/Bruce Coleman, Inc.; B49 (b) Roy Toft/Tom Stack & Associates; B50 Gary Braasch/Woodfin Camp & Associates; B53 MikeYamashita/Woodfin Camp & Associates; B54 (t) Frank Oberle/Stone; B54 (bl) David Woods/The Stock Market; B54 (bri) Stan Osolinski/Dembinsky Photo Associates; B54-B55 (b) Jeff Henry/Peter Arnold, Inc.; B55 (t) Milton Rand/Tom Stack & Associates; B55 (ti) Joe McDonald/Tom Stack & Associates; B55 (bi) Stan Osolinski/Dembinsky Photo Associates; B56 (t) Aneal Vohra/Unicorn Stock Photos; B56 (b) Merrilee Thomas/Tom Stack & Associates; B56 (bi) Tom Benoit/Stone; B57 Mark E. Gibson; B58 Tom Walker/Stock, Boston; B60-B61 (t) David Harp Photography; B60-B61 (b) Jason Hawkes/Stone; B61 (tr) Frans Lanting/Stone; B61 (br) Scott Slobodian/Stone; B62 (t) Mark E. Gibson;B62-B63 (b) Paul Chesley/Stone; B63 (t) J. Lotter/Tom Stack & Associates; B64 (t) David R. Frazier; B64 (b) Lori Adamski Peek/Stone; B65 Marc Epstein/Visuals Unlimited; B66 Jim Schwabel/New England Stock Photo; B69 (b) SuperStock; B70 (c) A. Bolesta/H. Armstrong Roberts, Inc.; B70 (r) IPP/H. Armstrong Roberts, Inc.; B71 (b) Mark Joseph/Stone; B72 (t) Gary Braasch Photography; B72 (b) Barbara Gerlach/Dembinsky Photo Associates; B73 Superstock; B74 (t) J. Blank/H. Armstrong Roberts, Inc.; B74 (bl) R. Kord/H. Armstrong Roberts, Inc.; B74 (br) Marc Muench/David Muench Photography; B75 (b) G. Ahrens/H. Armstrong Roberts, Inc.; B76 AP/Wide World Photos; B78 Earl Roberge/Photo Researchers; B80 (t) Jon Gnass; B80 (b) Connie Toops.

Unit C

Unit C Opener (fg) Francois/Gohier/Photo Researchers; C3 (b) Packwood, R./Earth Scenes; C4 Jock Montgomery/Bruce Coleman, Inc.; C8 Kenneth Fink/Bruce Coleman, Inc.; C9 Eric A. Wessman/The Viesti Collecton; C10-C-11 Kevin Schafer; C12 Wesley Bocxe/Photo Researchers; C14 Francois Gohier/Photo Researchers; C16 (t) Russell D. Curtis/Photo Researchers; C16 (bl) Tom McHugh/Photo Researchers; C16 (bc) Lee Foster/Bruce Coleman, Inc.; C17 Francois Gohier/Photo Researchers; C18 E.R. Degginger/Photo Researchers; C22-C23 C. C. Lockwood/Bruce Coleman, Inc.; C23 (t) Paolo Koch/Photo Researchers; C24 (t) Photo Researchers; C24 (b) H. Hannejdottir/Photo Researchers; C24 (bg) Ken Sakamoto/Black Star; C25 Krafft-Explorer/Photo Researchers; C26 Bill Ingals/NASA/Sygma; C27 Nancy Simmerman/Stone; C28 (t) Todd Bigelow/Black Star; C28 (b)Thomas Jaggar/NGS Image Collection; C32-C33 Gerd Ludwig/Woodfin Camp & Associates; C33 (t) The Westthalian Museum of Natural History; C33 (b) James Martin/Stone; C34 Murray Alcosser/The Image Bank; C36 (t) Beth Davidow/Visuals Unlimited; C36 (b) The Natural History Museum, London; C36-C37 (b) William E. Ferguson; C37 (c) The Natural History Museum, London; C37 (tl) Dr. P. Evans/Bruce Coleman Collection; C37 (tr) David J. Sams/Stone; C37 (l), C38 (l) William E. Ferguson; C38 (t) Peter Gregg/Color-Pic; C38-C39 (t) Bob Burch/Bruce Coleman, Inc.; C38-C39 (b) E. R. Degginger/Bruce Coleman, Inc.; C39 (ti) E. R.Degginger/Bruce Coleman, Inc.; C40, C42 (l) The Natural History Museum, London; C42 (li) William E. Ferguson ; C42-C43 (bg) Mark J.Thomas/Dembinsky Photo Associates; C43 (t) Runk/Schoenberger/Grant Heilman Photography; C44 (t) Phil Schofield/Stone; C44 (c) Phil Degginger/Bruce Coleman, Inc.; C45 Louie Psihoyos/Matrix International; C46 (t) Kevin Fleming; C46 (br) Breck B. Kent; C46 (b) David Hiser/PictureQuest; C47 (t), C47 (i) Layne Kennedy; C47 (b) Richard T. Nowitz/Corbis; C48 (t) Ted Clutter/Photo Researchers; C48 (b) J. C. Carton/Bruce Coleman, Inc.; C49 William E. Ferguson; C50 J.C. Carton/Bruce Coleman, Inc.; C52 (l) Larry Lefever from Grant Heilman Photography; C52 (r) Thomas Kitchin/Tom Stack & Associates; C53 (t) Kenneth Murray/Photo Researchers; C55 (t), C55 (b) Dr. E.R. Degginger/Color-Pic; C55 (tc), C55 (bc) Breck P. Kent/Earth Scenes; C58 (b) The Granger Collection, New York; C58 (tl) Alinari/Art Resource, NY; C58 (tr) The Granger Collection, New York; C58 (t) Bill Bachman/Photo Researchers; C59 (b) James King-Holmes/Science Photo Library/Photo Researchers; C60 (t) San Francisco State University/Department of Geosciences; C60 (b) AP/Wide World Photos; C64 (t)

J.F. Maxwell/Falls of the Ohio State Park; C64 (b) Sandy Felsenthal/Corbis.

Unit D

Unit D Opener (fg) Dorling Kindersley; (bg) FPG International; D2-D3 Warren Faidley/International Stock; D3 (t) Bob Abraham/The Stock Market; D3 (b) NRSC Ltd/Science Photo Library/Photo Researchers; D4 Keren Su/Stock, Boston; D6 Space Frontiers-TCL/Masterfile; D10 Bruce Watkins/Earth Scenes; D12 Peter Menzel/Stock, Boston; D14-D15 C. O'Rear/Corbis; D15 Warren Faidley/International Stock; D16 (b) Bill Binzen/The Stock Market; D18 J. Tapochaner/FPG International; D20 Sam Ogden/Science Photo Library/Photo Researchers; D21 (t) Breck P. Kent/Earth Scenes; D21 (b) B. Daemmrich/The Image Works; D22 (c) 1998 Accu Weather; D24 Geophysical Institute, University of Alaska, Fairbanks/NASA; D25 Pat Lanza/Bruce Coleman, Inc.; D26 (t) Clark Atlanta University; D26 (b) NASA/Science Photo Library/Photo Researchers; D30-D31 Warren Bolster/Stone; D31 (t) Warren Morgan/Corbis; D31 (b) Tom Van Sant, Geosphere Project/Planetary Visions/Science Photo Library/Photo Researchers; D32 Philip A. Savoie/Bruce Coleman, Inc.; D36 (tr) A. Ramey/Stock Boston; D36 (bl) Richard Gaul/FPG International; D38 John Lel/Stock, Boston; D40 E.R. Degginger/Photo Researchers; D41 (t) Fredrik Bodin/Stock, Boston; D41 (b) Peter Miller/Photo Researchers; D42 (t), D42 (c) Francois Gohier/Photo Researchers; D42 (b) Steinhart Aquarium/Tom McHugh/Photo Researchers; D46 Ralph White/Corbis; D49 (i) Dr. E.R. Degginger/Color-Pic; D49 (t) David R. Frazier; D50-D51 Marie Tharp/Oceanic Cartographer; D54-D55 Ben Margot/AP Photo/Wide World Photos; D55 Thomas Ives/The Stock Market; D56 (t) Erich Hartmann/Magnum Photos; D56 (b) Ron Sefton/Bruce Coleman, Inc.; D60-D61 Ton Kinsbergen/ESA/Science Photo Library/Photo Researchers; D61 NASA; D62 Dr. E. R. Degginger/Color-Pic; D68 Tom Till; D71 Frank Zullo/Photo Researchers; D72-D73 M. Agliolo/Photo Researchers; D74 NASA; D77 (t) U.S. Geological Survey/Science Photo Library/Photo Researchers; D77 (b) David Crisp and the WFPC2 Science Team (Jet Propulsion Laboratory/California Institute of Technology)/NASA; D77 (tc) NASA; D77 (bc) National Oceanic and Atmospheric Administration; D78 NASA; D78-D79 Erich Karkoschka (University of Arizona Lunar & Planetary Lab) and NASA; D79 (r) Dr. R. Albrecht, ESA/ESO Space Telescope European Coordinating Facility, NASA; D79 (c) Lawrence Sromovsky (University of Wisconsin - Madison), NASA; D80, D81, D82 NASA; D84 (r) Michael Freeman; D84 (tl) David Nunuk/Science Photo Library/Photo Researchers; D84 (bl) Omikron Collection/Photo Researchers; D85 (t) Simon Fraser/Science Photo Library/Photo Researchers; D85 (b) Robert Frerck/Stone; D85 (ti) Roger Ressmeyer/Corbis; D86 (bg) Shahn Kermani/Liaison International; D86, D87, D88, D89 NASA; D90 (r) Jean-Loup Charmet; D90 (l) NASA; D91 (t) The Granger Collection, New York; D91 (c) Sylvester Allred/Visuals Unlimited; D91 (b) Mark E. Gibson/Dembinsky Photo Associates; D92 J. Kelly Beatty; D92 (bg) Science VU/Visuals Unlimited; D96 (t) Mark E. Gibson; D96 (b) W. Metzen/H. Armstrong Roberts, Inc..

Unit E

Unit E Opener (fg); Dennis Yankus/Superstock; (bg); Pierre-Yves Goavec/Image Bank; E2-E3 Jon Riley/Stone; E3 Dr. E.R. Degginger/Color-Pic; E4 Superstock; E6 Michael Denora/Liaison International; E8 (b) Bob Abraham/The Stock Market; E10 (l) Lee F. Snyder/Photo Researchers; E14-E15 (b) Richard R. Hansen/Photo Researchers; E16 Stone; E20 (t) Kathy Ferguson/PhotoEdit; E20 (b) Doug Perrine/Innerspace Visions; E20 (bi) Felicia Martinez/PhotoEdit; E21 (b) Chip Clark; E22 (bg) Norbert Wu/Mo Yung Productions; E22-E23 Richard Pasley/Stock, Boston; E24 Stockman/International Stock; E29 (cl) Dr. E.R. Degginger/Color-Pic; E29 (br) Grace Davies; E29 (bl) Index Stock Imagery/PictureQuest; E30 (i) P. Degginger/H. Armstrong Roberts, Inc.; E30 (b) Jack McConnell/McConnell & McNamara; E30-E31 Paul A. Souders/Corbis; E32 Courtesy of J. G's Edible Plastic; E33 David R. Frazier; E34 (l) United States Nuclear Regulatory Commission; E34 (r) Tom Carroll/Phototake; E38-E39 Ray Ellis/Photo Researchers; E39 (t) Peter Steiner/The Stock Market; E39 (b) Murray & Assoc./The Stock Market; E40 Craig Tuttle/The Stock Market; E43 (t) Jim Zipp/Photo Researchers; E44 Ted Horowitz/The Stock Market; E48 D. Nabokov/Gamma Liaison; E50 (b) L. West/Bruce Coleman, Inc.; E50 (i) Jonathan Wright/Bruce Coleman, Inc.; E51 Gary Milburn/Tom Stack & Associates; E52 Jeff Foott/Bruce Coleman, Inc.; E56 (t) Craig Hammell/The Stock Market; E56 (b) Russell D. Curtis/Photo Researchers; E57 (tl) Stu Rosner/Stock, Boston; E57 (tr) John Mead/Science Photo Library/Photo Researchers; E57 (br) John Cancalosi/Stock, Boston; E58 (b) David Falconer & Associates; E58 (tr) Telegraph Colour Library/FPG International; E58 (cr) Charles D. Winters/Photo Researchers; E58 (bi) Montes De Oca & Associates; E59 Paul Shambroom/Science Source/Photo Researchers; E61 Danny Daniels/The Picture Cube; E62 Minnesota Historical Society; E62 (i) Peter Vadnai/The Stock Market; E66-E67 Stephen Dalton/Photo Researchers; E67 Carl R. Sams, II/Peter Arnold, Inc.; E68 A. Ramey/PhotoEdit; E71 (t) Summer Productions; E71 (li) Michelle Bridwell/PhotoEdit; E71 (tri) Peter Langone/International Stock; E72 (l) Ian O'Leary/Stone; E76 Randy Duchaine/The Stock Market; E78 (r) Jim Zipp/Photo Researchers; E78 Spencer Grant/PhotoEdit; E82 (t) Bose Corporation; E82 (b) Bose/Lisa Borman Associates; E84-E85 (b) NASA; E90-E91 Bruce Forster/Stone; E91 (i) Jon Riley/Folio; E96-E97 NASA; E97 (t) Chip Simons; E97 (b) David Madison/Bruce Coleman, Inc.; E100 (l) Mark E. Gibson; E100 (r) Bob Daemmrich/Stock, Boston; E103 Jan Butchofsky/Dave G. Houser; E105 (t), 105 (c) Richard Megna/Fundamental Photographs; E108 (b) Randy Duchaine/The Stock Market; E110 Tom Skrivan/The Stock Market; E111 (tr) David Woodfall/Stone; E113 Roy Morsh/The Stock Market; E114-F115 Paul Silverman/Fundamental Photographs; E115 (t) Ed Eckstein for the Franklin Institute Science Museum; E115 (b) Peter Angelo Simon/The Stock Market; E116 (t) Schomburg Collection; E116 (bl) Jim Davie; E120 (t) Sal Dimarco/Black Star; E120 (b) Jack Olson.

Unit F

Unit F Opener (fg) Steve Berman/Liaison International; (bg) Photone Disk #50; F2-F3 Pete Saloutos/The Stock Market; F4 Doug Martin/Photo Researchers; F9 Charles D. Winters/Photo Researchers; F10 Cosmo Condina/Stone; F15 Dr. E.R. Degginger/Color-Pic; F16 National Maritime Museum Picture Library; F19 Richard Megna/Fundamental Photographs; F20-F21 (t) Phil Degginger/Color-Pic; F22 Gamma Tokyo/Liaison International; F24-F25 Spencer Grant/PhotoEdit; F25 Tom Pantages; F27 (t), F27 (c) Phil Degginger/Color Pic; F27 (b) Bruno Joachin/Liaison International; F27 (bg) W. Cody/Corbis Westlight; F30 (t) PhotoDisc; F30 (b) Corbis-Bettmann; F31 Phil Degginger/Color-Pic; F32 (i) Fonar Corporation; F32 Jean Miele/The Stock Market; F36-F37 PictureQuest; F37 (t), F37 (ti) Dwight R. Kuhn; F37 (br) Tony Freeman/PhotoEdit; F38 (b) David R. Frazier; F40 (b) Mark E. Gibson; F42 (b) Bob Daemmrich/Stock, Boston; F44 (bl) Miro Vintoniv/Stock, Boston; F46 (bl) Jean-Marc Barey/Agence Vandystadt/Photo Researchers; F47 (tr) Daniel MacDonald/The Stock Shop; F49 Bernard Asset/Agence Vandystadt/Photo Research; F50 (t) Kathi Lamm/Stone; F53 Terry Wild Studio; F54 (b) William R. Sallaz/Duomo Photography; F57 (c) Photo Library International/ESA/Photo Researchers; F57 (cr) Photo Researchers; F58 (bl) Michael Mauney/Stone; F60 (b) Brian Wilson; F60 (t) PA News; F61 (b) Michael Newman/PhotoEdit; F62 (t) UPI/Corbis-Bettmann; F62 NASA; F66-F67 (bg) Dan Porges/Bruce Coleman, Inc.; F67 (tr) R. Sheridan/Ancient Art and Architecture Collection; F67 (tl) The Granger Collection, New York; F68 (bl) William McCoy/Rainbow; F70 (bl) Yoav Levy/Phototake/PictureQuest; F73 (tr) Michael Newman/PhotoEdit; F74 (tr) David R. Frazier; F78 (bl) Mark E. Gibson; F80 (b) Jeff Dunn/Stock, Boston; F82 (bl) Tom King/Tom King, Inc.; F84 (b) Aaron Haupt/David R. Frazier; F85 (tl) Dan McCoy/Rainbow; F85 (br) Michael Newman/PhotoEdit; F85 (cl) David Falconer/Folio; F86 (t) Superstock; F87 (r) Churchill & Klehr; F87 (bl) Staircase & Millwork Corporation, Alpharetta, GA; F88 (br) Tony Freeman/PhotoEdit; F90 (bg) Corel; F90 (l) Archive Photos; F90 (c) Noble Stock/International Stock; F90 (bl) Alexandra Guest/John F. Coates; F91 (l) Eric Sanford/International Stock; F94 (l) Archive Photos; F92 (r) Library of Congress/FPG International; F92 (bl) Library of Congress; F96 (t) Christian Heeb/Gnass Photo Images; F96 (b) Maxine Cass.

Health Handbook: R23 Palm Beach Post; R27 (t) Andrew Spielman/Phototake; (c) Martha McBride/Unicorn Stock; (b) Larry West/FPG International; R28 (l) Ron Chapple/FPG; (c) Mark Scott/FPG; (b) David Lissy/Index Stock.

All other photographs by Harcourt photographers listed below, © Harcourt: Weronica Ankarorn, Bartlett Digital, Victoria Bowen, Eric Camden, Digital Imaging Group, Charles Hodges, Ken Karp, Ken Kinzie, Ed McDonald, Sheri O'Neal, Terry Sinclair.

Art Credits

Mike Atkinson A85, B22, B23; Jean Calder A99, A100 - 101, A110, A111; Susan Carlson D22; Mike Dammer A33, A65, A91, A117, B45, B77, C29, C61, D27, D57, D93, E35, E63, E93, E117, F33, F63, F93; John Edwards E111; John Francis B14 - 15; Lisa Frasier E56-57; George Fryer C6 - 7, C20, C21, D20; Thomas Gagliano D48 - 49, E73, E78, E79, E80, F14; Patrick Gnan E60, F74; Terry Hadler E14, E19, E49, F78, F79; Tim Hayward C44, C48; Robert Hynes A16, A22, B28 - 29, B30 - 31; Joe LeMoniier A64, A90, E66; Mapquest A57, B40, C46; Janos Marffy D66; Michael Maydak B38 - 39; Sebastian Quigley D12 - 13, D44, D65, D76 - 77, D78 - 79, E6, E7, E8, E22, E72, F6, F7, F20, F24, F56; Eberhard Reinmann A98, A104 - 105, A106, A112, E74; Mike Saunders A7, A8, A20, A26, A27, A73, A84, B52 - 53, C7, C36, D8 - 9, D52 - 53, D70, D71, D72 - 73; Steve Seymour B7, B40 - 41, B62, B63, C8, C9, C10, C15, D14, D43, D86, E43, E44, E51, E52, E70, E85, E88 - 89, F8, F13, F49, F72; Shough E112; Bill Smith Studio D93; Walter Stuart A10 - 11, A14, A15; Steve Weston C14, C22, C23, D15, E72, E86 - 87, F18, F80, F86, F87, F88, F93